The Other Elites

The Other Elites

WOMEN, POLITICS, AND POWER IN THE EXECUTIVE BRANCH

edited by
MaryAnne Borrelli
Janet M. Martin

LYNNE
RIENNER
PUBLISHERS

BOULDER
LONDON

PB ISBN 1-55587-971-3

Published in the United States of America in 1997 by
Lynne Rienner Publishers, Inc.
1800 30th Street, Boulder, Colorado 80301

and in the United Kingdom by
Lynne Rienner Publishers, Inc.
3 Henrietta Street, Covent Garden, London WC2E 8LU

Library of Congress Cataloging-in-Publication Data
The other elites : women, politics, and power in the Executive Branch
     /   edited by MaryAnne Borrelli and Janet M. Martin.
     Includes bibliographical references and index.
     ISBN 1-55587-658-7   (hc   :   alk. paper)
     1. Women government executives—United States.   I. Borrelli,
MaryAnne.   II. Martin, Janet M.
JK721.085   1997
331.4'8135'0000973—dc20   96-43234
                                                                                                        CIP

British Cataloguing in Publication Data
A Cataloguing in Publication record for this book
is available from the British Library.

Printed and bound in the United States of America

The paper used in this publication meets the requirements
of the American National Standard for Permanence of
Paper for Printed Library Materials Z39.48-1984.

5 4 3 2

To
Joseph A. and Florence L. Borrelli, Damon J. Borrelli, and
Gertrude M. Karoghlanian

and to
Mary Martin, Judith Ann Bromberek, and Jean T. Martin

Contents

Tables and Figures

Tables

Figures

Acknowledgments

This book represents the first collection of articles on the presidency that addresses the issue of gender. The editors realized early the need for each contributor to write for two audiences—that of presidency scholars and that of women-and-politics scholars. Thus, the contributors had to look widely to literature beyond their own areas of expertise and craft arguments in language accessible to these different audiences. This volume has resulted from the shared vision and, more important, the collaborative and mutually reinforcing efforts of the scholars involved.

The extensive bibliography, painstakingly compiled by Cynthia G. Wilson, a student research assistant at Connecticut College, reflects the breadth of scholarship drawn upon for this volume.

A project of this sort also requires the support of an editor who shares the same vision. Don Reisman, editor-in-chief at Lynne Rienner Publishers, has been an enthusiastic and insightful supporter from the time we first proposed this project through to its completion. Bridget Julian, managing editor, and Steve Barr, director of production, did much to keep this project on track and guide it through to publication. The manuscript also benefited from the insightful comments of Michael A. Genovese.

We are very appreciative of the support we received at both Connecticut College and Bowdoin College. Throughout the project, Tina Falck and Sharon Moody at Connecticut College and Sarah Jensen at Bowdoin College provided expert clerical assistance. Joseph S. Calvo at Bowdoin College remained calm and patient in photocopying various forms of the manuscript, always on short notice. Tracy A. Barsamian, a Connecticut College student research assistant, cheerfully fielded an endless series of research questions and concerns. The crucial three-week period in the summer of 1996 when the final manuscript was to be submitted from Brunswick, Maine, to Boulder, Colorado, found the editors unexpectedly separated by half a continent. Without the secretarial talents of Charlotte Magnuson and expert research assistance provided by Erika Hafner at Bowdoin College, the final deadline could not have been met. Charlotte tirelessly responded to requests to revise and reenter parts of the manuscript to make our publication deadline. In spite of an endless series of glitches beyond her control, Erika could still remark, "This is a great summer job." We were grateful that her enthusiasm matched her administrative abilities.

For the editors, it is clear that this project will be only the first in their collaborative efforts, since both have benefited immensely from the sharing of insight and resources.

Janet M. Martin would like to thank John Winship, as ever, for all of his patient, unfailing, and encouraging support.

Finally, the book is dedicated to MaryAnne Borrelli's parents, Joseph A. and Florence L. Borrelli, her brother, Damon J. Borrelli, and her aunt, Gertrude M. Karoghlanian, and to Janet M. Martin's mother, Mary Martin, and sisters, Judy Ann Bromberek and Jean T. Martin, who have lovingly supported all of their endeavors.

1

Introduction

Janet M. Martin

In this collection the editors have compiled a series of research projects that bridge two previously distinct fields: that of executive politics and that of women and politics. Research in this area has been rapidly developing, and the contributors to this volume are among those who have been at the cutting edge of this emergent area of study.

Those of us who teach in the area of the American presidency have been asked increasingly by students of U.S. politics exposed to writings of feminist theorists or to gender as a framework for analysis or to women as a unit of analysis how women fit into presidency studies or how gender can be incorporated in our research. This volume can provide insight into those questions.

For example, the nomination of Madeleine Albright as secretary of state highlights the important fact that women are increasingly occupying positions involved in decisionmaking. In Barbara Hinckley's study of foreign policy making, *Less Than Meets the Eye,* she notes that often it is not the president but the presidency (e.g., those in the State Department or the Office of the Special Trade Representative) who make decisions in the area of foreign policy.

> When we say that the President makes foreign policy, what do we mean by "President?" Surely we do not mean the entire executive branch. Agencies have their own bureaucratic incentives and routines, while their ties to Congress and to clientele groups outlast any one sitting president. For every covert activity a president authorizes, we assume many others are going forward. Foreign policy is made within agencies at State, at points in Defense, Treasury, Agriculture, the Agency for International Development, the U.S. International Trade Commission, and the U.S. Information Agency, among others. It is made in the many intelligence agencies. . . . Presidents are chief in name only of such a vast operation.[1]

In turn, the role and influence of women may therefore be dependent upon the nature of the policy arena (e.g., crisis versus routine decisionmaking) and on the way the president structures his foreign policy decisionmaking apparatus. Although presidency scholars agree that the "president" is not the presidency, the virtual exclusion of women from most presidency studies seems to contradict this assessment.

The scholarship in this area is developing as a new subfield of study. We anticipate a proliferation of research in this area, as well as an incorporation of the work done by scholars in this emergent field, in the more traditional institutional, historical, and behavioral approaches to presidency research. This evolution would then parallel that of congressional scholarship. In the preface to the first edition of *Women as Candidates in American Politics,* for instance, Susan J. Carroll wrote, "In the mid-1970s when I first began the research that is reported in this book, there was little public interest in, and almost no systematic information about, women candidates and their campaigns."[2] In her pathbreaking study, Carroll systematically analyzed women emerging as candidates for congressional, statewide, and state legislative offices. In the past decade there has been a proliferation of studies building on the earlier work of Carroll and others.[3]

Presidency scholars have clearly lagged behind those in other areas in incorporating gender as a variable in analysis and women as a focus of study. The earliest studies have thus far focused primarily on numerical or descriptive representation, with an identification of how women have been included in executive branch posts.[4] Given the paucity of research on women and the presidency yet the proliferation of research on women and politics that can be broadened to include executive branch studies, the editors sought out presidency and executive branch scholars, as well as those who could expand their research to focus on the presidency, to contribute original scholarship to this volume. Other authors invited to participate in this project bring their own expertise and areas of specialization (e.g., Georgia Duerst-Lahti, feminist theory; Piper A. Hodson, comparative politics; Richard L. Pacelle, Jr., judicial studies; and Clyde Wilcox, voting and election studies).

The impetus for this project was a conversation between the editors in the summer of 1994 in which they discussed their work on the president's cabinet. Each had taken traditional studies and approaches to looking at the cabinet in a new direction that included women. Initially, the editors felt that perhaps their research would be duplicative in nature; however, they soon realized that, in fact, there was a need for cumulative research in this area similar to the proliferation of studies that have emerged on women running for elective office in the United States.

The research in this volume reflects the evolution and development of scholarship that not only builds on more traditional approaches and methodologies but takes them one step further to look at women and gender. As an example, not only does MaryAnne Borrelli build on the work of scholars such as Richard F. Fenno, Jeffrey E. Cohen, and Janet M. Martin, who have followed institutional and behavioral approaches in looking at the cabinet, but she also draws upon the research of feminist scholars in her study of the president's cabinet. Nancy E. McGlen and Meredith Reid Sarkees build on the work of those who have studied the leadership and management styles of a president to see how those styles include or exclude women in the making of foreign policy. Their focus is the Departments of State and Defense, two of the inner cabinet departments identified long ago by Thomas Cronin as having a special role in an administration. Likewise, in her chapter on the cabinet Borrelli offers a case study of another of the inner cabinet posts, that of the attorney general—a post long elusive to women. The comparative perspective of Piper A. Hodson adds two dimensions to presidential studies that are often overlooked by scholars—that of a comparative perspective, as well as a gender politics perspective. In addition, the contributors have worked to incorporate the scholarship of others in this volume to lay the foundation for cumulative research on gender and the presidency.

Theoretical and Comparative Perspectives: Women as Political Executives

The book begins with a theoretical and a comparative perspective of the modern presidency. In Chapter 2, Georgia Duerst-Lahti's analysis is of particular value in that it helps to remove the conceptual blinders that have prevented presidency scholars from including consideration of gender in their analyses. Some may still ask how women can be included in presidency studies if no woman has run as the nominee of a major party's presidential ticket, let alone served as vice president. Duerst-Lahti's work is particularly enlightening in this regard. In her chapter she includes analysis and discussion of Clinton Rossiter's familiar and classic list of "chiefdoms," as well as the less familiar but more theoretically enlightening construct of comity—useful in understanding the role of the White House staff—and discusses the appropriateness of gender analysis in presidency studies.

In Chapter 3, Piper A. Hodson explores the interesting phenomenon of why women in developing nations have experienced success in selection as a nation's chief executive in spite of the poor records of those same countries in the protection of women's rights. These countries also appear to have religious, social, and economic structures that would work against women's political or social advancement. Hodson examines the case of countries on the South Asian subcontinent where women have been particularly successful in achieving the post of chief executive, drawing upon a comparative framework that examines the socialization of women, the structure of the political system, and the political circumstances of the women leaders in each country to offer insight into how women have achieved the chief executive post in developing states but not in the United States.

Institutional Perspectives:
Women as Officeholders in the Executive Branch

The next section focuses on an institutional perspective. In Chapter 4, Janet M. Martin looks at presidential appointments to Senate-confirmed posts in departments and agencies throughout the executive branch. She builds on the work of David T. Stanley, Dean E. Mann, and Jameson W. Doig, whose study *Men Who Govern* was rather appropriately titled when published in the 1960s but is no longer appropriate in the 1990s.[5] Her database includes appointments from 1961 through the first two years of the Clinton administration, and her analysis adds to our understanding of career paths and the influence of generational change in understanding "Women Who Govern." Martin also examines presidential rhetoric in administrations' efforts to achieve symbolic and descriptive representation.

MaryAnne Borrelli's focus in Chapter 5 is on the president's cabinet and the issue of representation. It has long been observed that the cabinet has a strongly representative function. Borrelli builds on the work of Fenno and other scholars to look at the inclusion of new groups in the cabinet-building process, and she draws on Hanna Pitkin's conceptualization of representation and on the work of feminist theorists to enrich our understanding of descriptive and substantive representation. In particular, Borrelli includes a case study of the Justice Department and the appointment of an attorney general.

In Chapter 6, Kathryn Dunn Tenpas examines the White House Office in the Executive Office of the President, which has grown tremendously in both size and importance in the modern era. Given the importance of the White House Office in its role as adviser and agenda shaper for an administration, it is surprising that no systematic study of women in the White House Office has been done previously. Tenpas carefully identifies historical trends in the numbers and types of offices held by women on the White House staff and considers how these positions affect the women's ability to participate in presidential policymaking.

Foreign policy has long been identified as an area in which presidents play a dominant role, and the secretaries of state and defense serve as members of the president's inner cabinet. Therefore, it is particularly important to examine the inclusion of women in the shaping of foreign and defense policy. In Chapter 7, Nancy E. McGlen and Meredith Reid Sarkees examine the president's appointees and careerists in the Departments of State and Defense, as well as the president's role in setting the tone of an administration with respect to the inclusion of women and women's voices. But most important, this study addresses the management style of a president by examining how recent administrations have structured their foreign policy advising processes: (1) by centering decisionmaking in the White House and elevating the role of a national security adviser over the roles of those in the departments and agencies responsible for foreign policy, (2) by drawing upon and valuing the expertise of careerists in the bureaucracy, or (3) by relying upon the advice and information provided by noncareer political appointees over civil servants. Using case studies of the recent Reagan, Bush, and Clinton administrations, McGlen and Sarkees provide insight into how the leadership styles of presidents influence the extent to which women play a role in the foreign policy decisionmaking process.

Institutional Perspectives:
The President, Congress, and the Courts

In the next section the institutional perspective shifts to examine the president's relationship to the other branches of government—the Congress and the courts. One area that has received scholarly attention has been that of the constitutional role of the Senate to advise and consent to presidential nominations of individuals to head executive branch departments and agencies.[6] In Chapter 8, Jean Reith Schroedel, Sharon Spray, and Bruce D. Snyder examine the confirmation process, taking into account the changing nature of the Senate—which has become more partisan yet highly individualistic— and the shift in recent presidential administrations to make government "look more like America" through executive branch appointments. There is bound to be an inherent tension in these institutional approaches. Schroedel, Spray, and Snyder utilize a case study of the Senate's confirmation of Roberta Achtenberg as an assistant secretary in the Department of Housing and Urban Development to examine the increased politicization of the confirmation process.

In Chapter 9, Richard L. Pacelle, Jr., examines the role of the president in shaping the federal judiciary, an area that has long received both scholarly attention and public scrutiny. The impeachment and removal of federal judges is rare; thus, the judicial selection process becomes crucial. Although the courts avoid political questions, they nonetheless become influential institutional players in setting public policy, especially as a divided government has become the norm in recent decades and policy questions have moved onto the courts' agendas. The inclusion of women and women's voices in the selection process of federal judges and as nominees to the bench becomes critical when issues of policy that directly affect women—including issues of affirmative action, reproductive freedom, and domestic violence—come before the courts.

Policy and Participation:
Women as Executive Activists and as Citizens

The final section of the book addresses issues of participation and public policy, focusing on women as citizens and as executive branch activists. A key player, neglected in scholarly collections on the presidency, is the first lady. Some would argue that it is understandable that first ladies have been excluded from these studies, since they are not subject to election, as are the president and vice president, or subject to Senate confirmation, as are cabinet secretaries; have not attained their position through a meritorious rise up the career civil service hierarchy; and are not even subject to ethics guidelines as paid employees of an administration. Past studies of the presidency, however, have examined the role of "kitchen cabinet" advisers to the president and of the informal advisers brought in for substantive or strategic guidance. In these studies of advising systems, the Office of the First Lady has not received attention as an additional staff structure in the White House that contributes substantively in the policymaking arena. In Chapter 10, Barbara C. Burrell helps to expand the dimensions of examinations of the Executive Office of the President by including consideration of the Office of the First Lady. Given the emphasis of presidency scholars in addressing the symbolism of the White House and the role of formal and informal and hierarchical and collegial staffing arrangements, it is ironic that the Office of the First Lady has been neglected. Burrell provides a systematic analysis of the public policy role and involvement of the first lady and her office as part of the presidential advisory system.

As noted earlier, one way the president can influence judicial decision-making is through appointments to the federal courts. A second means is through the litigation of the solicitor general, the third-ranking post in the Justice Department. The solicitor general acts as the attorney of the government before the federal courts, deciding whether cases in which the U.S. government has been on the losing side should be appealed to the U.S. Court of Appeals or the Supreme Court and when the U.S. government should file an amicus curiae brief in a case before the Court. In fact, the solicitor general is an important player in influencing the Supreme Court's case agenda and its rulings. In Chapter 11, Richard L. Pacelle, Jr., examines the influence of the executive branch in the construction of judicial doctrine in the areas of gender discrimination and reproductive rights policy, through the role of the solicitor general. However, as is the case with cabinet secretaries, who are dependent on a bureaucracy for implementation of policy and on Congress for funds, the solicitor general's influence is shaped by his or her responsibility as an adviser to the Court and as a lawyer for Congress in defending legislation before the Court. Thus, the administration's influence on the Court in the area of women's rights will largely be determined by the solicitor general's office.

Finally, in Chapter 12, Clyde Wilcox explores the issue of a gender gap in political attitudes and partisanship and its implications for presidential elections and governing. Wilcox's study of gender and public opinion is especially important in understanding how presidents and their administrations may consider the interests of women as a group or a voting bloc in making their governing decisions.

Overview

The research in this volume does not represent a single dimension but is, rather, a broad cross section of the areas typically explored by presidency scholars. As a new subfield, scholarship is developing. As can be seen in the brief biographies of the authors included in this volume, however, much of the work presented here is part of larger research agendas that are laying the foundation on which scholarship on women and gender will evolve and develop in presidency studies. In time, the inclusion of women and gender issues will become an established part of the presidency literature, as has happened in the area of congressional studies over the past twenty years.

Notes

1. Barbara Hinckley. 1994. *Less Than Meets the Eye: Foreign Policy Making and the Myth of the Assertive Congress.* Chicago: University of Chicago Press (Twentieth Century Fund), pp. 15–16.
2. Susan J. Carroll. 1985. *Women as Candidates in American Politics.* Bloomington: Indiana University Press, p. xiii.
3. For example, see R. Darcy, Susan Welch, and Janet Clark. 1994. *Women, Elections, and Representation,* 2d ed., revised. Lincoln: University of Nebraska Press; Barbara C. Burrell. 1994. *A Woman's Place Is in the House: Campaigning for Congress in the Feminist Era.* Ann Arbor: University of Michigan Press; and Linda Witt, Karen M. Paget, and Glenna Matthews. 1994. *Running as a Woman: Gender and Power in American Politics.* New York: Free Press. Earlier studies include Kristi Andersen and Stuart Thorson. 1984. "Congressional Turnover and the Election of Women." *Western Political Quarterly* 37: 143–156; Susan Carroll. 1984. "Women Candidates and Support for Feminist Concerns: The Closet Feminist Syndrome." *Western Political Quarterly* 37: 307–323; R. Darcy and Sarah Slavin Schramm. 1977. "When Women Run Against Men." *Public Opinion Quarterly* 41: 1–12; and Diane Kincaid. 1978. "Over His Dead Body: A Positive Perspective on Widows in the U.S. Congress." *Western Political Quarterly* 31: 96–104.
4. For example, see Susan Carroll and Barbara Geiger-Parker. 1983. *Women Appointed to the Carter Administration: A Comparison with Men.* New Brunswick, NJ: Center for the American Woman and Politics, Eagleton Institute of Politics, Rutgers University; and Janet M. Martin. 1989. "The Recruitment of Women to Cabinet and Subcabinet Posts." *Western Political Quarterly* 42: 161–172. In addition, for a study of cabinet secretaries see Sue Tolleson Rinehart. 1988. "Madam Secretary: The Careers of Women in the U.S. Cabinet, 1932–1988." Paper presented at the Annual Meeting of the Southern Political Science Association.
5. David T. Stanley, Dean E. Mann, and Jameson W. Doig. 1967. *Men Who Govern: A Biographical Profile of Federal Political Executives.* Washington, D.C.: Brookings Institution.
6. For example, see G. Calvin Mackenzie. 1981. *The Politics of Presidential Appointments.* New York: Free Press.

PART 1

Theoretical and Comparative Perspectives: Women as Political Executives

2

Reconceiving Theories of Power: Consequences of Masculinism in the Executive Branch

Georgia Duerst-Lahti

More than any other kind of human activity, politics has historically borne an explicitly masculine identity. It has been more exclusively limited to men than any other realm of endeavor and has been more intensely, self-consciously masculine than most other social practices.[1]

With politics rooted in a public-private dichotomy,[2] the kingly patriarchal politics that spawned Locke's liberalism, governance that required a singular head of household, strong links between the military and politics, and more, one is hard-pressed not to agree with Wendy Brown's conclusion that the identity of politics is masculine. Within this masculinized arena, executive political power is arguably the most manly of all areas. Polls regularly show a belief that women have a tougher time winning executive office; the number of female CEOs in major corporations in the United States is a paltry 4 percent; and even casual scans of women's advancement in politics reveal the difficulty women have had penetrating executive levels in the United States. Only thirteen women have ever served as governors of states, and only nine of those were elected in their own right. Similarly, women in top Executive Office of the President posts were a rarity until the Carter administration. Only since the 1980s have women held top posts in trade (Carla Hills), economics (Laura D'Andrea Tyson), and the budget (Alice Rivlin). Only fourteen women have served as cabinet secretaries in U.S. history.

Explanations for the relative paucity of women in executive positions are plentiful. The most common one—the "pipeline effect"—combines time and credentials: Women have had too little time since the societal changes wrought by the women's movement for large numbers of them to develop the needed credentials. This explanation clearly has merit, as two of the three cabinet secretaries in the first term of the Clinton administration served in lesser posts during the Carter administration. Still, one should not ignore centuries of women's exclusion through law, custom, and other social regulations—the vestiges of which make women's full inclusion so difficult

11

today.[3] Students of executive power need to expand their conceptual base to include aspects of gender ideology, particularly the dynamics of masculinism, if they are to understand the paucity of women.

Although some women clearly have entered the prized elite ranks,[4] they have done so within the bounds set by gender ideology. To explore executive power in these terms, three arenas are especially fruitful: structural power arrangements in the executive, the implications of the singular executive leader, and comity. Few who study executive politics also study gender politics, however; thus, an introduction to concepts from the expansive new field of gender studies may be useful for readers in grasping the implications of the argument and the consequences of masculinism in executive power. Without such analysis, the effects of masculinism will continue to operate in an uncritically accepted fashion, and the transformative potential of a polity that is not under the sway of gender ideology will never be realized.

Gender: A Primer

In the past two decades gender analysis has developed into a sophisticated subfield, with gender emerging as a pivotal social concept. Within gender analysis, and critical to this chapter, is the seemingly new awareness that men have gender, too.[5] As a category for analysis, gender is not interchangeable with sex despite the rampant misuse of both terms, especially in quantitative analysis. For categories of analysis, sex denotes the limited knowledge of a respondent as a physiological male or female who presents himself or herself as a man or a woman. Gender, in contrast, is *relational:* To understand feminine requires understanding masculine.

Gender categories elaborate on the meaning of being in the category of male or female or of breaking the boundaries of the "given" sexes as a gay or a lesbian. Understanding the implications of gender is essential for understanding executive power because gender reveals that a female cannot enter a post previously held by a male and be entirely interchangeable with him—in meaning at least. Whereas job performance might be equally meritorious and the tasks performed the same, *gender shapes interpretation.* To acknowledge this fact does not diminish current "receptivity" toward women in positions of executive power. Rather, it accounts for the fact that as individuals shaped by society we still must contend with stored knowledge about "men" and about "women."

Much of gender analysis has focused on behaviors, roles, or traits and their appropriateness for males or females. This analysis grows out of structural-functional frameworks and, especially, strictly demarcated sex roles seen as complementary.[6] In this framework culture imposes "appropriate" behavior or conduct. To act outside of prescribed norms is to deviate from cultural standards and to "cross over" sex-role boundaries. Much of feminist activism has been directed toward opening options to women under a system that has dramatically constrained women's "proper" conduct.[7] Although enormous societal change has occurred since 1970 in terms of gender prescriptions, gender dualism remains deeply embedded in cultural expectations.

All of this suggests that political science must reconsider the use of the concept "gender neutral" in research findings and in thinking generally.[8] The term "gender neutral" is usually used to indicate that men and women report the same answer on a survey or achieve no statistical difference on some quantitative measure. But neutrality implies that gender has no effect, that it is indifferent or takes no part in interpretations of the behavior. One example illustrates the flaw in believing gender is neutral.

Consider a questionnaire about management style in which both women and men rate themselves as assertive at the same level, say, an average of 4.1 on a 5-point scale. This result would usually be reported as "gender neutral." Given societal changes, the boundaries of appropriate behavior for women now include assertiveness; finding female managers to be equally as assertive as male managers clearly represents a change from past gender constructions. Nonetheless, concluding that gender is indifferent or neutral to an assertive woman or an assertive man is simply inaccurate. Because of prior gender constructions, a woman's behavior is judged from an expectation of passivity, with assertiveness resting at the far boundary of acceptable conduct. In contrast, a man's behavior is judged from an expectation of aggressiveness, so assertive behavior is near the passive end of the continuum of appropriate behavior for him. Thoughts about male nurses or the distinction between "mothering" and "fathering" also illustrate different and gendered meanings. Gender is not neutral.

The concept of *transgendered* captures the dynamic of interpretation far better than does gender neutrality. The term implies that a biological male or female can cross past gender constructions and still be seen as appropriate, but it also implies that gender simultaneously continues to shape interpretations. Few doubt today, for example, that women and men can both serve well on school boards, although we might still expect men to gravitate toward the mechanics of building projects and women toward curricular matters. This distinction is crucial for understanding masculinism in executive power and for explaining why males and females are not fully interchangeable, in meaning at least.

Another closely related concept is *regendering,* or the reinscription of gender dualism in circumstances in which gender roles have broadened, weakened, or otherwise changed. With regendering, when a male has crossed into an occupation previously gendered as feminine or a female into a once-masculine occupation, conditions that were once strictly same sex no longer apply, and the practice of the occupation has gender reimposed upon it. This occurs even though no physiological reason exists to do so. Elaine Hall has written of the practice of requiring female Marine officers to undergo training in proper makeup while in dress uniform as an example of regendering a practice that no longer has a same-sex population.[9] In this case, femininity is reimposed upon women who cross into masculine practice, and female Marines become regendered. These women are not Marines but female Marines, with gender dualism reimposed by rules and practices.

These dynamics occur because gender is also a set of practices, a performance, something we "do."[10] As such, gender need not even be attached to a sex-specified human body. Transvestites and cross-dressers illustrate the point, as men, for example, don feminine garb and take on feminine body language and affectations. We all "perform" gender when we dress for the day and conduct our lives as men and women. And most of us do it willingly because these norms have become part of our own self-image and identity. Early in Clinton's term, some suggested that his presidency was suffering because he had not performed adequately as a "commanding" figure, with command being tied to manliness.

Importantly for executive power, gender is a set of practices and thus can be attached to the practices and not necessarily to the person doing the practice. Being a foot soldier is strongly gendered as masculine, but women in the military do many tasks only a whisker away from foot soldiering despite the resistance to women engaging in armed combat. The gender construction of any practice can change, and such changes often correspond with a redistribution of the "given" sex of those undertaking the practice.[11]

Posts in the executive branch are also gendered and can become regendered with changes in cultural interpretations. As long as the practice of being a public executive is gendered masculine, masculine privileges accompany the practice even as it is modified by transgendering and regendering processes. Whether these posts will become revalued remains to be seen.

Finally, much has been written about the relationship between gender and power. Often such writing suggests that men have the latitude to couple difference with dominance and to structure societal norms and belief systems to male advantage. Although this may be accurate, it is simplistic. Challenges to this characterization are easy to find and are often raised by the men's rights movement. Child custody awards in divorces, in which the mother has power superior to that of the father, or women's latitude to not be employed while also not being seen as failures provide examples. If women have power advantages in these circumstances, then they likely do in others as well; and if gender provides women with more power than men in some circumstances, then the larger claim of men's superior power can be refuted. Thus, if men's power is not absolute, then women can enter various power arenas by matching the positional demands. Executive power is such an arena.[12] Clearly, analysis of gender and power is complex.

The concept of gender power provides a more potent analytic tool than sexism or male dominance—commonly used analytic concepts—as it captures varied and fluid situational power. *Gender power* results from our (e)valuations of things and behaviors, of ways of being, behaving, and structuring social relations. Gender power permeates and follows from all facets of human interaction, operating at interpersonal levels and within institutions and social categories. Normative gender power shapes normative assessments as well. Gender power varies in every situation but can be identified and analyzed in any particular setting.

Important for executive power is the recognition that gender provides varying and alternative modes of power depending upon the situation. With this recognition, gender power might be greater for women in policy areas more closely aligned with feminine gender categories such as health and human services. Similarly, gender constructs for the military are highly masculine, so men would find gender power advantages in that area (see Chapter 7). And both of these exist within a larger framework of gender power in the executive branch because the concept also enables us to probe the differential possibilities of gender power in alternative settings of politics, contrasting the legislature with the executive, the House with the Senate, and so on.

Masculinism: Gender as Ideology

Kenneth Hoover has asserted that ideology is based on three elements: beliefs about human nature, normative decisions about the best way to structure power given those beliefs about humans, and a plan of action to put that structure into place.[13] Ideology is always connected to apparatus and practice—that is, to the actions that implement the structure. But what has this to do with masculinism?

The ideological concomitant to feminism is masculinism.[14] Masculinism operates as the guiding ideology of political life today and is difficult to deny once the possibility of its existence has been given any thought. An understanding of masculinism will help us understand the politics it shapes. Because of the nature of executive power, as is elaborated later, masculinism is particularly important, as it places men at the center of executing the form of public power that carries the most discretion,[15] much as it did with warrior kings of old.

Both masculinism and feminism fit within gender as an ideological structure. Feminists have long identified arrangements in which men (pre)dominate power resources and control power positions as ideological. For several decades, feminists have labeled the extant arrangements as patriarchy. These arrangements can be seen as the practices or actions that extend from decisions about who is suited to exercise political power, structure, and apparatus in the form of institutions and constitutions that shape the authority, laws, and rules that follow from those decisions. Under patriarchy, or the rule of fathers, men made decisions about the best way to structure power, who was suited to exercise that power, and the conditions under which it would be exercised.

Masculinism is a better name than patriarchy for the political ideology that structures current arrangements. Masculinism fits within the "structure of gender as ideology and myth," in which gender as ideology is relatively autonomous and hegemonic and is reinforced through an elaborate system of rules and punishments.[16] Laws that exclude women from political power, cultural practices that set norms and create the meanings of gender difference, and vestiges of past practice that spill over into present expectations constitute choices about human nature, power distribution, and the apparatus of masculinist ideology.

Masculinism as an ideology has been largely invisible, masking itself well, as any successful dominant ideology does. As Louis Althusser has elaborated, ideology "is profoundly unconscious" and functions through processes that escape those acted upon even as it functions to constitute its subjects.[17] Masculinism's cover runs deep in that only in recent decades has gender become a concept of social analysis.

Further, the clear conceptualization of masculinism as political ideology has been thwarted by the way political science has treated feminism as ideology. Throughout its evolution, feminism has been treated by most of political science as a political ideology comparable to liberalism, socialism, and the like—when it has been treated at all. Yet by the early 1980s, texts on feminist thought detailed variants of feminism that subsume these other ideologies: liberal feminism, socialist feminism, and so on. If feminism subsumes these ideologies, then how can it simultaneously be equivalent to them?

Feminism might more aptly be thought of as an overarching political meta-ideology that has approached political ideology from a gynocentric (women-centered) perspective rather than from the androcentric (man-centered) starting point of masculinism.[18] And if feminism subsumes well-known ideologies, it can logically be located in the ideological spectrum only as a political meta-ideology. If we assume feminism would not distribute political *dominance* to men,[19] then only another meta-ideology explains a distribution of power that favors men across all acknowledged ideologies except feminism. That ideology is masculinism, and masculinism fits within the larger framework of gender ideology.

Gender, then, is simultaneously ideology, categories of analysis, roles, a set of practices, and a source of power in its own right. With this tentative beginning, I now turn to an analysis of the executive branch and power.

The Executive Branch and Aspects of Power

When political scientists think about power in the executive branch, they usually focus on the president; the Executive Office of the President and its hub, the White House staff; and executive departments and agencies; and in passing they acknowledge a "kitchen cabinet." Power, however, is not uniform across various parts of the executive branch.

Each part of the executive branch has its own source of legitimate power, and the quality of that power varies greatly across parts. The president, or chief executive, holds the authority vested in an institution as well as in a person. The president is seen as the most powerful person in the world, at least in the textbook presidency.[20] The post holds considerable, if diminishing, referent power or public prestige.[21] From the post, a president has the power to persuade.[22] The position carries enormous constitutional authority derived from vague language and broad interpretation of powers over time and fueled by the use of extraconstitutional powers in times of crisis.[23] The paucity of precise constitutional limits on presidential power is consistent with the discretion often vested in executives.[24] Discretion, coupled with structural resources, provides a tremendous capacity to reward or coerce.

Important in presidential power are administrative units of the executive branch, most notably departments and agencies. These units have little constitutional basis; they derive their status by necessity and tradition from the single clause that the president "shall execute" laws. Somewhat ironically, the minor constitutional foundation for administrative agencies is greater than that which can be claimed by other executive institutions. In 1937 the Brownlow Committee issued its call that "the president needs help," and the staff posts of the Executive Office of the President (EOP) were born. This move began a continuing trend to centralize power in the White House.[25] The move has also had the effect, as Francis Rourke has described, of "presidentializing the bureaucracy."[26] And with the increased size and power of the EOP came the need to manage it—hence, the development of the White House staff[27] and the conversion of personal roles into institutional roles.[28] To manage an entire set of close advisers, the chief of staff was established, and the position's powers then expanded greatly.[29] With such concentrated power, "kitchen cabinet" advisers become the check on the chief of staff, as Nancy Reagan made evident with Donald Regan.

Some power dynamics are especially important within this enormous framework. Access to the president remains a source of power across all parts of the executive branch, with greater access providing more power. Differences among the power of cabinet departments are well-known, with State, Treasury, Defense, and Justice constituting the more powerful inner cabinet and all other departments relegated to the less prominent outer cabinet. Considerable EOP power flows from high levels of information, expertise, and access.

In terms of organization theory, the EOP functions as a direct extension of the president, much as the staff in Congress. John Hart has also argued that comity diminishes congressional oversight, with members understanding the need for personally loyal followers.[30] Because, as Chester Barnard noted long ago, the executive functions as a hub of communication,[31] the White House staff also derives power from the control of information. The "kitchen cabinet" derives its power from personal more than political sources—usually from long-standing friendships or other relationships, access, and trust. The members of a "kitchen cabinet" have no formal power and risk major criticism if they assume some, as became clear with health care and Hillary Rodham Clinton's assumption of a formal role in the Health Care Task Force (see Chapter 10).

Clearly, power manifests itself in multiple ways within the executive branch. This simple yet complex observation suggests that gender power also will manifest itself in multiple ways.

Women as the "Other" in Executive Power

The executive branch is arguably the most masculine branch of the government for several reasons.[32] Historically, executive power evolved from the close relationship between the military and the bureaucracy: The Anglo-Saxon nobleman and his warriors fought for the nobleman's expansion and control of territory. With the prospering of the nobleman came the prospering of the warriors, who could also become noble with success and sufficient fealty to the original lord.[33] The warrior king tradition precedes even Anglo-Saxon times and permeates politics generally, as Wendy Brown has detailed. Overlaying the military roots of executive power rests Weberian rationality, which also draws upon masculinity.[34] In both come a particular concern for domination consistent with constructions of manliness.[35]

The executive branch's power structure tends to be organized in a centralized, functionally distributed, and hierarchical arrangement. Certain behaviors accompany that structure. Consistent with this structure, the presidency operates on the great man model of leadership. Concomitant to both is the pervasive but elusive spirit of *comitatus,* a camaraderie that creates particular demands.

Much of executive power is derived from what we want from executives. In contrast, legislatures are fragmented, decentralized, laterally arranged, and intentionally slow because they are intended to be deliberative.[36] Executive power is characterized by unity of command, hierarchical arrangements, and—with centralized control—a capacity to act quickly and decisively when circumstances dictate.[37]

These factors create circumstances in which women are understood as "other" in contrast to a masculine norm, and they do so in a way that is predictable inside gender ideology. In a system constructed under masculinism, one would predict that the greater the power available in any particular part of the executive branch, the fewer women we will find. We would also expect women to emerge first and most often in functional areas associated with women and second in less powerful outer cabinets.[38] Because gender is constructed, however, it is fluid and subject to transgendering, regendering, and revaluation. As should become evident, particular factors produce gendered obstacles for women and opportunities for men.

Executive Branch Structure and Gender Power

Two aspects of the structural arrangements of the executive branch are most important for considerations of women's penetration of executive power: the regard for hierarchy and the functional distribution of agency work. Georgia Duerst-Lahti and Cathy Marie Johnson found that men in bureaucracies seem to expect and respect hierarchy much more than women, even though executive women also expect and understand how hierarchy works.[39] The point is simply that hierarchical modes of organizing accord more closely with masculinity than with femininity. Women are less likely to be seen by others as appropriate for top posts, at least in part because they are less likely than men to be present in the hierarchical chain of command.

But even more important than hierarchy is functional distribution. Women populate administrative agencies; often, nearly half of employees are female. However, women are not commonly found in command positions (e.g., administrators) within the executive branch because command posts do not accord with feminine gender expectations. Women are much more likely to be found in staff units or staff positions (clerical, bookkeeping, and so on) within line units. As such, they have little access to structural power resources—for example, authority to make critical decisions, to manage budgets, or to supervise personnel.

Critically, function is highly gendered. Gender influences what is seen as most valuable and hence as most powerful, as well as where women are most likely to enter executive power. As Meredith Newman demonstrated, even the way we think about policy areas and conditions in the agencies that administer them is shaped by masculinist assumptions.[40] Under masculinism, one would expect women's entrance to occur first in the least powerful parts of the executive agencies.

The inner cabinet departments related to the functions of State, Defense, Treasury, and Justice are considered the most important and most powerful. For this reason, the appointment of Janet Reno as attorney general had particular significance—she was the first woman to head an inner cabinet department. Because of gender power under masculinism, one would predict women's gains would occur largely in the outer cabinet.

However big in budget and personnel and however crucial to the lives of most Americans, the Department of Health and Human Services is frequently and narrowly characterized as the overseer of welfare and faces popular disfavor and congressional attacks as a result. Several women have headed the department, thus gaining access to the power of size but operating within the confines of an unpopular mission. Similarly, women have a history of heading the Department of Labor, but labor is less prominent in a system that favors capital. Since 1987, studies have confirmed the hypothesis that women will succeed best in agencies most consistent with gender expectations such as health, education, welfare, or other functions with which we associate women.[41]

Any appointment of a woman to a top post is important for changing gender power in the executive branch because each appointment contributes to changes in gender expectations and offers the opportunity to transform gender power. With a woman's appointment, the barrier of men's exclusive hold on the top executive posts is broken, and because of transgendering or regendering processes the office becomes less masculinized. Only time will reveal whether any post will become regendered into "a woman's post" or become transgendered, with an easy rotation of men and women serving as secretary. Predictably, women tend to repeat in posts either because the posts are originally seen as consistent with women or because once a woman has held the post it becomes regendered. It is not surprising, then, that Ann Dore McLaughlin, Elizabeth Dole, and Lynn Martin were appointed secretaries of the Department of Labor; they followed Frances Perkins by nearly half a century.[42]

Given all this, women's presence in top posts that have never been held by a woman and in agencies consistent with masculine expectations count as the most important gains. Because practices themselves are gendered, the possibility of achieving transgendered understandings is greatest with the first female appointment to a highly masculinized policy area.[43] The appointments of Elizabeth Dole as secretary of transportation and Hazel O'Leary as secretary of energy are therefore crucial and merit long-term study. These nominations upset our gender expectations more than the appointment of Donna Shalala as secretary of health and human services. Theories about executive power need to incorporate these gendered dimensions.

Only time will show whether women in top executive posts will remain the "other elites." If transgendering occurs, women will be seen as "normal" executive elites, and presumably over time the fact that they are not men will become unremarkable. The day a woman chairs the Joint Chiefs of Staff will mark such a time. Sheila Widnall's service as secretary of the air force in the Clinton administration demonstrates movement in the direction of transgendering even within the military.

Alternatively, regendering may occur. Regendering offers at least two options. Certain top executive posts might become associated so strongly with women that they become "the woman's slot." The attorney general position can be used for illustration. In terms of power, the attorney general continues to be seen as a crucial and close adviser to the president, and the Department of Justice remains within the inner cabinet. The value of the post remains high and unchanged.

The second option for regendering involves revaluation. Conceivably, the Department of Transportation might become "a woman's post," and the department could enter the inner cabinet. In this case, the post is regendered to the feminine, and its executive power increases. This scenario is unlikely both because of transportation policy's significance and because transportation is generally perceived to be a man's policy area. It is much easier to imagine a post becoming regendered to the feminine and then losing power. The attorney general, for example, could become "a woman's post," and concurrently the department could lose executive power by having its budget cut, its authority narrowed, its prestige diminished, and so on.

This revaluation exhibits the "contamination effect" described by Marxist feminists in the mid-1980s. The basic premise is that highly valued and prestigious work loses status once women perform it; the work becomes gendered in a way that is other than fully masculine and loses value in the process. Whereas cause and effect are often impossible to disentangle, work performed by women is reported as lesser in some way. Using this framework, one fears the post of ambassador to the United Nations—a post held by two women—has become less valued over time. Alternatively, we might conclude that two women have held this post because it is the least prestigious of all foreign affairs posts.[44] In any case, over time we will be able to map the relationship between gender and executive power.

The Chief Chief

A major arena of inquiry into the problems women experience in penetrating the executive branch focuses on the ultimate head of the executive branch as a single leader. Clinton Rossiter's classic list of presidential duties serves as a useful illustration: Chief of State, Chief Executive, Chief Diplomat, Commander-in-Chief, Chief Legislator, Chief of the Party, Voice of the People, Protector of the Peace, Manager of Prosperity, Leader of the Free World.[45] Whereas Rossiter, like many who have built on him, acknowledges the distance between constitutional and statutory powers and actual responsibilities, the titles themselves reveal the masculine assumption.

The term *chief* is seldom associated with traditional women's work, and women as commanders are even more rare. The "protector" role has been almost exclusively a masculine endeavor, beyond the image of a mother protecting her children. "Voice" is only recently something women have been known to have, although surely women have always spoken, often in very public ways. As advertising agencies and female candidates are well aware, authoritative voices are still ceded far more readily to men. This factor also figures centrally into a president's prime power: the power to persuade.[46] The elements that assist persuasion—such as a professional reputation, being seen as a commanding presence, and associated elements of public prestige—are also attributed more readily to men.

Imagining a female chief is sufficiently difficult; imagining a woman as the chief of all chiefs is even more difficult. The masculinist assumption-made-normal is strong and is made even stronger when it goes unnoticed for its gendered aspects.

In terms of our thinking about leadership, this singularity accords with the "great man" model. In this gendered construction of a singular leader, cause and effect are blurred and reinforcing; nevertheless, cultural constructions much more readily accord the possibility of individual accomplishment deserving of greatness—accomplishments earned in one's own right, without regard to connections or support—to men. Gender power gives the advantage to men in terms of the "great man" model of the lone leader at the top. In contrast, women are challenged in at least two ways: in the belief that a woman is or can be singular and in the possibility of be(com)ing "great."

Further, gender power arrangements make it far easier for men to become "great" in valued accomplishments and then to be seen as "great" by society. Since the mid-1960s, when such analysis was first conducted, training and occupational tracks for women have remained remarkably constrained. Although the percentage has dropped some, 80 percent of working women are still employed in twenty of nearly four hundred occupational categories.[47] This channeling of women largely eliminates 80 percent of working women from potential "greatness" and contributes to making the other 20 percent aberrations. And even though in March 1986 women constituted a majority in managerial positions for the first time in history, this change was achieved through most being managers within traditional feminine realms. These categories tend to be low paying, a critical signal of societal valuation of work.

One critical area in which women are not yet found in significant numbers is the military, particularly in combat roles, and this has ramifications for being perceived as "executive material." Important in presidential considerations is the value placed on military service in creating the image of presidential merit. Bill Clinton continues to suffer from not having a military record; he is the first modern president without military service.

Perhaps the most striking contrast of divergent gender interpretation can be found in the importance of connections or, said another way, in the myth that "great men" act alone.[48] The problem for women, however, is that men are assumed to be entitled to a helpmate wife who seldom threatens his stature, whereas a woman can have a helpmate only under unusual circumstances and in most cases will not be seen as uninfluenced by him.[49] This might be thought of as the assumption of autonomy for men and of heteronomy for women.[50] For example, 1984 Democratic vice-presidential candidate Geraldine Ferraro received severe scrutiny in her own right and emerged relatively unscathed. But her husband had some questionable dealings, and his actions were easily turned into an inordinately poor reflection of her. Clearly, with Hillary Rodham Clinton, attempts are under way to make the spousal reflection a transgendered reality. Paradoxically, however, to do so would mean acknowledging the power of presidential wives, which is itself upsetting.

These occurrences reflect, among others, vestiges of ideology made into law that placed the man as the head of the household and hence identified him as the singular important political actor. To some extent, it matters little that legally men are no longer automatically heads of households, as in Locke's day; the tradition continues as a powerful influence. Women struggle to be known as independent actors, whereas men are known as little else—even when they themselves acknowledge the supportive connections that make their performance possible. Although we cannot know if most women would choose a greater emphasis on connections if they had not been legally mandated to do so, we can conclude that the lone woman at the top has not yet become a transgendered image.

Comity, or the Palace Is Not Guarded by Women

Many scholars of the presidency worry about the centralization of power in the White House staff. Much of the danger rests in the inability to control the large number of staff—in excess of four hundred—who can wield the powerful words "the president wants" at least some of the time. Given this problem of accountability, trust and loyalty are essential. In such uncertainty, how are trust and loyalty assured? Comity, with its roots in *comitatus*, provides a crucial, if poorly understood, answer. And again, vestiges of the warrior king can be found in executive power.

> [The Anglo-Saxon] nobleman formed a group of warriors around him in an exclusive relationship known as the *comitatus*. He chose them to protect his lands and acquire new ones; they chose him to protect their lives and acquire status in their own realms. The symbiosis became known as the spirit of the *comitatus:* a special relationship of absolute, to-the-death fealty and archetypical camaraderie.[51]

Inside the contemporary presidency, we find such comity among the White House staff. The staff is often referred to as the "palace guard" or the "praetorian guard" because of its role of gatekeeper to the president.[52]

According to John Hart, comity is an understudied concept in political science. He says, "There is something elusive about it. Members of

Congress rarely discuss comity. It is quietly accepted by most of them and mentioned only when the 'informal understanding' is being challenged."[53] For issues of executive power, we need to understand how individuals become part of the trusted and loyal *comitatus*. For questions of the other elites, we need to understand how gender power operates within the comity of the White House staff. Few women presently gain power from the ability to say "the president wants."

Executive power is marked by discretion, and considerable ambiguity accompanies discretion. Because of this ambiguity, objectively determining who to trust is difficult. As Rosabeth Moss Kanter has found for such positions in organizations more generally, one of the best ways to select trusted others is to select those most like oneself.[54] Whereas many aspects of human existence contribute to high levels of comfort with another person, in a culture that constructs gender difference, comfort levels often increase in the homosociable conditions of the same sex. As long as the president is a man, he is likely to feel somewhat more comfortable around other men; because such comfort contributes to being selected for trust in conditions of ambiguity, women will continue to confront the problem of not being "like" the president. Women must find other grounds for entering the comity of the White House staff.

Within the White House staff, behavior is often characterized by loyalty bordering on sycophancy, arrogance, energy, ambition, and aggressiveness.[55] These traits should be considered for their gendered aspects. Some may be transgendered: Both women and men can be loyal, and both can be seen as highly energetic. Even though the interpretations may not be synonymous for women and men, neither would be seen as inappropriate.

On the other hand, arrogance, ambition, and aggressiveness are traits that carry negative connotations and hence are antistereotypes that shape women's behavior.[56] Even very talented and ambitious women seem to shy away from being seen as having too much of any of these traits, perhaps because they have been penalized for them in the past. If such traits are characteristic of White House staff and women have learned to avoid them, fitting into staff posts becomes difficult. The need to avoid certain behaviors is exacerbated by token status. With only token numbers of women in key posts, aggressive, ambitious, arrogant women find few others to confirm the appropriateness of their behavior.

The ability to retain power within the executive branch has been further exacerbated by another condition: Women become easy targets because men are less likely to see them as comrades. And as tokens, they lack female comrades; hence, they lack the "comraderie" so important to *comitatus*.

Gender analysis might further conclude that, by tradition, presidents have understood the need for loyal warriors to protect them. For those who protect the chief of all chiefs the stakes are highest, the power the greatest, and the elusive spirit of *comitatus* the strongest. Something more than a "boy's network" operates in comity. More study needs to be done of that spirit and its implications for women in the executive.

Consequences of Masculinism in Executive Power

Whereas ideally gender ideology will cease to dictate social constructs and hence social and political practices, the present imbalance between masculinism and feminism as determinants of gender power in politics creates immediate consequences. In more concrete terms, the consequences of masculinism in executive power include the following:

- *Loss of talent as the pool of those who aspire to work in positions that carry executive power is greatly diminished.*[57] With a substantial portion of the workforce directed away from executive power for reasons outlined previously, the nation loses a substantial portion of talent and hence experiences a loss of performance.
- *A constrained worldview that limits the framing of problems and their possible solutions to a narrow set of experiences.* With the full participation of women in executive power—much like changes found repeatedly in studies of legislative policy processes[58]—the agenda will shift, different options will emerge, and the possibility of deploying finite resources will improve. Worldviews may also change.
- *The legitimacy of the government itself.* As an increasing number of women participate as full citizens in the U.S. polity, the absence of visibly powerful women in the executive branch will increasingly create cynicism and disillusionment toward the government. The apparent symbolic importance of appointing at least some women to cabinet or other visible posts speaks to presidents' awareness of this dynamic,[59] as does heightened senatorial scrutiny (see Chapters 5 and 8). Making the body politic look like its citizenry has important implications for the legitimacy conferred upon the government (see Chapter 4) and for the support an administration garners among women.[60]
- *The future of gender relations, power relations, and the possibilities for transforming human interaction.* Minimally, women in visible positions of executive power provide role models for girls and boys alike.[61] More immediately, the absence of women in such positions perpetuates the belief that women are not qualified simply because male decisionmakers are not associated with them as collegial equals. *Comitatus* will continue to follow gendered lines unless the sustained experiences that build shared loyalties occur.

With a reinforcing pattern in place, masculinism remains a guiding force, an effective and largely invisible force that structures the polity and power within it. It is possible to move beyond the "masculine system" created by John Adams and the other founding fathers.[62]

Implications of "The Other Elites"

Women in the executive branch presently can—perhaps must—be seen as the "other elites." This construction, of course, posits the current occupants as the normal elites from which women as other are demarcated; it is a construct consistent with masculinism. Assuming that readers are not willful sexists who want to perpetuate a polity based on a gender power advantage for men, then the necessary first step toward developing another ideological foundation is to bring masculinist ideology into consciousness.[63] Unless the present "elites"—those with the least incentive to do so—acknowledge masculinism's existence, arrival at a different arrangement will be impossible—at least without coercive revolution.

The gender power of executive power will change only when a gender power balance permeates society and the polity. Full transformation, in the end, requires that gender power itself must become irrelevant because gender is no longer fixed into two "opposites," even if differences persist. Differences will need to flow along multiple individualized lines rather than mythically constructed gender opposites. Such is indeed part of the radical potential of liberalism, if liberalism is able to move beyond its inherent shortcomings.[64] Because gender is so deeply embedded in our consciousness that it is largely unconscious, transformation to a genuinely gender-irrelevant world will be an extraordinarily complicated and extended historical process.

Part of the process of transforming executive power clearly includes moving more women into "elite" executive positions for the reasons delineated earlier. As the number of women in visible positions of executive power increases, vigilance must be directed toward the interpretation of their presence. To make gender truly irrelevant, women's work as executive power wielders must be transgendered rather than regendered. If we allow regendering to occur, women's executive power work will unfortunately only succumb to different but still lesser (e)valuations. Through conscious efforts to create interpretations of executive women's work as transgendered—appropriate for both men and women—the boundaries of gender will expand. Even as gender continues to shape interpretation of male and female executive behavior, the importance of gender is weakened. Experience with more women in powerful positions should, over time, make powerful executive women unremarkable; that in itself will be an indicator of progress. Interacting with pervasive societal transgenderings, such a progression within executive power should produce conditions that truly transform thinking and relegate gender to the nonmeaningful.

Notes

1. Wendy Brown. 1988. *Manhood and Politics: A Feminist Reading in Political Theory*. Totowa, N.J.: Rowman and Littlefield, p. 4.

2. Jean Bethke Elshtain. 1993. *Public Man, Private Woman: Women in Social and Political Thought*, 2d ed. Princeton, N.J.: Princeton University Press.

3. Martha Minow. 1990. *Making All the Difference: Inclusion, Exclusion, and American Law*. Ithaca: Cornell University Press.

4. Kathleen Hall Jamieson. 1995. *Beyond the Double Bind: Women and Leadership*. New York: Oxford University Press.

5. Georgia Duerst-Lahti and Rita Mae Kelly, eds. 1995. *Gender Power, Leadership, and Governance*. Ann Arbor: University of Michigan Press. Because men have set the standard under masculinism, women are marked as having gender in contrast to normal humans—that is, men. As a result, gender analysis frequently focuses on women to the exclusion of men, leaving the impression ("knowledge") that only women have gender.

6. See ibid., chapter 2.

7. This is especially true of liberal feminism. Marxist feminism assumes that women have open options but that women are not compensated for the "reproduction of labor power"—that is, work at home—and hence would never attain an equal share of public power. Priorities and assumptions vary widely across strands of feminism but are not surprising, given knowledge of the other political ideologies.

8. For an example in which Cathy Johnson and I used "gender neutral" in this inappropriate manner, see Georgia Duerst-Lahti and Cathy Marie Johnson. 1990. "Gender and Style in Bureaucracy." *Women and Politics* 10(4): 67–120.

9. Elaine Hall. 1993. "Waitering/Waitressing: Engendering the Work of Table Servers." *Gender and Society* 7(3): 329–346.

10. Joan Acker. 1990. "Hierarchies, Jobs, Bodies: A Theory of Gendered Organizations." *Gender and Society* 4(2): 139–158; ibid.; and Judith Lorber. 1993. "Believing Is Seeing: Biology as Ideology." *Gender and Society* 7(4): 568–581.

11. For example, the practice of changing a baby's diaper has become transgendered in recent years, understood as normal for mothers and a demonstration of sensitivity for fathers.

12. The "proper" interpretation of advances for women is highly contested terrain within feminism. Take the case of a few women moving into executive posts, for example. If women must "out-masculine the males" to hold the positions and their numbers remain too few to constitute a critical mass for substantial change, then women's advance is arguably illusory, and their presence in executive posts results in a token co-optation that distracts from the larger effort of societal transformation. A contrary argument, probably the one most widely accepted outside of feminism, assumes that individual women must advance if all women are to advance. Without role models to pioneer the way, and women in positions of power and influence, the historical process of change will be extended dramatically. Women in power can and will make changes for all women, and the process begins with small advances. This debate, which has been primarily but not exclusively between radical and liberal feminists, has been highly divisive within feminism. For a poignant explanation, see Andrea Dworkin. 1988. *Letters from a War Zone*. New York: E. P. Dutton. See also Duerst-Lahti and Kelly, eds., *Gender Power, Leadership, and Governance*.

13. Kenneth Hoover. 1994. *Ideology and Political Life*, 2d ed. Belmont, Calif.: Wadsworth Publishing. For a cogent and sophisticated analysis of gender as ideology and myth that draws on Gramsci, Barthes, Durkheim, and Foucault, see Judith Grant. 1993. *Fundamental Feminism: Contesting the Core Concepts of Feminist*

Theory. New York: Routledge, especially pp. 160–184. See also Louis Althusser. 1979. *For Marx,* trans. Ben Brewster. London: Verso, p. 170; Roland Barthes. 1972. *Mythologies,* trans. Annette Lavers. New York: Noonday Press, pp. 109–159; Emile Durkheim. 1983. *Durkheim and the Law,* ed. Steven Lukes and Andrew Scull. Oxford: Basil Blackwell; Michel Foucault. 1979. *Discipline and Punishment: The Birth of the Prison.* New York: Vintage; and Antonio Gramsci. 1971. "State and Civil Society." In *Selections from the Prison Notebooks of Antonio Gramsci,* trans. Quintin Hoare and Geoffrey Nowell Smith. New York: International Publishers.

14. The term *masculinism* has emerged in the literature (e.g., Wendy Brown, Christine Di Stefano) as the rubric for an ideology that assumes men should control most power resources, although I have found no full treatment of it. The exact concomitants for ideology derived from females and males would be femininism and masculinism, or feminism and masculism. One can readily imagine distinctions that should be made between these rubrics. Since most works on theories of masculinity (e.g., Clatterbaugh, Brod) include conservatives such as George Gilder within masculinist thought, then femininism would also include Phyllis Schlafly and Beverly LaHaye within its thought. Many within feminism have cringed at the ready parallels between "feminine feminists" (Judith Grant's term), who focus on women's different voice and projects to revalue the feminine, and antifeminists like Schlafly, who defend clearly demarcated sex roles. Because the ideas of Schlafly and LaHaye are antifeminist (and arguably masculinist), they clearly should not be categorized as feminist. Yet, both claim that realms of female superiority (e.g., morality) and power for women through motherhood, control of sexual encounters and hence of men, and so on must be accounted for within gender ideology, thus recommending the value of femininism as a concept. The contours of masculist thought, in contrast to masculinist thought, have not yet solidified; masculists are often considered to be male feminists. The place of both masculinism and femininism within some form of humanism needs further contemplation. Theories of sexuality that start from homosexuality disrupt gender concepts even more. Theorizing political ideologies in these terms is nascent. For an extended discussion of these ideas, see Duerst-Lahti and Kelly, eds., *Gender Power, Leadership, and Governance;* Brown, *Manhood and Politics;* Kenneth Clatterbaugh. 1990. *Contemporary Perspectives on Masculinity: Men, Women, and Politics in Modern Society.* Boulder, Colo.: Westview Press; Christine Di Stefano. 1991. *Configurations on Masculinity: A Feminist Perspective on Modern Political Theory.* Ithaca: Cornell University Press; and Grant, *Fundamental Feminism.*

15. Charles Funderburk. 1982. *Presidents and Politics: The Limits of Power.* Monterey, Calif.: Brooks/Cole Publishing Company.

16. Grant, *Fundamental Feminism,* p. 160.

17. Althusser, *For Marx,* p. 233.

18. Many feminists would not agree with this characterization, as feminists have long disagreed about the defining elements of feminism. These disagreements support my contention that feminism is a meta-ideology that subsumes other acknowledged political ideologies. Only radical feminism has attempted to create theory outside the boundaries of known political ideology. For a discussion of fundamental feminism, see Grant, *Fundamental Feminism.*

19. Strands of feminist thought vary on how they would distribute power to men. Liberal feminists generally advocate sharing power equally with men, whereas cultural feminists tend to see women's approach as superior and hence generally favor giving women more power in public decisionmaking. Other emphases also exist. None, however, would give men dominance. Masculinist gendered social statuses are decidedly different from those feminism would construct.

20. Thomas Cronin. 1980. *The State of the Presidency,* 2d ed. Boston: Little, Brown.

21. Richard E. Neustadt. 1990. *Presidential Power and the Modern Presidents: The Politics of Leadership from Roosevelt to Reagan.* New York: Free Press. See especially chapters 1 and 5.

22. Ibid. See especially chapter 3.

23. Barbara Hinckley. 1985. *Problems of the Presidency: A Text with Readings.* Glenview, Ill.: Scott, Foresman.

24. Funderburk, *Presidents and Politics,* p. 192.

25. Here I cite only chapters on each topic, all drawn from Pfiffner's volume, *The Managerial Presidency.* Each area has developed a literature of its own, and the single citation is intended only to direct interested readers. James Pfiffner, ed. 1991. *The Managerial Presidency.* Pacific Grove, Calif.: Brooks/Cole Publishing Company, p. xviii.

26. Francis Rourke. 1991. "Presidentializing the Bureaucracy: From Kennedy to Reagan." In *The Managerial Presidency,* ed. Pfiffner, pp. 123–124.

27. Samuel Kernell. 1991. "The Evolution of the White House Staff." In *The Managerial Presidency,* ed. Pfiffner.

28. Matthew Holden Jr. 1991. "Why Entourage Politics Is Volatile." In *The Managerial Presidency,* ed. Pfiffner, pp. 70–76.

29. Richard E. Neustadt. 1991. "Does the White House Need a Strong Chief of Staff?" In *The Managerial Presidency,* ed. Pfiffner, p. 29.

30. John Hart. 1995. *The Presidential Branch: From Washington to Clinton,* 2d ed. Chatham, N.J.: Chatham House Publishers.

31. C. I. Barnard. 1938. *The Functions of the Executive.* Cambridge, Mass.: Harvard University Press.

32. Those who study executive power may know the most about masculinism because the executive is particularly masculinized, but paradoxically they are also the least likely to acknowledge its existence. They know the most because their thinking about executive power is imbued with its assumptions, their behaviors are predicated on its standards, and their ideals of organization are reified in its structures. Their values and norms make masculinism normal. Many students of executive power, however, will likely not acknowledge the existence of masculinism because to do so would call into question the advantages masculinism affords the masculine; further, the concurrence between masculinism and their own worldview makes it difficult for them to see it at all. To do so would require conscious and serious self-reflection. Like any adherent to an ideology, the masculinist views masculine as normal, right, proper, and good. It is familiar and therefore invisible without conscious scrutiny.

33. The case presented here is far too simplistic. For more sophisticated accounts, see Brown, *Manhood and Politics,* Kathy E. Ferguson. 1984. *The Feminist Case Against Bureaucracy.* Philadelphia: Temple University Press; and Henry Jacoby. 1973. *The Bureaucratization of the World.* Berkeley: University of California Press.

34. Brown, *Manhood and Politics.* See especially chapters 1, 7, and 8.

35. For a discussion of power, domination, and bureaucracy, see also Ferguson, *The Feminist Case Against Bureaucracy.*

36. Malcolm Jewell and Marcia Lynn Whicker. 1994. *Legislative Leadership in the American States.* Ann Arbor: University of Michigan Press.

37. These principles apply to both administrative agencies and staff agencies, although considerable variation can be found situationally and by function and history. Research divisions of NASA, for example, are structured differently than the

procurement division of the Department of Transportation, even though both are administrative agencies. Much of the evolution of public administration contends with these distinctions. These ideas nonetheless survive from the early days of public administration with the work of Max Weber and Luther Gulick especially. For key summaries of these and related ideas, see Jay M. Shafritz and Albert C. Hyde. 1987. *Classics of Public Administration,* 2d ed. Chicago: Dorsey Press.

38. K. M. Bartol. 1978. "The Sex Structuring of Organizations: A Search for Possible Causes." *Academy of Management Review* 3: 805–815.

39. Georgia Duerst-Lahti and Cathy Marie Johnson. 1992. "Styles, Stereotypes, and Advantages." In *Women and Men of the States: Public Administrators at the State Level,* ed. Mary Ellen Guy. Armonk, N.Y.: M. E. Sharpe. See also Kathleen P. Iannello. 1992. *Decisions Without Hierarchy: Feminist Interventions in Organization Theory and Practice.* London: Routledge.

40. Meredith Ann Newman. 1995. "The Gendered Nature of Lowi's Typology: Or Who Would Guess You Could Find Gender Here?" In *Gender Power, Leadership, and Governance,* ed. Duerst-Lahti and Kelly.

41. Georgia Duerst-Lahti. 1987. "Gender Power Relations in Public Bureaucracies." Ph.D. dissertation, University of Wisconsin; Duerst-Lahti and Johnson, "Styles, Stereotypes, and Advantages"; and ibid.

42. Secretary of labor during the period 1933–1945, Frances Perkins was the first woman cabinet member in U.S. history. Elizabeth Dole held two cabinet positions: secretary of transportation in the Reagan administration and secretary of labor in the Bush administration.

43. Duerst-Lahti and Johnson, "Styles, Stereotypes, and Advantages."

44. Race also plays into the power of this and other posts in a manner similar to gender power. Of course, as a superpower the United States has had an ambiguous relationship with the United Nations since its inception. In this scenario, the post was prime for someone other than prestigious white males because it was less significant than, say, secretary of state.

45. Clinton Rossiter. 1956. *The American Presidency.* New York: Harcourt, Brace, pp. 3–24.

46. Neustadt, *Presidential Power and the Modern Presidents.*

47. Kelly discusses related dynamics in considerable detail, especially in Part 1. See Rita Mae Kelly. 1991. *The Gendered Economy: Work, Careers, and Success.* Newbury Park, Calif.: Sage Publications.

48. The idea of connections is central to the purported differences between women and men in Carol Gilligan's work. See Carol Gilligan. 1982. *In a Different Voice.* Cambridge, Mass.: Harvard University Press. See Christine Di Stefano for a compelling critique of the flaws in liberalism through the absence of (m)other. She reveals the extent to which our foundation on individuals is itself misguided. With it she indicts the "great man" understanding of leaders. Di Stefano, *Configurations on Masculinity.*

49. One suspects that much of the vitriolic fervor directed toward Hillary Rodham Clinton revolves on her inevitable challenge to these assumptions in that she clearly won the competition in standing at Yale Law School from her husband, the president, and that her competence as a political actor is difficult to deny. Jamieson, *Beyond the Double Bind.* See especially chapter 7.

50. Autonomous comes from *auto,* self, and *nemein,* to hold sway. Heteronomous comes from *hetero,* the other of two, another, other. Autonomous individuals hold sway over themselves, whereas heteronomous individuals are in the sway of another. Prior laws denied autonomy to women, even defining them as not human so that they could legally be the property of their husband or father. Although

most such laws disappeared in the 1970s (a mere blink of an eye compared with centuries of their enforcement), present abortion debates demonstrate the strength of the political unwillingness to give women sway over themselves.

51. Maxine Berman. 1994. *The Only Boobs in the House Are Men: A Veteran Woman Legislator Lifts the Lid on Politics Macho Style.* Troy, Mich.: Momentum Books, p. 1.

52. Congressional staffs are also disproportionately male, especially at their highest advisory levels. Thus, the problems that are seen in the White House permeate the larger legislative structure as well. Hart, *The Presidential Branch,* p. 145; and Dan Rather and Gary Paul Gates. 1974. *The Palace Guard.* New York: Harper and Row.

53. Hart, *The Presidential Branch,* p. 187.

54. Rosabeth Moss Kanter. 1977. *Men and Women of the Corporation.* New York: Basic Books.

55. Hart, *The Presidential Branch,* p. 146.

56. Duerst-Lahti and Johnson, "Gender and Style in Bureaucracy."

57. The belief that the Soviets won the first round of the space race because their women were educated and worked throughout the economy may have been a critical catalyst for the second wave of the women's movement. The gendered implications of this argument proffered four decades later in terms of executive power are both sad and ironic. See Georgia Duerst-Lahti. 1989. "The Government's Role in Building the Women's Movement." *Political Science Quarterly* 104(2): 249–268.

58. The most recent such study was done by Debra L. Dodson, Susan J. Carroll, Ruth B. Mandel, Katherine E. Kleeman, Ronnee Schreiber, and Debra Liebowitz of the Center for the American Woman and Politics, Rutgers University, New Brunswick, N.J., in *Voices, Views, Votes: The Impact of Women in the 103rd Congress,* 1995. The study documents, as earlier studies have, that women pursue an agenda that differs from that of men and expand it to new areas. Further, they shape the content of legislation in new ways, expand the terms of debate, and shape the way issues are framed. Given women's and men's different experiences of life, the fact that women bring something different to politics should come as no surprise. Hence, their presence matters substantively as well as symbolically.

59. Janet M. Martin. 1991. "An Examination of Executive Branch Appointments in the Reagan Administration by Background and Gender." *Western Political Quarterly* 44: 173–184.

60. The dynamic of symbolic appointments and heightened scrutiny seems to occur with anyone who is not a white male. A systematic study of relative scrutiny by the Senate demonstrates this contention. See MaryAnne Borrelli. Forthcoming. "Gender, Credibility, and Politics: The Senate Nomination Hearings of Cabinet Secretaries-Designate, 1975–1993." *Political Research Quarterly;* and ibid. Dayna Verstegen and I explore the meaning of representation, and the consequences of women's visible absence, in "Making Something of Absence: The 'Year of the Woman' and Women's Representation." In *Gender Power, Leadership and Governance,* ed. Duerst-Lahti and Kelly.

61. A joke from Britain told late in the Thatcher administration is revealing in this regard. Kindergarten boys and girls were playing. A girl asked a boy what he wanted to be when he grew up. "The prime minister," he responded. Immediately the girl retorted, "Prime minister? You can't be prime minister. Only girls are prime minister."

62. John Adams explicitly stated that they were creating a "masculine system" in a letter to his wife, Abigail, on April 14, 1781; "Remember the Ladies." In *The Feminist Papers,* ed. Alice Rossi. New York: Columbia University Press, 1973.

63. A quarter century after the initial women's consciousness-raising groups, I suggest a need for raised consciousness with some trepidation, fearing instant dismissal by readers of a book on executive politics. It is entirely possible that under a different ideological arrangement the hierarchical and dominating understanding of elite will change. Space does not allow even a cursory exploration of this topic here.

64. See Zillah Eisenstein. 1981. *The Radical Future of Liberal Feminism.* New York: Longman, on the potential of liberalism; and Di Stefano, *Configurations on Masculinity,* for a critique of liberalism.

3

Routes to Power:
An Examination of Political Change,
Rulership, and Women's Access to
Executive Office

Piper A. Hodson

Contrary to what we might expect, women have held the position of chief executive in more "developing" than "developed" states. In Western Europe female prime ministers have provided strong, ideologically based political leadership; one example is Margaret Thatcher, former prime minister of Great Britain. However, many of the world's female national chief executives are found in the developing world. The traditional economic, social, and religious structures that continue to exist in these states pose serious challenges to the advancement of women. In spite of, and sometimes because of, these traditional structures, women have risen to the pinnacle of executive power.

In the South Asian subcontinent, women have led all but one of the republics.[1] Indira Gandhi was prime minister of India during the periods 1966–1977 and 1980–1984. Sirimavo Bandaranaike was prime minister, which is to say then–chief executive, of Sri Lanka from 1960 to 1965 and 1970 to 1977 and is the current prime minister of Sri Lanka. The country's new constitution identifies the president as chief executive, and since 1994 this office has been held by Chandrika Kumaratunga, Bandaranaike's daughter. Khaleda Zia was prime minister of Bangladesh from 1991 to 1996.[2] Benazir Bhutto was the prime minister of Pakistan (1988–1990 and 1993–1996).[3] This chapter presents case studies of Bhutto, Kumaratunga, and Zia.

When one examines the executive branch in comparative perspective, it is important to distinguish between the role of head of state and that of chief executive. Whereas the U.S. president functions in both capacities, other constitutions frequently assign these responsibilities to separate offices. The head (sometimes called the chief) of state is the ceremonial leader; the chief executive, however, is the center of political power in the executive branch. Identification of the chief executive requires careful attention to the division of duties, as in a mixed system either the president or the prime minister may wield executive power. In some developing countries, the role of chief executive has changed from one position to the other in recent history, as occurred when Sri Lanka adopted a new constitution in 1978. In the three cases studied here, the president is the chief executive in Sri Lanka, whereas the prime minister is the chief executive in Bangladesh and Pakistan.

The Chief Executive in Comparative Perspective

A study of the executive from a comparative perspective provides insight into how chief executives emerge. One could limit a comparative analysis to the experiences in Western democracies, but the advancement of women to the chief executive office has occurred most frequently in the developing countries. In looking to these countries, this examination provides *models* for the advancement of minority groups—particularly women—within a democracy. If scholars and practitioners of executive politics understand the factors that account for political success in other democratic states, they may be more successful in their efforts to advance women toward the U.S. presidency.

Comparative study of the chief executive also allows us to explore structural barriers to minority representation and government leadership in the United States. Existing research has explored the impact of various representational and electoral systems on women politicians, and this study builds on that work.[4] Of particular importance is the information to be gained about the competition for power in different governmental structures.

In addition, the cases of Zia, Kumaratunga, and Bhutto provide insight into the puzzle that surrounds the existence of women chief executives in the developing world. Women have achieved the highest political office in governments that continue to struggle to control such problems as killing wives and infant girls, allowing child brides, and discriminating against females in nourishment. The effect of traditional societal arrangements and practices has yet to be fully determined.

Similarly, the case studies of Zia, Kumaratunga, and Bhutto reveal the effects of a mixed presidential-parliamentary governmental structure, often referred to as the French model, on women's political endeavors. Existing research has examined the influence of both parliamentary and presidential systems on the ability of women to gain political power, but the mixed system remains largely unexplored.[5] And yet, the mixed system provides the opportunity to investigate how gender affects the ability of a woman political leader to exercise her constitutionally granted powers. Current research on women chief executives suggests that their election or appointment is sometimes engineered by men who have no intention of allowing them to exercise actual executive power.[6] If this is true in mixed systems, as in South Asia, power struggles should occur between the president and the prime minister.

Paths to Power

Whereas the experiences of the three women discussed here share certain similarities, their emergence as chief executives did not follow identical paths. This section provides brief political biographies of Bhutto, Kumaratunga, and Zia.

Benazir Bhutto was raised to be her father's assistant and successor. Bhutto's father, Zulfikar Ali Bhutto, founded the Pakistan People's Party (PPP)—which she now leads—and served as the prime minister of Pakistan from 1973 until 1977, when he was overthrown and arrested by General Zia ul-Haq. He was executed by General Zia's regime in 1979.

Bhutto was born in 1953 and was educated at Radcliffe (1969–1973) and Oxford (1973–1977), where she was president of the Oxford Union in her final year. In addition to educating her abroad, Zulfikar Ali Bhutto gave his daughter political experience, such as taking her to meetings of the UN Security Council. The clearest example of her political training was her inclusion at the 1972 Simla meetings, which officially ended the 1971 war between India and Pakistan. Bhutto believes her father intended her to take over the PPP and to continue his opposition to General Zia.[7]

Bhutto first became prime minister of Pakistan in 1988. General Zia had promised to allow elections, which were held on November 16, 1988. Bhutto and her mother, Nusrat Bhutto—the official head of the party—led the PPP to victory at the polls. On December 1, 1988, Bhutto became the first woman to be named prime minister of an Islamic state. Her first term ended less than two years later, in 1990, when President Ghulam Ishaq Khan dissolved the National Assembly and asked the leader of the opposition to form a caretaker government until elections were conducted.[8] Accused of corruption and unable to maintain law and order, the PPP lost its parliamentary majority in the 1990 election.[9] The new government proved no more successful, and when the PPP organized a workable majority coalition following the 1993 elections, the president again named Bhutto prime minister.

Chandrika Kumaratunga, born in 1945, was directly elected to her six-year term as president of Sri Lanka in 1994. Although she was also raised in a political family, she confronted different expectations from those faced by Bhutto. Her father, S.W.R.D. Bandaranaike, was prime minister of Sri Lanka from 1956 until his assassination in 1959. Her mother, Sirimavo Bandaranaike, was prime minister from 1960 to 1965 and from 1970 to 1977 and was appointed prime minister by Kumaratunga in 1994. Involved in politics throughout her adult life, Kumaratunga became a national figure in 1993 when she became chief minister of the politically important Western Province.[10] In August 1994 the People's Alliance (PA), a coalition of parties to which Kumaratunga's Sri Lankan Freedom Party (SLFP) belonged, and the Sri Lanka Muslim Congress won 50.7 percent of the valid vote. These parties subsequently formed a coalition to constitute a parliamentary majority, and Kumaratunga was then appointed prime minister. In the presidential election held three months later, Kumaratunga won easily, receiving 62.3 percent of the valid vote.[11]

Khaleda Zia, born in 1945, was the daughter of a businessman. Unlike Bhutto and Kumaratunga, she did not grow up as a member of her country's political elite. Zia's path toward political leadership began when she married Ziaur Rahman, then a captain in the Pakistan army. (Bangladesh was a part of Pakistan at the time.) After the war for independence, Rahman became a member of the Bangladeshi political elite and served as president from 1977 until 1981, when he was killed in the coup that brought Lieutenant General H. M. Ershad to power. In 1990 Ershad ended his dictatorship, called for elections, and resigned as president. Zia led the Bangladesh National Party (BNP) to a parliamentary majority in the 1991 elections and was named prime minister by the acting president.[12]

Having outlined their careers, I now seek to determine the role of socialization in these female chief executives' paths to power. I then investigate the influence of the governmental systems in which the women rose to power, and finally, I explore the influence of particular circumstances on their political careers.

The Influence of Socialization

Rita Mae Kelly, Mary Boutilier, and Mary Lewis, in their comparative study of achieving, public, and private women, argue that four stages of socialization must occur for a woman to achieve political leadership: (1) As a girl, she must "develop an activist modern sex-role ideology" that will enable her to envision herself in nontraditional roles, (2) she must attain a sense of personal control over her life, (3) politics must become salient to her, and (4) she must experience some political success at critical points in her life.[13] Although this model was developed through an examination of Western women, it is relevant to the experiences of Zia, Kumaratunga, and Bhutto— all of whom seem to have passed through these stages, albeit in different ways and at different points in their lives.

Modern Sex-Role Ideology and Personal Control

The three major agents of socialization—religion, education, and family upbringing—are especially relevant to the first two of these stages. Family upbringing and education are closely tied because the family chooses the kind of education the girl receives; they are also highly specific to the individual. Religion, on the other hand, produces a general cultural atmosphere that helps to shape the girl's sense of control of her life.

Hinduism, Islam, and Buddhism—the three major religions in South

Asia—contain images of powerful women. For instance, the Hindu goddess Kali both gives life and destroys it, although she is more commonly associated with destruction.[14] Hindus also believe women are the source of creative energy. Buddhism views the power of women through the same dual lens of creation and destruction.[15] Benazir Bhutto's autobiography cites several positive images of powerful public Muslim women in Islamic history and notes that "Muslim history was full of women who had taken a public role and performed every bit as successfully as men. Nothing in Islam discouraged them, or me, from pursuing that course."[16] Western religions offer no similarly pervasive images of female power.

In addition to this support, Hindu and Muslim social structures give substantial power to women. According to Gail Minault, women have traditionally had roles of potential political importance within the family, particularly as they grow older. Through their ability to influence important family decisions, such as marital or political alliances, "women exercized power, both as individuals and as members of the group, to the degree that decisions made in the private sphere—the women's realm—influenced the fortunes of the family in the public sphere, dominated by men."[17] Marriage, which represents a possible route to business and political alliances and advancement for a family, gives South Asian women influence in those public spheres because they play a significant role in identifying appropriate prospective spouses for their children, grandchildren, nieces, and nephews. This role allows them to help shape the financial and political future of the family. Bhutto, Kumaratunga, and Zia grew up in societies in which their mothers exercised this kind of influence. Wives and mothers in leading U.S. political families have power within their private sphere, but the absence of arranged marriages diminishes the influence of that private power on the public realm.

Even more important, U.S. chief executives do not routinely emerge from political families. In contrast, in South Asia the private role of wife or daughter has led to the public role of party and government leader after the death of a male family head. The frequency with which this has occurred now plays its own socialization role. Girls and women in political families have role models of women emerging as national chief executives, which has made national political leadership an option for them.

The history of the nationalist movements on the South Asian continent provides some insight into the development of the activist identification and the sense of personal control. In fact, it may help to explain why the majority of female chief executives have emerged in former colonies. The struggle for independence led nationalist organizations to encourage that girls and young women be educated in an effort to modernize in preparation for independence. This education was conservative and taught the women to become good Western housewives; it was also contingent upon family wishes, as the girl's education was planned by her parents. Still, national educational initiatives "brought bourgeois women out of their homes and into various professions, into social work, and into the political sphere claiming the right of suffrage."[18] In fact, in these states women gained the right to vote at independence (in 1947 and 1948). The education initiative also fueled the feminist movements that socialized South Asian women to political activity.

For Zia, however, neither education nor life in her parents' household socialized her to expect or want an active political role. Her father was a businessman who raised his daughters to be good wives, and she was educated to be a homemaker. As the first lady of Bangladesh, "She was only a devoted, loyal housewife always maintaining a low profile. She was seldom seen in public."[19]

Until she assumed the chair of the BNP in 1984, Zia closely resembled the prototype of the passive political woman who engages in politics primarily through the man in her life. Her rise to leadership closely resembles that of early female members of the U.S. Congress who succeeded their deceased husbands.[20] After the death of her husband, Zia's conceptualization of her public role changed to encompass possible political leadership.

Kumaratunga's family socialized her to expect a more activist role than did Zia's, but her socialization was not as purposeful as Bhutto's. Both her father and her mother were Sri Lankan prime ministers. With her husband, Vijaya Kumaratunga, she was cofounder of the Sri Lanka Mahajana Party.[21] Kumaratunga has been politically active throughout most of her adult life, but she did not seem to expect to rise to the pinnacle of power. The United National Party dominated Sri Lankan politics for seventeen years prior to her success in 1994, and her mother, not Kumaratunga, was the leader of the SLFP, which was Kumaratunga's party within the coalition of parties known as the People's Alliance. Kumaratunga had always played a supportive role to other members of her family until her 1993 appointment as chief minister of Western Province.

Bhutto, unlike Kumaratunga, has played a leading role in the PPP throughout her adult life. Substantial evidence indicates that Bhutto's father intended for her to spend her life in public leadership. According to Bhutto, he was careful to educate her about political life.[22]

All three women thus experienced the first two stages of political socialization, although in different ways and at different times. Each developed a modern sex-role ideology and a sense of personal control, events also linked to the processes by which they began their careers in political leadership.

Politics Becomes Salient

All three of these women experienced the third stage of socialization, the salience of politics, in a violent and personal way. All are widows, daughters, or both of slain political leaders—a fact that is important to the discussion of circumstance later in this chapter.

In addition, all have suffered persecution for their own or their relatives' political activities. Zia's husband was killed in a coup, and Zia spent time in prison during the 1971 war because of her husband's activities. Kumaratunga's father was assassinated, as was her husband, and she was driven into exile in 1988. Bhutto's father was executed by General Zia. Her brother, Shah Nawaz Bhutto, died from poisoning while in exile in France, and Bhutto believes his death may have been arranged by the Afghan mujahideen in hopes of pleasing General Zia.[23] These experiences promoted not only a salience but a centrality of politics in the lives of these three women.

Political Success

The final stage of socialization involves the political success of the women at key points in their careers. For Zia, one of those points came in 1984, not long after she had assumed the chair of the BNP. Although Ershad was in power and would be until 1990, a poll taken in 1984 revealed that Zia had substantial popular support. Asked to choose among the top three likely candidates for the presidency, Zia secured 41 percent of the support, compared with 31 percent and 28 percent, respectively, for the other two potential candidates.[24] After only a year as chair of the BNP, a post she had assumed reluctantly, the poll reassured Zia that there was popular support for her leadership and the party.

Kumaratunga's success came after she had returned from exile and rejoined the SLFP in 1991. According to Howard Schaffer, she "was soon widely regarded as her mother's choice to take over the party reins when the time came for 'the Lady' to step down. In May 1993 she led the PA in provincial council elections in the important Western Province, which includes Colombo."[25] In other .words, Kumaratunga not only experienced political success, she also gained experience and exposure that were useful for a presidential bid.

Bhutto was a leading member of the PPP from the beginning of her father's imprisonment in 1977. From the time her mother left Pakistan for medical treatment in 1982 until her own exile in 1984, Bhutto served as her mother's spokesperson and as the spokesperson for the party in Pakistan, even though she was either in prison or under house arrest throughout that time. In exile in London, Bhutto helped to lead the PPP there and mounted an international publicity campaign against General Zia's regime. She returned to Pakistan in 1986 to lead the resistance against General Zia's government. During this time, Bhutto increased her popularity at home and her exposure internationally.

These three cases provide a continuum of early socialization experiences—ranging from Zia, who expected no political role, to Bhutto, who was guided into political leadership. The violence in South Asian politics, as demonstrated by the assassinations of so many political leaders, caused politics to become salient for these women in a particularly powerful way.[26] The structure and circumstance that constitute the environment in which these women have competed for political power are likely to provide further insight into the disproportionate number of female chief executives in South Asia.

The Influence of Structure

Bangladesh, Pakistan, and Sri Lanka all have a mixed parliamentary-presidential government. The effects of the mixed system seem to be very similar to those of the parliamentary government.[27] The party structure funds individual campaigns, even in presidential races. Consequently, elite women in South Asia do not face all of the structural disadvantages present in the U.S. presidential system, in which candidates run independently to win the nomination and the party then plays a secondary role that is dictated by the nominee.

It is unlikely, however, that the campaign funding advantage would hold true for women attempting to work their way up the party structure rather than beginning their political careers at the elite level, as Zia, Kumaratunga, and Bhutto did. Although campaigns at all levels are funded by the parties, the legal limits on spending for lower-level, particularly municipal, campaigns are so low that individuals must bring in unreported money to be chosen as a party candidate. This places most South Asian women at the same disadvantage as American women. The upper-class women, who begin political life as leading members of the party, are the ones who enjoy the advantage provided by party financing of elections.

The design of the chief executive office also has important implications for the acquisition and retention of power. In most Western mixed systems, either the presidency or the prime ministership is primarily a subordinate or even a ceremonial role. In South Asia, however, both roles have true potential political power. The structure of the governments is new, and the constitutional division of power can be unstable. Prerogative power is used in the same way early U.S. presidents set precedents that more clearly established their vaguely defined constitutional powers. These states have little precedent to prevent struggles for executive power between the two offices, which allows one to consider whether (and under what circumstances) women chief executives are able to wield or even expand their constitutionally prescribed power.

In assessing this aspect of the chief executive's performance, gender has clearly affected Bhutto's political reign more than it has that of

Kumaratunga or Zia. In 1990 she was removed from office by President Ghulam Ishaq Khan. Citing the government's corruption, abuse of power, and general incompetence, he dissolved the National Assembly, declared a state of emergency, and called for a general election. Although many of the charges were accurate, at least some of Bhutto's problems stemmed from her gender. In 1990 Pakistan faced significant foreign policy concerns when Saddam Hussein invaded Kuwait. According to one analyst, "Pakistan's military leaders did not believe they could leave matters in the hands of a young woman perceived to have limited capacity. Moreover, the times called for personal contacts in the Gulf states that would be awkward for a Muslim woman."[28]

Bhutto did return to the prime ministership in 1994, however, when the Pakistan People's Party won 86 of the 211 seats in the National Assembly. She struggled to maintain the coalition government in the face of stringent opposition by Nawaz Sharif and the Pakistan Muslim League. Still, this return to power weakened any claim that she was a mere figurehead who was in power only because of her father's memory.

Bhutto's second dismissal, however, does not exhibit the obvious gender bias found in her 1990 fall. This time, the charges of corruption are substantial, credible, and without the apparent additional motivation of removing her because she is a woman. While gender has played a role in Bhutto's problems as chief executive, it is important to realize that her government has failed to address a number of serious national problems effectively.

Zia's relationships provide some evidence that gender was not a central factor in her political difficulties. The president, currently Abdur Rahman Biswas, is elected by the National Assembly and is thus unlikely to launch an expansionist bid, since he is dependent upon the prime minister's (majority) party. Instead, Zia's political challenges, which were substantial, came from the parliamentary opposition headed by Sheikh Hasina Wajed, the daughter of a prominent politician who had been assassinated.

Kumaratunga has had the least difficulty of the three women in establishing her rule. As noted earlier, in 1994 Kumaratunga's party won the majority of parliamentary seats and established a coalition government three months before the presidential election. Many worried that then-President Dingiri Banda Wijetunga would take advantage of his constitutional powers as head of both the state and the government and strengthen the position of his own party. Instead, "Wijetunga became a virtually invisible figure,"[29] essentially turning the government over to Kumaratunga. She was subsequently elected president, and her gender does not appear to have weakened her ability to establish leadership.

This examination of the governmental and electoral structures of these countries demonstrates that whereas women chief executives do confront political challenges, those challenges are not always gender driven. In spite of the political struggles in these relatively young mixed systems, only Bhutto's leadership was threatened because she was a woman. Clearly, women do act as independent chief executives, successfully wielding the political power of their offices.

The Influence of Circumstance

The final characteristic to be examined is the circumstance that surrounds the electoral success of female chief executives. Every candidate's election depends on a favorable configuration of circumstances. Candidates are assisted by their competitors' mistakes, by their own powerful supporters, by correct strategic calculations, and by events that reinforce issue choices.

The current literature suggests that circumstances are especially important for women. In particular, Michael Genovese has argued that worldwide, "Very few of the women rose to power 'on their own.' Most of the women who have become leaders came to power in periods of social or political turmoil, and 'inherited' power from family, father or husband."[30] Although Zia, Bhutto, and Kumaratunga benefited greatly from their family connections, readers should not assume that this means their ascension to power was less competitive than is the case for those without such connections. These women often compete *with other relatives* for the "inheritance," and even with the name recognition and sympathy an "inheritance" provides, these women and their parties must still compete with opposition parties.

When a leader of a party dies, he or she does not always leave a single obvious successor. Of the three women discussed here, only Zia's leadership has not been challenged by a relative. Kumaratunga's entire family is involved in Sri Lankan politics. She inherited her political role most immediately from her mother, Sirimavo Bandaranaike. During the 1994 parliamentary elections, there were reports of a power struggle between Kumaratunga and Bandaranaike. These reports may have been politically motivated and were silenced by Bandaranaike's announcement that Kumaratunga would become prime minister if the People's Alliance formed the government.[31] Kumaratunga and Bandaranaike have also faced a political challenge from Kumaratunga's brother. Formerly the chief organizer of the SLFP, he led a defection from the party prior to the parliamentary elections.[32] This move, however, ultimately left Kumaratunga at the head of the SLFP—with her mother—and unified the People's Alliance.[33]

Bhutto has faced very strong challenges to her leadership of the PPP. Her brother Murtaza, supported by their mother, claimed he was the rightful successor to their father in the PPP until he was killed in September 1996.[34] In December 1993, Benazir removed her mother, Nusrat, from the chair of the PPP and took her place. In response, Nusrat began to claim that Benazir should stop using Bhutto as her surname and should take her husband's name instead.[35]

The inheritance effect in South Asia is unusually strong, primarily because of the tremendous struggles and hardships with which the families become identified. Candidates in the United States also seek to inherit the positions of their family members. Linda Witt, Karen M. Paget, and Glenna Matthews recount the following story:

> Kathleen Brown, the daughter of one former California governor and the sister of yet another, ran for treasurer in 1990 not under the name of either her first or second husband but under the slogan "A Brown of a Different Color." . . . It made her a legitimate heir to the positive feelings voters might still have for either her father, Edmund G. "Pat" Brown, or her controversial brother, Jerry Brown (Edmund G. Brown Jr.), while subtly enabling voters to distinguish her from the latter.[36]

Americans may not recognize the process of inheritance as a part of their political system, but it does exist for both sexes.

Inheritance is obviously neither nonpolitical nor noncompetitive. In the United States it primarily provides money, name recognition, and campaign organization. In South Asia, in addition to these benefits, inheritance identifies candidates with the struggle to gain freedom from oppression. Inheritance is a valuable source of power and, consequently, is a political resource for which politicians compete. Acquisition of the inheritance is an achievement.

Once held within the party, the inheritance must be utilized in the national political arena, in which the female chief executives of South Asia compete with other politicians—both men and women—who possess their own political inheritances. The candidate who opposed Kumaratunga for the presidency was the widow of the original opposition candidate who had been assassinated during the campaign.[37] In Bangladesh, Zia's parliamentary opposition was led by Sheikh Hasina Wajed, the daughter of an assassinated politician, who has substantial political experience and, like Zia, is strongly identified with the suffering under and opposition to the former dictatorship.

For all of these reasons, the acquisition and use of a political inheritance should be viewed as a test of a leader's effectiveness. It is not presumptive evidence of political weakness.

Two conclusions can be drawn about the role of circumstances. First, Michael Genovese's argument that female chief executives rise to power in unusual times is an accurate description of the three situations described here.[38] In fact, these cases fit the pattern of women emerging as leaders of the opposition. Zia led her party to victory in the first parliamentary election following the resumption of democracy. Bhutto initially gained power under the same circumstances and regained power when the dominant political coalition was dissolved. Kumaratunga won both of her elections largely because of public dissatisfaction with the ongoing failure of the ruling party to achieve peace with the Tamil separatist movement. Although new male leaders often emerge under similar conditions, it seems important that in these newly independent countries women leaders have emerged *only* under these circumstances.

The second lesson to be gained from an examination of circumstance is that inheritance, although an important feature of South Asian politics for both men and women, does not automatically lead to power for either sex. Women compete for and win their inheritance. The inheritance itself is not the key to understanding the success of women in South Asia, however; rather, the key is the underlying social system of which the inheritance is a product. In these countries, a limited number of people have access to political power, which limits the pool from which leaders have been recruited. This fact combined with the increased turnover in leadership caused by frequent assassinations has allowed women to gain access. The positive identifications provided by political inheritance, which are now enjoyed by the relatives of men who fought for freedom, will likely fade with time. By then, however, women will have become so prevalent in South Asian politics that they may endure.

Conclusion

This study has examined the role of socialization, structure, and circumstance in the emergence of three recent female chief executives in South Asia. The existing literature on women political leaders highlights these factors as central, and this study demonstrates that all three were important in the rise of Zia, Kumaratunga, and Bhutto. Each factor contributed to the advancement of each woman, but none was experienced identically by the three.

Socialization provided the drive and the skill to pursue political office, but the socialization experiences of these three leaders lie on a continuum of intensity. Whereas Bhutto was purposefully groomed for political leadership, Kumaratunga's socialization seems to have been comparatively inadvertent. Zia's childhood socialization did not prepare her for political leadership; the experiences of her adult life seem to have instilled her desire to pursue political power. There is obviously no one method of successful socialization for leadership, and socialization alone does not fully explain the emergence of these women as chief executives.

The governmental structure was the environment within which these actors sought political power. All three women emerged in mixed presidential-parliamentary systems, and the election processes provided certain advantages women in presidential systems do not enjoy. On the other hand, the existence of both a president and a prime minister provided a potential challenge to their rulership.

Again, the three cases were not identical. Whereas Bhutto suffered strong challenges to her leadership, some of which were gender driven, Zia's similarly serious leadership problems were unrelated to her gender. Kumaratunga's leadership appears much more secure than that of the other two, but structural differences contribute greatly to her success. She is a president elected to a six-year term, whereas the terms of prime ministers can be ended with a vote of no confidence or a president's call for elections. Government structure thus clearly plays a significant role in the emergence and performance of women as chief executives.

Finally, for these women circumstances provided the actual opportunities for participation in the political system and for political success. Two circumstances are common to the emergence of all three women: They all "inherited" a political role from a family member, and they all emerged in times of great national instability. The inheritance—which Kumaratunga and Bhutto acquired after competition and struggle—provided name recognition, status, and symbolic identifications that allowed them to compete in the political arena when national instability opened the door for their opposition parties. Political circumstance is therefore vital to understanding the achievements of these three female chief executives.

Khaleda Zia, Chandrika Kumaratunga, and Benazir Bhutto illustrate an important fact about political leadership. Patricia Sykes has written that "it proves as difficult to generalize about women as it is to generalize about men when it comes to the subject of leadership."[39] In the cases considered here, socialization, structure, and circumstance all acted to allow—perhaps even to promote—the advancement of these women, but each woman is an individual with her own experience and her own unique configuration of events and influences. Women in the United States who aspire to political power will be affected by their socialization, structure, and circumstance, but they will be individuals pursuing power within the distinctive constraints and opportunities of these three factors.

Notes

1. Maldives is the only republic that has not had a woman as chief executive. The other two states on the subcontinent, Nepal and Bhutan, are monarchies.

2. Zia's Bangladesh National Party swept the elections in February 1996, but only 10 percent of the eligible voters turned out because of an opposition boycott. Zia resigned as prime minister in April 1996 to allow a neutral ruling coalition to be formed to run the government until new elections could be held. The Bangladesh National Party lost its parliamentary plurality, and Zia consequently lost the prime ministership to Sheikh Hasina Wajed's Awami League in the elections held June 12, 1996.

3. Bhutto was ousted from the prime ministership when, on November 4, 1996, President Farooq Leghari dissolved the National Assembly and called elections for February 1997. Leghari cited several reasons for his decision, including corruption, nepotism, and the government's lack of response to rising political violence.

4. See, for instance, Linda C. Gugin. 1986. "The Impact of Political Structure on the Political Power of Women: A Comparison of Britain and the United States."

Women and Politics 6: 37–56; and Wilma Rule and Joseph F. Zimmerman, eds. 1994. *Electoral Systems in Comparative Perspective: Their Impact on Women and Minorities.* Westport, Conn.: Greenwood Press.

5. Gugin, "The Impact of Political Structure on the Political Power of Women."

6. Michael A. Genovese. 1993. "Women as National Leaders: What Do We Know?" In *Women as National Leaders,* ed. Michael A. Genovese. Newbury Park, Calif.: Sage Publications; and Michelle A. Saint-Germain. 1993. "Women in Power in Nicaragua: Myth and Reality." In *Women as National Leaders,* ed. Genovese.

7. Bhutto's understanding of her father's wishes is made clear throughout her autobiography. Benazir Bhutto. 1989. *Daughter of Destiny: An Autobiography.* New York: Simon and Schuster.

8. In some mixed presidential-parliamentary systems, the president may require that the opposition parties form a ruling coalition to govern the state as a "caretaker" in the period preceding elections. The majority party in a parliament has considerable freedom of action because these systems do not include the strong checks and balances found in the U.S. presidential system. The caretaker government is meant to decrease the ability of the majority party to manipulate election rules, government policy, and funding to influence the outcome of the elections.

9. Lawrence Ziring. 1991. "Pakistan in 1990: The Fall of Benazir Bhutto." *Asian Survey* 31: 113–124.

10. Gamini Keerawella and Rohan Samarajiva. 1995. "Sri Lanka in 1994." Asian Survey 35: 155.

11. Howard B. Schaffer. 1995. "The Sri Lankan Elections of 1994: The Chandrika Factor." *Asian Survey* 35: 409.

12. S. Abdul Hakim. 1992. *Begum Khaleda Zia of Bangladesh: A Political Biography.* New Delhi: Vikas Publishing House.

13. Rita Mae Kelly, Mary Boutilier, and Mary Lewis. 1978. "Studying Women in Politics." In *The Making of Political Women: A Study of Socialization and Role Conflict,* ed. Rita Mae Kelly and Mary Boutilier. Chicago: Nelson-Hall, pp. 5–6.

14. Margaret Stutley and James Stutley. 1977. *Harper's Dictionary of Hinduism.* New York: Harper and Row Publishers.

15. Diana Y. Paul. 1985. *Women in Buddhism: Images of the Feminine in the Mahayana Tradition,* 2d ed. Berkeley: University of California Press, pp. xxiv–xxv.

16. Bhutto, *Daughter of Destiny,* p. 44.

17. Gail Minault. 1981. "Introduction: The Extended Family as Metaphor and the Expansion of Women's Realm." In *The Extended Family: Women and Political Participation in India and Pakistan,* ed. Gail Minault. Delhi: Chanakya Publications, pp. 5–6.

18. Kumari Jayawardena. 1986. *Feminism and Nationalism in the Third World.* London: Zed Books, p. 19.

19. Hakim, *Begum Khaleda Zia of Bangladesh,* p. 3.

20. Diane D. Kincaid. 1978. "Over His Dead Body: A Positive Perspective on Widows in the U.S. Congress." *Western Political Quarterly* 31: 96–104; and Kelly, Boutilier, and Lewis, "Studying Women in Politics," pp. 5–6.

21. Keerawella and Samarajiva, "Sri Lanka in 1994: A Mandate for Peace," p. 155.

22. See, for instance, Bhutto, *Daughter of Destiny,* p. 75.

23. Ibid., p. 292.

24. Hakim, *Begum Khaleda Zia of Bangladesh,* p. 13.

25. Schaffer, "The Sri Lankan Elections of 1994: The Chandrika Factor," p. 412.

26. This is not universally true in all South Asian examples of female national chief executives. Indira Gandhi's socialization did not include the violent death of an immediate family member. Her father, Jawaharlal Nehru (Indian prime minister from 1946 to 1964), died of natural causes. Gandhi had, however, grown up watching British security come into her home to arrest members of her family.

27. For a discussion of presidential and parliamentary systems, see Gugin, "The Impact of Political Structure on the Political Power of Women," p. 37. For a similar conclusion, see also Matthew S. Shugart. 1994. "Minorities Represented and Unrepresented." In *Electoral Systems in Comparative Perspective,* ed. Rule and Zimmerman.

28. Ziring, "Pakistan in 1990: The Fall of Benazir Bhutto," p. 114.

29. Schaffer, "The Sri Lankan Elections of 1994: The Chandrika Factor," p. 420.

30. Genovese, "Women as National Leaders," p. 214.

31. Schaffer, "The Sri Lankan Elections of 1994: The Chandrika Factor," pp. 417–418.

32. Ibid., p. 412.

33. Keerawella and Samarajiva, "Sri Lanka in 1994: A Mandate for Peace," p. 154.

34. Murtaza Bhutto's motorcade was stopped near his home in Karachi on September 20, 1996. According to official reports, his bodyguards opened fire on the police and he was killed in the cross fire. Many Pakistanis believe that Benazir Bhutto's supporters, or perhaps even she herself, arranged for his death, a fact that contributed to President Leghari's decision to dissolve the National Assembly and remove Bhutto.

35. Ahmed Rashid. 1994. "My Mother, My Enemy: Bhutto Family Feud Explodes into the Open." *Far Eastern Economic Review* (January 20): 18. Bhutto's use of the family name highlights a particular problem of circumstance women everywhere face because of their gender. If a woman who is working from a political power base established by one of her parents or who has amassed her own power base marries, she faces the dilemma of whether to take her husband's name. Name recognition is vital in politics, but in many societies women are expected to relinquish their name upon marriage. Benazir Bhutto wants to run as a Bhutto, with all that name implies about a history of suffering at the hands of a dictator and about dedication to the people of Pakistan. Taking her husband's name would mean something else. She could run as Benazir, which provides connotations of her own suffering and dedication. Her opposition hopes she would have to run as a Zardari (her husband's name), which could weaken her name recognition and potentially increase the political disadvantage at which she is already placed by her gender.

36. Linda Witt, Karen M. Paget, and Glenna Matthews. 1994. *Running as a Woman: Gender and Power in American Politics.* New York: Free Press, p. 80.

37. Schaffer, "The Sri Lankan Elections of 1994: The Chandrika Factor," p. 422.

38. Genovese, "Women as National Leaders," p. 214.

39. Patricia Lee Sykes. 1993. "Women as National Leaders: Patterns and Prospects." In *Women as National Leaders,* ed. Genovese, p. 224.

PART 2

Institutional Perspectives: Women as Officeholders in the Executive Branch

4

Women Who Govern:
The President's Appointments

Janet M. Martin

"Bean counters," a term of derision used by President-Elect Bill Clinton in his assault on those who keep track of the numbers of men, women, and minorities appointed to cabinet-level posts, is now a part of the political lexicon. At the time, Clinton angrily noted that women's groups were "playing quota games and math games" in scrutinizing the formation of a new government.[1] The presidential use of the term "bean counting" was new in 1992, but Clinton is not the first and will not be the last president who has engaged in a ritualistic dance with the media, political observers, and various interested parties in taking on the challenge of forming a new government that is more representative of America than the previous administration.

Forming a Government

The president's formation of an administration is watched the most closely in the weeks immediately following an election. The people the president selects for seats at the cabinet table or as heads of governmental agencies to help shape and move his new legislative agenda receive close scrutiny and are the focus of a barrage of news reports and editorials. Will the president turn to those from an earlier administration who have prior government service and build on the past legacy of a party and its leader? Or will the president reach out to include representatives from different ideological camps within a party to help heal wounds left from a bruising intramural nomination contest? If the new president campaigned as a Washington outsider, will efforts be made to include those with experience from inside the Beltway? Will states, the breeding ground of innovative policy in an age of devolution, be a source of federal policymakers? Or will efforts be made to lay the foundation for a repeat electoral college win by strategizing the choice of cabinet members to mute divided state party factions?

To this list a new dimension has been added in the past twenty years.

Although the rhetoric differs by administration, since Jimmy Carter presidents have pledged to make their governments more inclusive by reaching out to women and minorities—groups that have found themselves underrepresented among high-level Senate-confirmed presidential appointments. The promise of "fresh faces" by Jimmy Carter, the pledge of "new faces" by George Bush, and a commitment to an administration that "looks more like America" by Bill Clinton encouraged close monitoring of the presidents-elect by the press, political observers, and women's groups. Even President Reagan, who did not appoint a woman to head a cabinet department until 1983, emphasized diversity in his selection of appointees by prominently featuring Jeane Kirkpatrick, ambassador to the United Nations. Having elevated her position to cabinet rank, the administration's inclusion of Kirkpatrick in the center of the official White House portrait of the cabinet conveyed the notion that this otherwise all-male administration was also inclusive of women.[2]

The rest of this chapter provides an analysis of presidential appointment patterns from both the president's and the appointee's perspective. From the presidential perspective, presidents have long claimed and advertised to be organizing a more inclusive presidency than their predecessors. Presidents thus demonstrate an attentiveness to the electorate through descriptive representation (e.g., appointing people of different ethnicities, races, and genders), as well as through symbolic representation by prominently featuring any and all of these diversity appointments.

The first part of this chapter examines the presidential rhetoric that has led to enhanced scrutiny and monitoring of recent administrations for "diversity" appointments, especially by the media. This discussion is followed by an assessment of the truthfulness of these claims. Whereas the amount of descriptive representation can be assessed through quantitative statistics, the impact of symbolic representation cannot be so easily measured. In fact, a president may achieve a greater degree of symbolic representation when fewer women are included in an administration than occurs when women are selected for a large number of posts. This is especially true in cases where few women may be appointed but those who are receive the highest administration posts.

In the remainder of the chapter, the perspective shifts to that of the appointee. Differences in the career paths and political ambition of women and men are examined within the context of wider societal trends (e.g., increasing access of women to educational opportunities and other political resources). The development of a pool from which women can be recruited for government posts highlights reasons presidents may have more or less success in efforts to diversify their administrations. Finally, the interrelations between women's "personal" and public lives are considered. Although research in this area has been limited, the area has not escaped presidential attention.

Presidential Rhetoric

The analysis of presidential rhetoric begins with the Carter administration, which is the first administration in which gender begins to be addressed systematically in the administration's consideration of descriptive representation.

President Carter

In mid-November 1976, President-Elect Jimmy Carter invited enhanced media scrutiny. He "instructed his talent scouts to provide him with the names of at least one experienced Washington insider, someone from outside the capital, a woman and a black for each position in his Cabinet."[3] When there were no women among Carter's early cabinet nominees, he had to defend both his talent search and his choices.

Jane Cahill Pfeiffer's withdrawal from consideration as secretary of commerce in mid-December prompted a flurry of discussion, and Pfeiffer soon felt impelled to explain her actions. A former vice president at IBM, she had married Ralph Pfeiffer one year earlier and gained a ready-made family of ten stepchildren. Her first priority was her marriage, and she stated that "I did not feel I could take on the responsibility of an assignment in Washington without my husband with me and that just wasn't possible."[4]

In a news conference shortly after Pfeiffer's remarks, Carter commented,

> When a woman has become a pre-eminent leader in the business or professional world, she can demand and receive superb salaries. . . . In addition to that, quite often a woman who has become prominent becomes a member of the boards of directors of five, six, seven, eight major corporations.
>
> Each one of those corporations pays stipends of 10 to 20 thousand dollars each. . . . So there's a tremendous salary level for women who are well-known and who serve in major positions; and this has made it difficult for some of them to decide to come into government.
>
> Women have a much more difficult time telling the other members of their family that they're going to move to Washington than do men; and I've had several women who have expressed some concern that they would like to serve in the Government, and they just couldn't split their family, and their husband was not willing to move.[5]

A few days later, Carter found himself under attack by prominent women leaders, including Juanita Kreps, the first woman nominated to the cabinet by the president-elect. She gently "twitted" Carter "for suggesting . . . he had found a paucity of qualified women to serve in his administration."[6] Bella Abzug, a member of Congress who commuted between her home in New York and work in Washington, D.C., noted that "the problem of jobs that call for travel had usually been met by women of achievement long before they were recruited for the government."[7] And many professional women have relocated to follow a husband's career move to Washington, D.C.[8]

As we will see later after we examine the rhetoric of each of his successors, President Carter eventually appointed four women to cabinet posts and a number of women to other posts. Carter thus provided a marker against which the press and others could measure success in regard to descriptive representation.

President Reagan

Reagan did not lay down the same challenge and invitation to close scrutiny as had Carter, yet he did receive such attention in 1982. Responding to a question posed by longtime Washington correspondent Sarah McClendon at a news conference dealing with a Justice Department report on discrimination against women in the executive branch, Reagan stated, "I don't know of any administration that in the first 16 months that it was here placed as many women—certainly not the last administration—in high positions, a great number of them requiring confirmation."[9]

With this challenge, media scrutiny resumed. In a press conference a year later, Chris Wallace of NBC News asked why women had not been appointed to the newly formed Kissinger Commission on Central America, adding, "Doesn't that add to the perception that you're insensitive to women?" The president replied by listing his administration's accomplishments for women in the areas of tax policies and tax credits for child care. Reagan then observed, "I noticed the other night that someone on the air was comparing our record to that of the previous administration. . . . And when you compare our first 2 years with their first 2 years, well, we're quite a ways out ahead."[10]

When a reporter persisted in getting an answer to the question "Why [are] no women on this commission?" Reagan replied, "Maybe it's because we're doing so much and appointing so many that we're no longer seeking a token or something. It just came out that these were the 12 we selected. . . . But we've appointed over 1,000 women in executive positions here in government . . . it's just a case of our record isn't known."[11]

President Bush

President-Elect George Bush followed Carter's lead in seeking to diversify his administration. Bush invited media scrutiny when, during the 1988 presidential campaign, he joined Democratic nominee Michael Dukakis in a commitment that each would appoint more women in his administration than had ever been appointed before.[12] Craig Fuller, the transition co-director, noted that Bush wanted "to bring to his Cabinet 'men and women, different ethnic groups and, above all, the best people that he can find.'"[13] The transition team, however, faced certain problems in its search for diversity and "fresh new faces" that did not constrain the incoming Carter, Reagan, or Clinton administrations.[14] As the first president in sixty years to succeed a president of the same party without having been elevated from the vice presidency because of death or resignation, Bush inherited a government of party loyalists.

> The fact that the transition to a Bush administration was a "friendly takeover" was a mixed blessing. . . . On the one hand, there was no rush, as there would be with a party-turnover transition, to ensure that the opposition political party was out of office as soon as possible. . . . On the other hand, since they were loyal Republicans and had supported George Bush, many hoped and expected to stay on into a Bush administration.[15]

As is shown later, Reagan's appointment of relatively few women throughout his two terms[16] added a constraint in that the administration inherited by Bush was not broadly reflective of the diversity in the United States. Dissatisfied with the number of women and minorities included on short lists, Bush called upon Betty Heitman, a former president of the National Federation of Republican Women, to help locate women; Jose Martinez, a former Air Force officer and aide to former Senator John Tower, to assist in recruiting Hispanics; and Constance Newman, a former official in the Department of Housing and Urban Development, to identify African Americans for top posts.[17]

The record of the Reagan administration, however, gave President-Elect Bush some leeway. In spite of his campaign pledge to include more women, Bush did not receive the criticism that came to his successor in the White House. The press noted that this expanded transition team was designed to both "expand his base of political support [and] head off the impression that the new administration will be dominated by the white male."[18] In fact, "The reaction of some feminists and civil rights advocates was a mixture of skepticism and hope that Mr. Bush's policies in both recruiting and governing would be more acceptable to them than President Reagan's."[19] Chase Untermeyer, head of the transition team's personnel office, in a response to a question from the press on how many women and minority group members Bush would appoint, simply replied "more." Untermeyer went on to note that the president-elect "has set that standard. Certainly more than the past administration."[20]

President Clinton

Four of Clinton's first eleven appointees were women. The unveiling of these appointments, however, revealed the conflicting goals and objectives of any new administration. With a preinaugural economic conference scheduled for the second week in December 1992, Clinton had first moved to form and announce his economic team.[21] On December 10, Clinton introduced Senator Lloyd Bentsen as his secretary of the treasury; Representative Leon E. Panetta as director of the Office of Management and Budget (OMB); Alice Rivlin, former director of the Congressional Budget Office, as deputy director of OMB; investment banker Roger Altman as deputy secretary of treasury; and Robert E. Rubin, cochair of Goldman, Sachs and Company, as senior economic adviser.[22]

Clinton ran into trouble the next day. December 11's appointees were Laura D'Andrea Tyson, chair of the Council of Economic Advisors (CEA); Robert Reich, secretary of labor; Donna E. Shalala, secretary of health and human services; and Carol M. Browner, head of the Environmental Protection Agency (EPA).[23] Clinton was criticized for separating the appointment of CEA Chair Tyson from the rest of the economic advisers and moving it to a day when two other women were announced, one to head a cabinet department and the other to head an independent agency. Although Browner's appointment was elevated to cabinet rank, it was unusual to announce the administrator of the EPA before the secretaries of state, defense, and justice. Those who closely scrutinize cabinet formation noted the sudden urgency in announcing these three women. December 11 was identified as the "day of diversity and change."[24]

Clinton thus learned that in addition to the overall picture of diversity in his government, he would have to pay attention to the symbolism associated with the order and status of the positions filled. During the next two weeks the diversity drama played itself out in the media, and I found myself with a small role. As a longtime student of presidential appointments, a "bean-counter," as it were, I was quoted in the *Christian Science Monitor* as questioning the unusual order of the Clinton appointments and wondering why all the women were announced en masse.[25]

As the drama continued, "The Governor's mansion in Little Rock was flooded with faxes requesting more women appointees" during the weekend of December 19–20.[26] Clinton received criticism from a number of quarters—including Harriet Wood, chair of the Coalition for Women's Appointments,[27] and Eleanor Smeal, president of the Fund for a Feminist Majority, "who urged the President-elect to 'shatter the glass ceiling' and surpass President Bush's record of appointing three women to Cabinet positions."[28] Clinton responded testily on December 22, calling the leaders of women's groups "'bean counters' who were more interested in quotas than competence."[29]

The incoming administration's ability to set the stage for maximum dramatic effect was clearly demonstrated when Clinton responded to his critics in a news conference at which the appointment of Hazel R. O'Leary as secretary of energy was announced. Clinton noted that O'Leary's name had come to his attention through a "friend in the energy industry"[30] and gestured to O'Leary, stating that her name had not been on lists of cabinet recommendations submitted by women's and black groups.[31] O'Leary, an African American, was in fact included on the list of potential nominees submitted by the Coalition for Women's Appointments.[32] Clinton stated that

He was particularly unhappy that two of his appointees—Laura D'Andrea Tyson as chairwoman of the Council of Economic Advisors and Carol M. Browner as administrator of the Environmental Protection Agency—were being treated by some women's advocates as less important that [sic] other appointees because their jobs were not Cabinet level.

"I believe that if I had appointed white men to those jobs, those people, those same people would have been counting those jobs in a very negative way . . . against our Administration, those bean counters who are doing that, if I had appointed white men to those positions."[33]

When questioned on the "glass ceiling of three women in the Cabinet," Clinton observed that women would be "more powerful in terms of substantive impact than ever before," leaving him room to distinguish his record from those of his predecessors even if he failed to appoint four women. However, this statement opened the door for a new challenge and a new set of criteria by which to evaluate his administration.[34]

Women in the Executive Branch, 1961 to 1994

In the analysis that follows, the rhetorical claims of these presidents will be tested against the statistical record of their appointments. Thus, we have a measure by which to assess presidential rhetoric with presidential action. In this study the focus is on the nature of posts to which women have been appointed, as well as the number of women appointed in each administration. Following this analysis, the career development and career paths of women appointees are explored, as is the influence of the Washington, D.C., community on the recruitment and appointment of women. The effects of familial life on women are also addressed, since this area has been raised by presidents as a concern in their efforts to diversify their administrations.

The data in this chapter build on the study of presidential appointments begun by the National Academy of Public Administration in the 1980s. The data consist of biographical characteristics of all full-time presidential appointments to posts in executive branch departments, agencies, and regulatory commissions—with the exception of ambassadors, U.S. marshals, and U.S. attorneys—appointed and confirmed by the Senate during the period 1961 to 1994.[35]

In the last three decades the appearance of administrations has changed, with an increasing percentage of women recruited for high-level posts in successive decades. Since 1961, every administration, with the exception of those of Presidents Nixon and Reagan, has had a greater percentage of women serving in high-level posts than the preceding administration, as illustrated in Table 4.1.

Table 4.1   Percentage of Appointments Going to Women, 1961–1994

Administration	Percentage of Appointments Going to Women	
Kennedy	2.1	(N=331)
Johnson	4.8	(N=270)
Nixon	3.0	(N=301)
Ford	6.0	(N=151)
Carter	15.0	(N=360)
Reagan	13.2	(N=826)
Bush	21.4	(N=641)
Clinton	30.5	(N=476)

Source: Compiled by author.

How has this diversity been achieved? What credentials have women brought to these posts? The rest of this chapter provides an overview of who these women are, the experience they have brought to their jobs, and similarities and differences of women replacing men in high-level posts, using a number of different measures for assessment. Other authors in this volume explore the potential policy significance of women moving into these posts and issues of substantive representation (in particular, see McGlen and Sarkees's study of women in foreign and defense policy roles in Chapter 7 and Pacelle's analysis of the Office of the Solicitor General in Chapter 11). The focus here is on issues of descriptive and symbolic representation.

The "Thickening of Government"

The number of positions to which presidents make appointments has grown steadily each year. In Paul C. Light's detailed study of the increasing layering of government, he noted that

> between 1960 and 1992, the number of department secretaries increased from 10 to 14, the number of deputy secretaries from 6 to 21, under secretaries from 14 to 32, deputy under secretaries from just 9 to 52, assistant secretaries from 81 to 212, deputy assistant secretaries from 77 to 507, administrators from 90 to 128, and deputy administrators from 52 to 190.[36]

The proliferation of posts to fill—inevitably added below the highest ranks of secretary, deputy, and under secretary—has occurred at the same time the number of women appointed has increased. It is not surprising, therefore, that women might find their ranks increasing in these expanded positions rather than at the highest levels. Whereas the percentage of appointments going to women has increased, the increase is not seen at the highest levels. From 1977 through 1994, the Carter and Reagan presidencies—with the fewest number of women appointees of the four most recent presidents— nonetheless appointed the highest percentage of women to the highest department offices (see Table 4.2).

Table 4.2   Type of Posts to Which Appointments Have Been Made (%)

	Carter		Reagan		Bush		Clinton	
	Women	Men	Women	Men	Women	Men	Women	Men
Secretary, deputy secretary, under secretary	13.0	18.6	9.3	15.5	5.9	13.0	5.6	16.3
Assistant secretary	44.4	41.5	33.9	34.5	35.8	28.0	34.5	27.5
Regulatory boards and commissions	20.4	13.7	31.1	19.0	24.0	17.1	15.8	7.5
Other posts	22.2	26.2	25.7	31.0	34.3	41.9	44.1	48.7
Total	100.0	100.0	100.0	100.0	100.0	100.0	100.0	100.0
Number	54	306	109	715	137	504	145	331

Source: Compiled by author.

Issues of symbolic representation have seemed important, especially when the number of women in high-level posts has been small. As the first woman in the cabinet and a part of a network of women whose "friendship and cooperation . . . maximized their influence in politics and government," Frances Perkins helped to bring women into the government, including into the Labor Department.[37] However, "Perkins could only go so far in making the Labor Department a female enclave. As the first woman Secretary of Labor, Perkins did not feel she could appoint another woman as head of one of Labor's main divisions."[38] The substantive role of women was correspondingly limited, as was the descriptive representation of the Labor Department in terms of the population it served. (See Borrelli's extensive discussion of issues of descriptive and substantive representation, focusing especially on the cabinet, in Chapter 5.)

The increase in the number of women appointed has not resulted in an increased percentage of women moving into the highest policy posts in the cabinet departments. Rather, the women are appointed to regulatory boards and commissions; to posts such as deputy administrator or agency administrator or bureau director; and to the post of assistant secretary. However, the assistant secretary post and other lower-level posts may provide the experience needed for vertical movement within departments. As President Carter noted, there is a sequencing of posts: "I'm going to make a special additional effort at the Under Secretary, Deputy and Assistant Secretary level to take into the administration those who are now in a process of being trained for a higher position."[39]

Although overall there has been a proliferation of positions, the post of cabinet secretary continues to have special significance, and the number of department heads, although increasing over time, has remained small. Thus, this post merits special consideration when examining the appointment of women to executive branch posts.

The President's Cabinet

In the last two hundred years only sixteen of over six hundred cabinet appointments have gone to women.[40] Not until President Franklin Delano Roosevelt appointed Frances Perkins secretary of labor in 1933 did a woman serve in the cabinet. Perkins left her cabinet post in 1945, and there was an eight-year gap before a second woman, Oveta Culp Hobby, served in the cabinet. Hobby, who headed the newly created Department of Health, Education and Welfare, was appointed in 1953 by President Eisenhower—twenty years after the appointment of Perkins. It was another twenty years until the third woman was appointed—Carla Anderson Hills, appointed in 1975 to head the Department of Housing and Urban Development (see Table 4.3).

Table 4.3 Women in the Cabinet

Name	Appointing President	Department	Term of Office
Perkins	F. D. Roosevelt	Labor	1933–1945
Hobby	Eisenhower	HEW	1953–1955
Hills	Ford	HUD	1975–1977
Kreps	Carter	Commerce	1977–1979
Harris	Carter	HUD	1977–1979
Harris	Carter	HEW	1979–1980
Hufstedler	Carter	Education	1979–1981
Heckler	Reagan	HHS	1983–1985
Dole	Reagan	Transportation	1983–1987
McLaughlin	Reagan	Labor	1987–1989
Dole	Bush	Labor	1989–1990
Martin	Bush	Labor	1991–1993
Franklin	Bush	Commerce	1992–1993
O'Leary	Clinton	Energy	1993–
Reno	Clinton	Justice	1993–
Shalala	Clinton	HHS	1993–

Note: HEW - Health, Education and Welfare; HHS - Health and Human Services; HUD - Housing and Urban Development.

In a number of ways, few differences are found between the men and women appointed to the cabinet. For example, the median age of the fourteen women who served in the cabinet from 1961 to 1994 is 52.5 years, whereas the median age for men is 53.0. A majority of men and women are recruited to the cabinet directly from service in the public sector, with 54.0 percent of the men and 57.1 percent of the women moving from a post in government at the local, state, or federal level to a post in the cabinet.

With cabinet secretaries often having prior experience in the departments they head, especially for posts in the inner cabinet, it becomes important to examine whether women are in the pool of those considered when the highest posts to the cabinet are chosen. One notable difference between the men and women who have served in the cabinet since 1961 is that whereas nearly equal percentages of men and women have had some executive branch experience (57 percent for women, 62 percent for men), only one woman had gained that experience in the department she was heading (Hazel O'Leary, Clinton's secretary of energy).

In contrast, over a fourth of the men (26 percent, N=138) had such continuity of experience. Prior research has shown that for the inner cabinet posts, there has been a tendency to draw from those who have had previous government service in the department (e.g., elevating a deputy secretary to secretary, as in the case of William Perry, Clinton's secretary of defense) or from those who have served as deputy or under secretary in an administration (e.g., moving them to the post of secretary in a subsequent administration as with Warren Christopher, deputy secretary of state under Carter and secretary of state under Clinton).[41] Given the paucity of women in high-level posts over the past twenty years, it is not surprising to see so few women in the cabinet—especially in the inner cabinet, where Attorney General Janet Reno has been the first woman. As the numbers of women increase in a variety of positions, especially in the subcabinet, the number of women in the cabinet will likely correspondingly increase.

Continuity and Change: The Washington Community

Presidents enter the White House following one of two scenarios: (1) party succession, that is, an individual succeeds a president of the same party through either election or the elevation of a vice president upon the death or resignation of an incumbent president; or (2) party transition, that is, control of the White House changes from one party to another following an election. The way presidents come to the White House affects their ability to structure an administration. A president who comes in as the leader of the "out party" will have greater leeway in fulfilling campaign pledges by bringing in "new faces" than will a president whose party remains in control of the White House. This structural aspect is similar to that facing presidents once in office—that is, as an administration progresses, the tendency is greater to draw upon those in the Washington community for service.[42]

As the president and administration work with those in the Washington community—careerists in the departments and agencies, members of Congress, and interest group lobbyists—there is an increased sense of trust and enhanced respect for the members of the Washington community. Moreover, once an administration has been in office for a year or two, there grows a pool of individuals who have gained experience in lower-level appointed posts—for example, as assistant agency heads—who may be tapped for advancement to a higher post.[43]

Table 4.4   **Recruitment of Women and Men from the Washington, D.C., Area (includes Virginia and Maryland) (Percentage Employed in Washington)**

	Carter	Reagan	Reagan First Term	Reagan Second Term	Bush	Clinton
Women	57.7	76.0	64.7	82.2	75.8	55.6
Men	48.3	60.1	47.8	70.2	66.3	51.3

Source: Compiled by author.

In the period from 1961 to 1994, the presidents who drew most heavily from those in the Washington area in making their initial appointments were Presidents Johnson, Ford, and Bush.[44] Each of these men succeeded presidents of the same party, and many of their appointees had past government experience in the federal sector. The Washington community has also proved fertile for presidents in their recruitment of women as both initial and midterm replacements.[45] Of the Senate-confirmed presidential appointments from 1961 through 1994, 64.9 percent of all women (N=482), in contrast to only 54.1 percent (N=2,938) of men, came from the Washington, D.C., area. It therefore appears that women who are already living and working in the Washington, D.C., area are tapped for executive branch posts. Thus, presidents avoid revisiting the "Pfeiffer dilemma" of recruiting women whose personal lives preclude their relocating to the capitol.

There is an expectation that any difference between men and women in geographical mobility would lessen over time to reflect changes in society in which dual-career households maintain homes in different parts of the country or in which it becomes more common for the wife's rather than the husband's career path to influence the part of the country in which a family resides. Table 4.4 provides some evidence of such an evolution. For instance, in both the Carter and Bush administrations, a greater percentage of women than men came from the Washington, D.C., area. The Reagan administration needs special consideration in that whereas the gap is 16 percent, much greater than that for either the Carter or Bush administrations, few women were among the initial round of appointments. As has been noted, as an administration establishes itself, the tendency is greater to turn to the Washington community for job candidates. Therefore, women appointed well into an administration are more likely to come from the Washington area.

In the Clinton administration, the 9 percent gap seen for both the Carter and Bush administrations is cut in half, with only 4 percent more women than men coming from the Washington area. Whether this reflects increasing societal acceptance of women following independent career paths or partisan effects of presidential succession is an interesting line of inquiry for future research.

In addition to societal influences, a second explanation for these differences lies in the nature of how names come to the presidents-elect and presidents for consideration. Journalists and scholars have long identified an "old boy's" network, no matter how elaborate the recruitment structure. Dom Bonafede has described the ad hoc nature of the appointment process—a process whereby readily available advisers, often close associates from the recent campaign, suggest and seek out names from past associates.[46]

Political scientists, however, have often overlooked the "old girl's" network" at work in appointment decisions. Certainly a factor in Franklin D. Roosevelt's administration, this phenomenon is only now beginning to be systematically explored. For example, in his study of the White House Personnel Office, *The Politicizing Presidency,* Thomas J. Weko noted the role of the National Women's Political Caucus in forming the Coalition for Women's Appointments—which represents the interests of fifty women's organizations—to suggest names to the incoming Carter transition team in 1976, "the first independent effort of women's organizations to collect resumes and lobby for the appointment of women."[47] In fact, the Coalition for Women's Appointments existed during the Nixon and Ford administrations, but it did not play an influential role in the appointment process until Carter's election,[48] since presidents and their staffs structure the advice received and used in the decisionmaking process.

As Susan Carroll and Barbara Geiger-Parker observed in looking at Carter's appointment process, "The lobby effort by the Coalition, combined with a presidential commitment to appoint substantial numbers of women, created a climate of expectations about women's appointments far more optimistic than in the past."[49] Whereas the structure of the decisionmaking process and the president's receptivity to advice from a number of different sources are important, it is also true that the political resources of any outside group seeking to play a role is a determinative factor in whether representatives of that group will be selected for administration posts. G. Calvin

Mackenzie's observation that the response of the Carter administration in increasing the number of women appointed was the result not of "any substantial alteration in the operation of the appointment process, but rather of a change in the relative political strength of the actors who compose its environment" is a key consideration, one that has often been overlooked in studies of the appointment process.[50]

The political strength of women and women's groups in shaping decisionmaking in the White House has probably received more attention from historians than from political scientists.[51] Susan Ware's analysis of the role of Molly Dewson in the Democratic Party and of Eleanor Roosevelt in the White House in facilitating the appointment of women to administrative posts in the 1930s is particularly insightful.[52]

The Washington Community: The Role of Education

Presidents Bush and Clinton present a contrast in generations; Bush is a veteran of World War II, and Clinton is the first president born after the end of World War II. The different generations mirror changes in society, especially in terms of educational opportunities available for men and women. As expected, presidential appointees overall are highly educated, with three-fourths having advanced degrees at the time of appointment. And as seen in Table 4.5, in each administration beginning with that of President Carter, a greater percentage of men than women held advanced degrees, which reflects patterns found in society. With the Clinton administration, however, that pattern changes, and women now hold the greater percentage of advanced degrees.[53]

Table 4.5   Percentage of Appointees with Advanced Degrees, 1977–1994

	Women	Men
Carter	78.7	83.5
Reagan	63.8	76.3
Bush	65.7	75.7
Clinton	83.9	81.7

Source: Compiled by author.

Bush drew heavily from those in government and in the Washington, D.C., area in filling posts in his administration. As a result, it is not surprising that overall, more men and women in the Bush administration received advanced degrees from one of the Washington universities than from more prestigious graduate programs, such as Harvard and Yale. In the case of Clinton, who drew widely from across the country and chose more appointees with no prior service in the executive branch, the pattern is reversed—with a greater percentage of both men and women receiving degrees from Harvard and Yale than from Georgetown, American University, and George Washington University. (See Table 4.6.)

Table 4.6   Graduate Schools Attended, 1989–1994 (% of total)

	Women	Men
Bush appointees		
Washington, D.C. universities (American,		
George Washington, Georgetown)	17.2	10.4
Harvard, Yale	8.8	12.0
Clinton appointees		
Washington, D.C. universities (American,		
George Washington, Georgetown)	12.6	4.5
Harvard, Yale	14.0	21.4

Source: Compiled by author.

These patterns are similar to those found in earlier decades. David Stanley, Dean Mann, and Jameson Doig observed in 1967, in looking at appointments made from 1933 through April 1965, that a large percentage of those selected for high-level posts had received advanced degrees from Harvard (22.2 percent) and Yale (8.1 percent).[54] Another 8 percent had earned advanced degrees from either Georgetown or George Washington, "where the men went to night classes" and worked during the day.[55]

The Bush and Clinton administrations, with substantial inclusions of women, allow more intensive study of the career paths of men and women political appointees. As noted earlier, evidence supports the theory that because of job mobility that traditionally has been less available to women than to men, presidents have tended to draw more heavily from women already in Washington, D.C., whereas the search for men has covered a wider geographic sweep. There may be another explanation for the geographic difference, however. Of the graduate schools attended by men and women, a far greater percentage of women than of men in both the Bush and Clinton administrations received advanced degrees from one of the prominent universities in Washington, D.C. (i.e., American, Georgetown, or George Washington).

These institutions may be selected because they provide the easiest access for pursuit of a career in Washington, D.C., and therefore are part of a long-term career strategy that involves selecting an institution based in part on its geographic location. Often, those with master's and law degrees will choose to work in the area where the degree was obtained. These same institutions also have programs that allow career professionals to receive master's and law degrees in extended-year and evening programs. Regardless of the reason, these institutions are providing the credentials that facilitate upward mobility.

The Clinton administration, which has a record number of women and a more detailed recording of information, can more precisely indicate the influence of the most prestigious educational institutions in the recruitment of women as high-level public servants.[56] In looking at the undergraduate education of the Clinton appointees, nearly a fourth of the women and men were educated at the most selective eastern private colleges,[57] with 18.7 percent of the women having a degree from one of the Seven Sisters schools.[58] This is similar to the pattern Susan Ware identified in looking at the network of women in politics and government who were influential in the 1930s (yet who were not necessarily serving in a high-level post). A fourth of these women had attended one of the Seven Sisters colleges. A noticeable difference, however, between the influential women of the 1930s and those in the 1990s is that a number of the prominent women in the 1930s never attended college (including Eleanor Roosevelt), whereas virtually all of the women appointed in the 1990s have done so.[59] First Lady Hillary Rodham Clinton not only has a degree from Wellesley but also has a law degree from Yale.

In fact, although women may represent members of society not heretofore represented, the women in the Clinton administration—even more than the men—are less representative of society. Of the Clinton appointees, 83.9 percent of the women and 81.7 percent of the men have advanced degrees. In contrast, in overall patterns in society, of persons who are at least twenty-five years of age 24.5 percent of men but only 18.1 percent of women have attended at least four years of college.[60] Thus, the pool of potential appointees remains small. As educational opportunities have become available to women, however, advanced degrees are providing the same credentials for women as they have for men to move into the pool of eligible candidates. And for both men and women, the appointees are not descriptively representative of the educational levels found in the general population.

The Washington Community: Party Succession, Party Transition

As prior research has shown, those "administrations with the greatest percentage of appointees with experience in the federal sector have all succeeded an administration of the same party."[61] This includes any full-time work in the bureaus and in the federal civil service (see Table 4.7).

The fact that presidents grow more comfortable with the Washington community as their terms progress is reflected in their increasing elevation of those with federal government experience to executive posts. This creates an opportunity path for women. As noted earlier, even though an "old girl's network" has been identified, it has not had the constancy seen with the "old

Table 4.7　Past Federal Administrative Experience, by President, 1961–1994

Administration	Percentage of Those with Federal Administrative Experience	
Kennedy	61.3	(N=331)
Johnson	68.3	(N=271)
Nixon	59.9	(N=302)
Ford	64.2	(N=151)
Carter	54.4	(N=364)
Reagan	69.8	(N=827)
First term	59.5	(N=358)
Second term	77.8	(N=464)
Bush	78.8	(N=641)
Clinton	57.1	(N=476)

Source: Compiled by author.

boy's network." The circumstances that facilitated its role in the New Deal have not been repeated, and not all presidents have been receptive to the Coalition for Women's Appointments. With women underrepresented in the inner circle of campaign advisers throughout the twentieth century, the women a president and his advisers have turned to are those from the Washington community who have the federal administrative experience that gives them one type of credential needed for a high-level post.

Table 4.8　Past Federal Administrative Experience of Women and Men, 1977–1994

Administration	Percentage of Those with Federal Administrative Experience			
	Women		Men	
Carter	50.0	(N=54)	56.0	(N=306)
Reagan	74.0	(N=109)	69.0	(N=716)
Bush	81.0	(N=137)	78.0	(N=504)
Clinton	49.0	(N=145)	61.0	(N=331)

Source: Compiled by author.

Table 4.8 presents data on the past federal administrative experience of men and women who have served in high-level posts since the Carter administration, the first administration that included a sizable number of women in executive posts. Same-party succession, rather than gender, appears to be a factor in the career paths of political appointees, with a far greater percentage of Republican than Democratic men and women having federal government experience. This finding suggests different opportunity structures for Republicans and Democrats, largely because of Republican control of the White House for all but six years in the period from 1977 to 1994.

In the past government service of all of those appointed during the period 1961–1994, 26.2 percent (N=489) of the women and 32.2 percent (N=2,981) of the men served in more than one appointive post. The Clinton administration is typical of the pattern whereby party transition administrations look outside Washington in forming a new administration. After twelve years of Republican rule, President Clinton searched widely and selected few who had served in the highest levels in previous administrations. Only 17 percent (N=331) of the men and 9 percent (N=145) of the women Clinton chose had served previously in a Senate-confirmed post.

In addition, in the cases of the Carter and Clinton administrations—both of which entailed a party transition—a greater percentage of *men* than women came from the federal sector, as opposed to the pattern found in the Republican administrations, where a greater percentage of *women* had served previously in one of these top-level posts. The Clinton administration was not only diverse, it was also a new administration—especially in terms of bringing more women into the highest levels of government, few of whom had previously served in a high-level Senate-confirmed post.

The Clinton administration presents a stark contrast to the case of Bush, who had inherited a government already in place. Although Bush pledged to bring in "new faces," the task was not so simple when he faced loyal Republicans already serving in the administration and hoping to continue to do so.[62] And in fact, Bush showed a greater tendency to look within government, at those who had already been tapped for a government post, in recruiting women. In the Bush administration, over a third of the women and over a fourth of the men had served in prior posts.

Conclusion

Recent presidents have done much to stimulate discussion on issues of the descriptive representation of women in high-level appointive positions. Even when the rhetoric has been absent, as in the case of Reagan's first year in the White House, the imagery has been present.

Since 1977, each succeeding administration has striven for "diversity" in its appointments, which has resulted in the recruitment and appointment of increasingly greater numbers of women. This increase is the result not just of evolving abstract political values but also of the rise in effectiveness of women's network groups.

Women political executives selected for these high-level posts have been drawn more heavily from the Washington community than have their male cohorts. Possible explanations include greater societal constraints on career mobility for women, especially those with children and with husbands who do not have jobs in the Washington, D.C., area; the role of women's networks centered in Washington, which recommend those women most familiar to the network—that is, those in the Washington community; and finally, the influence of Washington-area universities in both attracting and helping to credential women who are appropriate for these positions.

Finally, with the thickening of government, more posts have become available, thus opening up slots for women. These appointments, made at lower levels, provide an opportunity structure for the advancement of women to cabinet posts. They have also worked to lessen the showcasing aspect of appointments of women, whereby only a few women were appointed in an administration, but they were given very visible and high-level posts. Accordingly, presidents have expanded their focus to address the requirements of both symbolic and descriptive representation.

Notes

1. Gwen Ifill. "Clinton Chooses 2 and Deplores Idea of Cabinet Quotas." *New York Times,* December 22, 1992, sec A.

2. *New York Times,* December 2, 1987, sec B.

3. Hedrick Smith. "Carter Urges Aides to Find a Broad 'Mix' for Posts in Cabinet." *New York Times,* November 19, 1976, sec A.

4. "Jane Cahill Pfeiffer Expected to Be Announced as Secretary of Commerce." *New York Times,* December 15, 1976, sec A.

5. James T. Wooten. "Carter Considering Splitting CIA Post Between 2 Persons." *New York Times,* December 19, 1976, sec. A.

6. James T. Wooten. "Carter Names Friend as Attorney General and Selects Woman." *New York Times,* December 21, 1976, sec. A.

7. Lawrence Van Gelder. "Women Leaders Differ with Carter on the Difficulties of Taking U.S. Job." *New York Times,* December 23, 1976, sec. A.

8. For example, in the Clinton administration the congressional careers of some husbands have brought families to Washington and facilitated the selection of women to high-level posts. Assistant Attorney General Ann Bingaman moved her law practice to Washington when her husband, Jeff Bingaman, was elected to the U.S. Senate. Ruth Harkin, selected president of the Overseas Private Investment Corporation, was an attorney with a Washington law firm for a number of years while her husband, Tom Harkin, served in the House of Representatives and then in the U.S. Senate.

9. Ronald Reagan. 1982. *Public Papers of the Presidents of the United States.* Washington, D.C.: U.S. Government Printing Office. "The President's News Conference," July 28, 1982, p. 988.

10. Ibid., July 26, 1983, p. 1088.

11. Ibid.

12. Judith Havemann. "Bush to Get 2,500 Conservative Resumes." *Washington Post,* November 15, 1988, sec A.

13. Frank Swoboda and Judith Havemann. "The Search for New Faces Continues." *Washington Post National Weekly Edition,* December 12–18, 1988.

14. Ibid.

15. James P. Pfiffner. 1990. "Establishing the Bush Presidency." *Public Administration Review* 50 (Jan./Feb.): 67–68.

16. Janet M. Martin. 1991. "An Examination of Executive Branch Appointments in the Reagan Administration by Background and Gender." *Western Political Quarterly* 44: 173–184. The appointment of women as a percentage of total appointments from 1961 through 1988 is as follows for each administration: Kennedy 2.1 (N=331), Johnson 4.8 (N=270), Nixon 3.0 (N=301), Ford 6.0 (N=151), Carter 15.0 (N=360), and Reagan 13.2 (N=826).

17. Ann Devroy. "Bush Likely to Tap Black for Cabinet." *Washington Post,* December 10, 1988, sec A; and Bernard Weinraub. "Bush Plans a Drive to Recruit Minorities." *New York Times,* December 4, 1988.

18. Bernard Weinraub. "Bush Plans a Drive to Recruit Minorities."

19. Ibid.

20. Ibid.

21. Thomas Friedman. "Experts Gather for Conference on the Economy." *New York Times,* December 14, 1992, sec B.

22. Thomas L. Friedman. "Clinton Team Takes Shape with Bentsen and 4 Others Named to Economic Posts." *New York Times,* December 11, 1992, sec. A.

23. Ann Devroy and Al Kamen. "Social Policy Posts Filled by Clinton." *Washington Post,* December 12, 1992, sec A.

24. Marshall Ingwerson. "Clinton Stresses Diversity, Fiscal Probity in Cabinet." *Christian Science Monitor,* December 14, 1992.

25. Ibid.

26. Catherine S. Manegold. "Clinton Ire on Appointments Startles Women." *New York Times,* December 23, 1992, sec. A (electronic).

27. Ibid.

28. Ifill, "Clinton Chooses 2 and Deplores Idea of Cabinet Quotas"; and Ingwerson, "Clinton Stresses Diversity, Fiscal Probity." [President Carter also named three women to cabinet posts, with Harris serving in two posts.]

29. Ifill, "Clinton Chooses 2 and Deplores Idea of Cabinet Quotas."

30. Jeffrey H. Birnbaum and Timothy Noah. "Clinton Picks Female Energy Secretary, O'Leary, but Criticizes Women's Groups." *Wall Street Journal,* December 22, 1992, sec. A.

31. Ifill, "Clinton Chooses 2 and Deplores Idea of Cabinet Quotas."

32. Birnbaum and Noah, "Clinton Picks Female Energy Secretary, O'Leary, but Criticizes Women's Groups."

33. Ifill, "Clinton Chooses 2 and Deplores Idea of Cabinet Quotas."

34. Ibid.

35. I am extremely appreciative of the assistance provided by Cal Mackenzie, Linda Fisher, and Paul Light of the National Academy of Public Administration's Presidential Appointee Project in making the project's data available. For full information on the project, see G. Calvin Mackenzie, ed. 1987. *The In-and-Outers: Presidential Appointees and Transient Government in Washington.* Baltimore: Johns Hopkins University Press. Student research assistants who have worked on this project include Marty Malague, John Dougherty, Tim Blakely, Melissa Koch, Stephanie Fine, Erika Hafner, Deirdre Griffin, and Sean Cronin.

36. Paul C. Light. 1995. *Thickening Government: Federal Hierarchy and the Diffusion of Accountability.* Washington, D.C.: Brookings Institution, p. 8.

37. Susan Ware. 1981. *Beyond Suffrage: Women in the New Deal.* Cambridge: Harvard University Press, p. 2.

38. Ibid., p. 54.

39. Wooten, "Carter Considering Splitting CIA Post Between 2 Persons."

40. Herbert F. Weisberg. 1987. "Cabinet Transfers and Departmental Prestige." *American Politics Quarterly* 15: 238–253.

41. Janet M. Martin. 1985. "Cabinet Secretaries from Truman to Johnson: An Examination of Theoretical Frameworks for Cabinet Studies." Ph.D. dissertation. The Ohio State University.

42. Martin, "An Examination of Executive Branch Appointments in the Reagan Administration by Background and Gender," p. 175.

43. Janet M. Martin. 1992. "George Bush and the Executive Branch." In *Leadership and the Bush Presidency,* ed. Ryan J. Barilleaux and Mary E. Stuckey. Westport, Conn.: Praeger, p. 43.

44. Initial appointments are those made during the first six months of an administration, except in the case of Lyndon Johnson, who inherited an administration and retained most of the Kennedy appointments until November 1964. For Johnson, the initial appointments are those made before November 1964.

45. This discussion includes those working in Washington, D.C., Virginia, or Maryland at the time of appointment.

46. Dom Bonafede. 1987. "White House Personnel Office from Roosevelt to Reagan." In *The In-and-Outers: Presidential Appointees and Transient Government in Washington,* ed. Mackenzie.

47. Thomas J. Weko. 1995. *The Politicizing Presidency: The White House Personnel Office, 1948–1994.* Lawrence: University Press of Kansas, p. 84.

48. Arvonne S. Fraser. 1983. "Insiders and Outsiders: Women in the Political Arena." In *Women in Washington: Advocates for Public Policy,* ed. Irene Tinker. Beverly Hills: Sage Publications,.

49. Susan J. Carroll and Barbara Geiger-Parker. 1983. *Women Appointed to the Carter Administration: A Comparison with Men.* New Brunswick, N.J.: Center for the American Woman and Politics, Eagleton Institute of Politics, Rutgers University, p. viii.

50. G. Calvin Mackenzie. 1981. *The Politics of Presidential Appointments.* New York: Free Press, p. 257.

51. I am addressing this issue in a larger study that examines the influence of the women's movement on the presidency. In addition, see Susan Ware's study, *Beyond Suffrage.* Ware does much in providing evidence of a women's network that "recruited women for prominent government positions, demanded increased political patronage, and generally fostered an awareness of women as a special interest group with a substantial role to play in the New Deal." p. 7.

52. Ibid. See especially chapters 1–3.

53. By 1982, women were earning over half of all degrees awarded (including associate's, bachelor's, master's, first professional degrees, and doctor's); and a third of doctorates. See the U.S. Bureau of the Census. 1991. *Statistical Abstract of the United States, 1991 (111th ed.).* Washington, D.C.: Table no. 283, p. 167; and *1989–90 Fact Book on Higher Education.* 1989. Compiled by Charles J. Anderson, et al. New York: Macmillan. Table 128, p. 205.

54. David T. Stanley, Dean E. Mann, and Jameson W. Doig. 1967. *Men Who Govern: A Biographical Profile of Federal Political Executives.* Washington, D.C.: Brookings Institution, p. 128.

55. Ibid., p. 23.

56. The study done by the National Academy of Public Administration recorded the prestigious men's colleges but not the prestigious women's colleges by name. The women's colleges were coded as "other."

57. The colleges include Smith, Wellesley, Vassar, Radcliffe, Bryn Mawr,

Barnard, Sarah Lawrence, Amherst, Columbia, Dartmouth, Princeton, Wesleyan, Williams, Brown, Cornell, Harvard, and Yale.

58. Smith, Wellesley, Vassar, Radcliffe, Mount Holyoke, Barnard, and Bryn Mawr.

59. Ware, *Beyond Suffrage,* p. 23.

60. U.S. Bureau of the Census, *Statistical Abstract of the United States, 1991 (111th edition),* Table no. 225, p. 139.

61. Martin, "George Bush and the Executive Branch," p. 50; also see Martin, "An Examination of Executive Branch Appointments in the Reagan Administration by Background and Gender."

62. Pfiffner, "Establishing the Bush Presidency," pp. 64–72.

5

Campaign Promises, Transition Dilemmas: Cabinet Building and Executive Representation

MaryAnne Borrelli

In his classic work on the cabinet, Richard Fenno noted that this institution has fulfilled a representative function by drawing "social constituencies" into closer relationships with the presidency. A concern for "balance" among those constituencies was taken as evidence of a president's desire to ensure an equitable representation of society's "pluralism and diversity."[1] Without denying the continuity associated with these political calculations, a present need remains to assess how the battles for cabinet representation are changing as women and people of color become more influential within both the electorate and the Washington community.[2]

In the past, negotiations for cabinet representation were restricted to organized or semiorganized interests—the business community for Treasury and Commerce appointments, unions for Labor, and so forth. Today, however, women and racial and ethnic groups are gaining the electoral strength to demand presidential resources.[3] Chief executives have begun to recruit "diversity" appointees for their administrations.[4] But a willingness to practice more inclusive appointment politics does not necessarily alter the substantive representation provided by presidential nominees.[5] Certainly, it does not require that the president-elect welcome a diversity of voices, as "voice" has been defined by gender politics scholars.

This chapter argues that cabinet representation of women and of people of color has significantly affected the process and substance of cabinet formation during the presidential transition. Presidents-elect must consult (or, minimally, consider the wishes of) those once invisible to political institutions. At the same time, long-established cabinet constituencies must be reassured that their own power is not waning. It is not enough under these circumstances to say that cabinet building has become more contentious. One must note instead that the contenders have changed and that the communications and relationships that create representation are continuing to do so.

Specifically, a detailed case study of the Clinton cabinet-building experience suggests that "diversity" appointees are most acceptable as descriptive representatives whose presence does little to modify the established patterns of substantive representation within the cabinet. When descriptive representation potentially challenges Washington's established power brokers, the representatives' influence is delimited. Ultimately, the "diversity" appointees' contributions to descriptive representation may be lost.

Building the Clinton Cabinet

During his 1992 campaign, Clinton promised to build a more inclusive government that would prioritize domestic issues. He won the election by a plurality vote, with a coalition of frustrated liberals and beleaguered centrists.[6] As the Clinton advisers later acknowledged, there was no sense of relationship or coherence among these constituents. Meanwhile, Clinton was about to undergo the postelection scrutiny reserved for Democratic presidents-elect who are perceived as presiding over a coalition of societal groups.[7] Clinton would find his campaign promise of an administration that "looks like America" well remembered by the press and the public. The president-elect therefore entered his transition, a time in which expectations are unusually high and public oversight is unusually detailed, having raised hopes and interests even further.

Clinton wanted cabinet members with whom he could work constructively and comfortably, and he therefore conducted the recruitment interviews himself. He then checked his impressions with a small number of close advisers: Hillary Rodham Clinton, Al Gore, Bruce Lindsey (later assistant to the president and deputy counsel to the president), Roy Neel (later Gore's chief of staff), Thomas McLarty (later chief of staff), and Warren Christopher (later secretary of state).[8] Confining deliberations to so small and loyal a group prevented leaks and protected Clinton from early criticism.

In some respects, the maneuvering of Clinton cabinet candidates appeared similar to that observed in previous presidential transitions. Campaign relationships and debts were noted, Clinton's status as a Washington outsider was taken as evidence of his need for insiders, and influential actors were consulted. Commentators ascribed the Clinton appointments of Lloyd Bentsen (Treasury), Robert Reich (Labor), Ron Brown (Commerce), Warren Christopher (State), and Les Aspin (Defense) to these machinations.[9]

Also similar to previous transitions were the efforts of departmental issue networks and clienteles to secure cabinet secretaries who would substantively represent their interests. Their success was not unequivocal. Clinton had promised that he would not be dictated to by "special interests," and he wanted advisers whose first loyalty was to himself.[10] In several instances, therefore, he appointed an individual who was acceptable to—although not well-known by—the relevant groups. Robert Reich, Hazel O'Leary (Energy), and Richard Riley (Education) fit this profile.[11] At other times, Clinton did appoint an established advocate. The choice of Jesse Brown (Veterans Affairs), then-executive director of the Disabled Veterans of America, was an effort to improve relations with veterans.[12] Bruce Babbitt (Interior) was strongly endorsed by the conservationist lobby.[13] Henry Cisneros (Housing and Urban Development [HUD]) was a former mayor, appointed to a department of interest to mayors.[14] In the end, segments of the Labor, Energy, Education, HUD, Veterans Affairs, and Interior networks assured themselves of substantive representation within the president's cabinet.

As always, there were more idiosyncratic explanations for other appointees. Donna Shalala (Health and Human Services [HHS]), for example, was a liberal Democrat appointed to head the department in which the most extensive and liberalizing reforms were to be effected. But arching over these considerations, and also over the politicking of long-established interests and individuals, was a mobilization by women and people of color to hold the president-elect to his promise of a more inclusive government. When the cabinet was finally complete, Clinton had appointed proportionately fewer white males than had his predecessors in the modern presidency. The count was six white men, two white women, three African American men, one African American woman, and two Latino men.

The circumstances surrounding Clinton's appointment of women to the cabinet make for an unusually intriguing and illustrative study. The sometimes confrontational exchanges between the president-elect and the women's appointments activists received considerable press coverage and became an important aspect of the secretarial selection process. A study of the dynamics surrounding Clinton's women secretaries-designate, therefore, educates us in the agenda-setting politics of cabinet building.

The Coalition for Women's Appointments, which has lobbied presidents-elect since the Nixon transition, reconstituted itself in fall 1992. Approximately 70 "women's issues" interest groups joined "to promote women for top-level policymaking positions in the federal government."[15] Establishing task forces according to policy subfield, the Coalition generated a list of women whose political experience it considered sufficient to merit a presidential appointment. This annotated list was forwarded to the president-elect on November 10.[16] Subsequently, the Coalition circulated press alerts that tallied and evaluated the Clinton appointments.[17] Prominent Coalition members met with Vernon E. Jordan Jr., Clinton's Washington-based transition director.[18] At the same time, the National Political Congress of Black Women formed the nonpartisan Commission for the Presidential Appointment of African American Women.[19]

Reviewing the Coalition list, one is immediately aware that the endorsed women strongly advocated antidiscrimination measures. Otherwise, considerable diversity of policy interests and stances was found. The prospective appointees did have ties within the "women's issues" network, but those alliances were viewed as entirely congruent with the policy positions of the president and his party. Thus, the network arguably assessed its candidates in terms of their individual political ideology and partisanship, as one would expect of liberal feminists. There was no distinctively "feminine voice" to be represented, only individual talents to be exercised and respected.

A cultural or radical feminist would argue against delimiting a woman's attentiveness to her own gender and also against accepting so much of the prevailing political order. At best, these thinkers view descriptive representation as an interim step toward the desired goal of substantive representation. For liberal feminists, however, creativity is individualistic rather than gendered. From this perspective, the presidential appointment of women proves the presidency is accessible to women. When Clinton equaled the Bush record of three women department secretaries and appointed similarly substantial numbers of women to subcabinet posts, the liberals considered the Coalition a successful venture (see Chapter 4).

Media Coverage and the Depiction of Representation

Perhaps the greatest difficulty in practicing descriptive representation divorced from substantive advocacy lies in communicating the value of that representation. Notwithstanding his efforts to detail his nominees' qualifications, Clinton did not entirely succeed in communicating the caliber of his appointments. His emphasis on an administration that "looks like America" quickly degenerated into a simplistic counting of sexes, races, and ethnicities. Formal announcements of the cabinet appointments were highly self-conscious: White male nominees were always presented in company with at least one "diversity" appointee.

To further assess Clinton's performance as an image maker, one can turn to the media coverage. A comparison of *New York Times* and *Washington Post* accounts of the Carter, Reagan, and Clinton party turnover transitions revealed that Clinton's cabinet-building efforts received the most supportive coverage during those weeks. For example, editorials at that time uniformly praised both Clinton and his appointees.[20]

When one undertakes a more detailed analysis, however, this coverage is found to contain the full complement of biases. Consider, for example, the political biographies of each appointee. Accounts of white male nominees focused on their policy priorities and roles. Christopher was described as complementing National Security Adviser Anthony Lake, Bentsen as a senior statesman, Aspin and Babbitt as policy intellectuals, Reich as an innovator, and Riley as a consensus builder.[21] "Diversity" appointees, however, were presented in terms more reassuring than supportive. Reporters emphasized that these individuals would not challenge accepted relationships and offered few insights about the secretaries-designate's political or programmatic commitments.

The *New York Times* coverage is particularly interesting in this regard. *Times* headlines inventoried "diversity" appointees by sex, race, and ethnicity. Meanwhile, political biographies downplayed the relevance of that identity to the nominees' politics and ideology in three ways. First and most obviously, articles argued that the secretary-designate's sex, racial, or ethnic identity would not yield extensive change or reform. Ron Brown's political biography, for example, mentioned four times that race was "only part of his political identity." Also stressed were his extensive contacts throughout the Washington establishment and his willingness to mediate among such "unruly elements" as African American interest groups and with such "confrontational persons" as Jesse Jackson.[22]

The treatment accorded Mike Espy (Agriculture) indicates the second method of introducing "diversity" appointees. Espy was described as "black" at three points in the article that announced his appointment *and* was described as very similar to Clinton in his politics.[23] Thus, he became acceptable through his political resemblance to the elected and, at the time, increasingly well-endorsed white president-elect.[24] The women also found their establishment ties heavily accented. A gushing *Times* editorial entitled "Looks Like America" is illustrative.[25]

> In a Cabinet designed to look like America, Zoe Baird, the Attorney General–designate, has the bearing and credentials of what America would like to look like. Personable and smart, experienced in the ways of the Justice Department and White House, Ms. Baird more than vindicates President-elect Clinton's determination to put a woman at the head of the Federal legal establishment.

The heightened scrutiny Senators accord "diversity" appointees during their hearings suggests that this coverage may carry some benefits to the extent that it legitimizes the secretary-designate. Unfortunately, it also fails to distinguish the appointee from white male nominees, thus eradicating the benefits of the descriptive representation promised by the president-elect.

The third and final response was evidenced in those articles that made absolutely no mention of the secretary-designate's "diversity." This occurred in biographies of Jesse Brown, Henry Cisneros, and Federico Peña (Transportation).[26] One would otherwise have expected commentaries on the political alliances and policy implications of this more inclusive government.

Coverage by omission was also accorded the women secretaries-designate. Their sex was noted only in association with the politicking that surrounded their nomination and not in connection with their political identity. Donna Shalala's nomination was pushed forward to balance the already announced white male economic team, Hazel O'Leary seemed to have been chosen only for her sex and race, and Zoe Baird was the promised woman attorney general–designate.[27] Given the mobilization of "women's issues" interest groups on behalf of women cabinet appointees and the media's attentiveness to this lobbying, one might have expected women nominees to be assessed as representatives of this interest network or voting group. After all, Shalala's ties to the "Washington sisterhood" were notable.[28] They were also ignored in all early political biographies.

The transition is no easier for the media than for the president-elect. Campaign reporters offer one perspective on the president-elect, and the Washington press corps holds to another. Meantime, editors reach their own conclusions. Daily coverage reflects these negotiations and, consequently, reveals how well the president-elect is interacting with those whose business is communication. In this instance, the *Times* seemed to presume its readers would consider "diversity" appointees a threat. The articles rushed to reassure readers of the contrary, even to the point of rendering invisible the "diversity" that occasioned the concern. The significance of descriptive representation was therefore not merely discounted in the *New York Times;* it was ruthlessly suppressed. Similar practices were evident in the *Washington Post* and the *Los Angeles Times.* If Clinton intended to introduce a new standard of descriptive representation, he failed to convince the press of its value.

The Confirmation Hearings

Little changed during the weeks of confirmation hearings. Of course, deference to the prevailing institutions of power is expected at this time. Clinton's comparatively heavy recruitment from Congress meant some secretaries-designate would merely nuance already long-standing relationships. Several other cabinet nominees had been governors or mayors; as such, they were experienced veterans of media and legislative scrutinies. Among the members of Congress, former governors, and former mayors, therefore, Clinton could anticipate (ceteris paribus) noncontroversial hearings for seven of his fourteen cabinet secretaries-designate. Jesse Brown was similarly well respected.

The six remaining appointees—Warren Christopher, Zoe Baird, Ron Brown, Robert Reich, Donna Shalala, and Hazel O'Leary—were viewed with varying degrees of optimism by the press and the Washington community. Christopher was a product of the Carter administration, with its associated strengths (a thorough and detailed approach to foreign policymaking) and limitations (a lack of conceptual breadth and creativity). His confirmation hearing would reveal as much, without undue controversy.[29] The nomination of Commerce Secretary–Designate Ron Brown, a former corporate lobbyist and chair of the Democratic National Committee, appeared initially to compromise Clinton's campaign promise of tight ethical regulations. Brown's reluctance to name his former clients or to recuse himself from future policy decisions seemed questionable. Still, his hearing progressed smoothly until harshly critical editorials in the *New York Times* spurred Senate Republicans to make more detailed inquiries. Even so, these exchanges did not halt his progress toward confirmation.[30] Reich's hearing was uneventful.[31]

Introduced by a bipartisan coalition of two senators, a governor, and a representative, Shalala was challenged less for her history of "political correctness" than for the limited scope of her introductory statement. Committee members reminded her that HHS was concerned with more than health reform and that Clinton had promised more than a single-issue legislative agenda.[32] O'Leary was also introduced by an array of legislators, including several who freely admitted to having found her a worthy adversary in old environmental policy battles. Her hearing was uncontentious.[33]

Zoe Baird, however, dominated the Clinton confirmation scene. Observers now generally attribute the Baird nomination to the new administration's rush to meet artificial deadlines (Clinton had promised a complete cabinet by Christmas) and to hubris (Clinton's advisers maintained that the president-elect should be able to appoint whomever he wished).[34]

These qualities, however, were at work in other, successful cabinet appointments. Only in Baird's case was the nominee's representational contribution also in question. Political analysts noted that a "diversity" appointee had never before been named to the inner cabinet. When the nominee was a comparatively young woman whose legal experience was limited largely to corporate law, her qualifications became an issue.[35] Baird also had no ties to the Washington interest groups or issue networks and had no contacts outside the Clinton administration. Her only constituent was the president-elect, with whom she had a somewhat attenuated relationship. Unlike many previous attorney generals, Baird was neither a long-time friend of, nor a high-level campaign activist for, the new president.[36]

As already noted, the Coalition for Women's Appointments wanted women appointees who would be descriptive representatives for women, witnesses to the talented nature of women as individuals. There was no expectation that women appointees would speak with a "different voice" or that their policy positions would manifest a distinctively feminine nature, as would be expected of descriptive representatives who also adhered to the cultural feminist school of substantive representation for women. And yet, the appointment of a woman attorney general revealed that descriptive and substantive representation were interrelated practices for liberal feminists and for the Coalition. Because liberal feminists seek to end sex discrimination, their expectation of representation contains an element of substantive representation. As a result, the "women's issues" network implicitly hoped the woman attorney general–designate would be both a descriptive and a substantive representative for women, albeit under a firmly rights-centered liberal feminist philosophy.

Clinton, however, rejected the Coalition's recommendation of Brooksley Born and nominated Zoe Baird.[37] A corporate attorney whose ties to presidential politics came through her affiliations with white male elites—Lloyd Cutler and Warren Christopher—Baird could be presumed to have little interest in mediating the discrimination concerns of the "women's issues" network; consequently, those organizations made little effort to support her confirmation. When Clinton also failed to give her rigorous support, Baird proved unable to weather the public controversy surrounding her child-care arrangements, and the appointment was withdrawn. Although appointees are always expendable from a presidential perspective, Baird was dropped primarily because she was a representative without constituents.[38]

Baird also lacked constituents in the wider polity, again for reasons that mixed issues of descriptive and substantive representation. There was the concern that Baird was a person who had broken the law and who was now being appointed to a law enforcement position. An ABC News/*Washington Post* poll conducted the day before Baird's withdrawal found that 58 percent of respondents felt she should not be confirmed.[39] *USA Today* reported that her actions were taken as indicating that she viewed herself as above the law (56 percent of respondents) and as undermining her ability to enforce the law (59 percent).[40] On the day of her withdrawal, 75 percent of those surveyed by Gallup believed Baird had lied in claiming an inability to hire legal workers.[41] These judgments appeared to weigh Baird according to liberal feminist standards, examining her as an individual (transgendered) officeholder. A second set of public evaluations, however, judged Baird's femininity.

Critics repeatedly described Baird as an uncaring and neglectful mother.[42] Although supporters argued that these discussions were discriminatory—the child-care arrangements of Clinton's male appointees had not been investigated[43]—one can argue that these assessments were made in anticipation of Baird's performance as a representative. If, as the *New York Times* had averred, Baird had "the bearing and credentials of what America would like to look like,"[44] then America wanted to know what that "bearing" was: As a descriptive representative, a role model, and a standard of success, her values and behavior were of interest. At the same time, the attention paid to Baird's mothering abilities definitely raised matters of substantive representation insofar as her priorities in this role were taken as indicative of her future performance as a presidential adviser. At the least, Baird was perceived as contradicting the expectations of woman-as-nurturer. Whether these assessments were based on stereotypes or on the promises of cultural feminism remains a matter for future research. For now, it is enough to note that the public, like the "women's issues" network, rejected this first prospective woman attorney general.

The Representation of Women in the Clinton Cabinet

The Baird nomination is fascinating because it reveals the complexities that attend the descriptive and substantive representation of women by women. Although Shalala and O'Leary are also intriguing studies, their nominations do not reveal the same tensions and contradictions. First and foremost, both of these women were endorsed by the Coalition for Women's Appointments, which meant the "women's issues" network had identified them as acceptable even before they were selected for the Clinton cabinet.[45] Shalala's appointment may also have occasioned less comment because women had previously served as HHS secretary.[46] O'Leary was the first woman Energy secretary–designate, but her policy arena was less central to the "women's issues" network. (See also Chapter 2 for a contrast of the Shalala and O'Leary nominations.) When O'Leary's qualifications were challenged, she mustered bipartisan support for her confirmation.[47] In brief, O'Leary presented herself as a descriptive representative for women, particularly African American women, while also reassuring nuclear and environmental networks of her sensitivity to their substantive concerns. Although this required considerable skill, O'Leary's relations with the "women's issues" network were never as problematic or as complex as those of Zoe Baird.

If the appointment of a woman attorney general raises unusually intriguing issues of descriptive and substantive representation, then what conclusions are to be drawn about Janet Reno? She was also evaluated in traditionally gendered terms. Considerable attention was given to her guardianship of two teenagers and to the care she had personally given to her recently deceased mother. Additionally, Reno herself depicted familial relationships as crucial to her own life experience. In describing her policy priorities, she spoke of drawing criminal offenders back into constructive relationships with their communities. This attorney general–designate thus appeared to be a cultural feminist; she expressed herself in traditionally feminine terms of nurturance and discipline, a rhetoric acceptable to the wider society.[48] If Reno promised a form of substantive representation the Coalition's liberal feminists did not necessarily advocate, it was nonetheless one that did incorporate their concerns for antidiscrimination initiatives.[49]

Reno was also satisfactory as a descriptive representative. Five times elected to serve as a Democratic states attorney in Republican Dade County, Reno was widely respected for her legal professionalism and her political abilities. If some questioned her limited experience in corporate and tax law, her frank appreciation of the complexities of the Justice Department agenda was at once disarming and reassuring.[50] Reno, in brief, seemed a good role model who was well able to demonstrate the capacity of women for political excellence.

Issues of descriptive and substantive representation surface with great consistency in regard to every "diversity" appointee because the political identities and priorities of these elites occasion concern. But the appointment of a woman attorney general revealed previously latent tensions within the liberal feminist sponsorship of women appointees, thereby uncovering ways in which otherwise individualistic liberal feminists presumed their descriptive representatives would advance women's concerns. Thus, the interactive aspects of descriptive and substantive representation were revealed. The Baird and Reno appointments are also interesting for what they reveal about the Coalition for Women's Appointments as a critic of Democratic presidential administrations.

The policy preferences of the "women's issues" network and of women voters generally are more congruent with the Democratic than the Republican Party (see Chapters 9, 11, and 12). Practicing opposition politics in response to those who are otherwise one's allies is a complex matter. The Coalition's ardent support of Brooksley Born for the attorney general appointment, its subsequent (nonverbal) shunning of Zoe Baird, and its acceptance of Janet Reno suggest a network that is still negotiating its own identity. The Coalition was a strong supporter but a quiet critic, indicating a greater consensus regarding women who merit support than regarding women who should be criticized.

More generally, the wider case study of the Clinton cabinet-building experience permits an assessment of descriptive and substantive representation in the cabinet. The traditional form of representation within the cabinet—particularly the outer cabinet—is substantive representation as understood by liberal feminists. In these instances, the political executive provides clients and networks with access to the president and mediates their interests with the legislature and the wider executive branch. The difficulty, of course, is that presidents expect secretaries to evidence this degree of support for presidential priorities. Substantive representation as anticipated by the cultural feminists appears more difficult to conceptualize because it is premised on the appointees' socialization and consequent personality traits. Descriptive representation is the task of serving as a role model for those from the same sociopolitical group. Just as any new undertaking is refined through repeated practice, so also one must anticipate that presidents-elect and secretaries-designate will encounter some difficulties in filling these roles and responsibilities.

It does seem, however, that presidents-elect and Washington power brokers have made certain calculations about cabinet representatives and representation. Providing women with descriptive representation allowed Clinton to increase what was otherwise a finite resource, namely, the number of cabinet secretarial nominations. Hazel O'Leary provided African American women with descriptive representation and the nuclear power utility companies with substantive representation. Predictably, cabinet secretaries-designate encounter the greatest difficulties when they are mostly unknown to, or distant from, a department's clients and networks. This balancing of descriptive and substantive representation, therefore, may also be dictated by the current balance of power within the Washington community. Certainly, the possibility that descriptive representation signals a forthcoming change in substantive representation has worried the political establishment. Although the new chief executive had promised a more inclusive government, journalistic accounts suggested that readers were more at ease with exclusivity.

Descriptive representation is, in brief, a difficult undertaking. Unless political executives can explain this role to the media in a way that establishes both their image and their agenda, descriptive representation will degenerate into a superficial inventory of sexes, races, and ethnicities. At the same time, this case study reveals that descriptive and substantive representation are sometimes closely intertwined. Activism to secure descriptive cabinet representation may establish the foundations for more substantive representation in the future.

In more general terms, this analysis demonstrates that members of both the executive branch and the Washington community are increasingly aware that the presidential appointment of a "diversity" nominee ends one set of negotiations only to begin another. How the nominee's descriptive representation will be communicated and the types of substantive representation that will be provided are matters of concern to the appointee, her or his constituents, department networks, and the president. What cannot be presumed is that the appointment will inevitably provide descriptive representation or that substantive representation will naturally follow descriptive representation. Securing any form of representation requires ongoing attentiveness to political and presidential relationships.

Conclusion

In recent presidential administrations, previously marginalized issue networks and voting groups have mobilized on behalf of securing representation within the cabinet. And yet, this representation has been qualitatively different from that which has traditionally been associated with the cabinet. "Diversity" appointees have typically provided their sociopolitical groups with descriptive representation, thereby demonstrating the opportunities available to all talented individuals and proving the president-elect's receptivity to such persons. With specific regard to the ideologies of the women secretaries-designate, the nominees adhere to the doctrines of liberal feminism, accepting the current institutional arrangements while seeking to eliminate sex discrimination.

Considerable evidence suggests that members of the various voting groups often expect only descriptive representation. To suggest otherwise would be to presume a commonality of interests that edges into a controversial political ideology at best (as with cultural feminism) or stereotyping at worst. At the same time, evidence is also found of an expectation that the "diversity" appointee will act as a role model. The presentation of these women and men in ways that either reduce or submerge their sex, race, and ethnicity immediately challenges their ability to be so identified and thus to fulfill this responsibility.

The experiences of the Clinton nominees suggest that a secretary-designate must mobilize supportive constituencies to secure confirmation, particularly when the secretary-designate is a "diversity" appointee subject to higher levels of scrutiny. This circumstance should cause presidents-elect to carefully consider their appointment criteria. Presidents should determine the kinds of descriptive representation in which they are willing to invest. The "diversity" appointees themselves must be capable of mobilizing the issue networks and voting groups they presumptively represent. Such calculations will recast the politics of cabinet building and oblige participants to assess the cabinet's deeper responsibilities, opportunities, and powers. Ultimately, such reflections will also require that the appointees and their constituents reflect critically upon their own standards of cabinet representation.

Notes

1. For the purposes of this chapter, the "cabinet" refers only to the departmental secretaries and not to those others who may be accorded "cabinet rank" in a particular presidential administration. Richard F. Fenno. 1959. *The President's Cabinet, An Analysis in the Period from Wilson to Eisenhower.* Cambridge, Mass.: Harvard University Press, pp. 21–25, 67–68; Janet M. Martin. 1988. "Frameworks for Cabinet Studies." *Presidential Studies Quarterly* 18: 795–798; and Jeffrey E. Cohen. 1988. *The Politics of the U.S. Cabinet: Representation in the Executive Branch, 1789–1984.* Pittsburgh: University of Pittsburgh Press.

2. I appreciate that many women are also people of color. This listing, however, seemed at once the most brief and most accurate reference to all of these marginalized groups.

3. In the 1992 election, for example, Voter Research and Survey exit polls revealed that 57 percent of the Clinton vote was provided by women. More specifically, 40 percent of the Clinton vote came from white women, 11 percent from African American women, and the remaining 6 percent from Asian American and Hispanic American women. This statistical information was provided by Mary Bendyna of Georgetown University.

4. The members of all marginalized groups, taken together, constitute a majority of the U.S. population. "Diversity" is accordingly placed in quotation marks.

5. Throughout this chapter, the author utilizes the classification schema created by Hanna Pitkin, namely, that representation may be formal, descriptive, symbolic, and/or substantive. See Hanna Fenichel Pitkin. 1972. *The Concept of Representation.* Berkeley: University of California Press.

6. Gerald M. Pomper. 1993. "The Presidential Election." In *The Election of 1992: Reports and Interpretations,* by Gerald M. Pomper et al. Chatham, N.J.: Chatham House Publishers, p. 138.

7. See Chapter 4 for a discussion of the ways in which presidents invite media scrutiny. My survey of *New York Times* coverage of the Carter, Reagan, Bush, and Clinton transitions also noted that Republican presidents-elect encountered a more hierarchical and organizational standard of assessment. Although the *Times* is the newspaper of record for the United States, I am presently extending my content analysis to include other print sources. Preliminary analysis indicates that the trends identified in association with the *Times* are typical.

8. Elizabeth Drew. 1994. *On the Edge: The Clinton Presidency.* New York: Simon and Schuster, pp. 21, 28–29; Thomas L. Friedman. "Clinton Is Taking Big Role in Picking Cabinet Deputies." *New York Times,* November 18, 1992, sec. A; Gwen Ifill. "People in Line for Jobs: The 'Short List' Grows." *New York Times,* November 23, 1992, sec. A; Gwen Ifill. "The Baird Appointment." *New York Times,* January 23, 1993, sec. A; *The White House Staff* (listing), posted by the Office of the President-Elect, January 14, 1993; and *The United States Government Manual 1995/1996.* Office of the Federal Register, National Archives and Record Administration.

9. Drew, *On the Edge: The Clinton Presidency,* pp. 25–29; Adam Clymer. "Insider for the Treasury." *New York Times,* December 11, 1992, sec. A; Douglas Jehl. "Clinton Names Bentsen, Panetta to Economic Team." *Los Angeles Times,* December 11, 1992, sec. A; Steven Mufson. "Reich Hopes to Revitalize, 'Expand the Vision' of Labor Dept." *Washington Post,* December 12, 1992, sec. A; Thomas L. Friedman. "Democratic Leader and Clinton Friend Gain Major Posts." *New York Times,* December 13, 1992, sec. A; and Thomas L. Friedman. "Clinton to Name Two More to Cabinet." *New York Times,* December 17, 1992, sec. B.

10. Drew, *On the Edge: The Clinton Presidency,* pp. 25–29. See also Bob Woodward. 1994. *The Agenda: Inside the Clinton White House.* New York: Simon and Schuster.

11. Ann Devroy and Al Kamen. "Social Policy Posts Filled by Clinton." *Washington Post,* December 12, 1992, sec A; James Risen. "Reich May Become New Kind of Labor Secretary." *Los Angeles Times,* December 12, 1992, sec. A; and David G. Savage. "Riley Reforms Won Applause of Experts." *Los Angeles Times,* December 11, 1992, sec. A.

12. Paul Richter and David Lauter. "Clinton Appoints Cisneros and Brown to Cabinet Posts." *Los Angeles Times,* December 18, 1992, sec A; and Felicity Baringer. "Clinton Selects Ex-Mayor for HUD and Ex-Marine for Veterans Affairs." *New York Times,* December 18, 1992, sec. A. For a discussion of Clinton's lack of military service and the veterans' vote during the 1992 election, see Kathleen A. Frankovic. 1993. "Public Opinion in the 1992 Campaign." In *The Election of 1992: Reports and Interpretations,* by Pomper et al., p. 123.

13. Gerald F. Seib. "Babbitt's Vision: A Changing West, Changed Politics." *Wall Street Journal,* December 29, 1992, sec. A; and Timothy Egan. "The (Bruised) Emperor of the Outdoors." *New York Times Magazine,* August 1, 1993, pp. 21–22.

14. Richter and Lauter, "Clinton Appoints Cisneros and Brown to Cabinet Posts"; and "Nailing Down More Cabinet Diversity." *Los Angeles Times,* December 18, 1992, sec. A.

15. Although commonly used, "women's issues" is a misnomer insofar as it suggests that only women would be concerned about such matters as social welfare and reproductive rights. Throughout this chapter, therefore, the term is placed in quotation marks. Coalition for Women's Appointments, Statement of Purpose and Policies, September 1992. (Provided to author by the National Women's Political Caucus.)

16. Coalition for Women's Appointments, Initial List of Recommendations, November 10, 1992.

17. *The Mirror,* dated December 16, 1992; December 17, 1992; December 21, 1992; December 22, 1992; December 24, 1992. Also Coalition for Women's Appointments, Project Report, August 1993 (provided by the National Women's Political Caucus).

18. Gwen Ifill. "Clinton Chooses Two and Deplores Idea of Cabinet Quotas." *New York Times,* December 22, 1992, secs. A and B; and Catherine S. Manegold. "Clinton Ire on Appointments Startles Women." *New York Times,* December 23, 1992, sec. A.

19. Dorothy Gilliam. "Black Women Need a Seat at the Table." *Washington Post,* December 19, 1992, sec. B. Further information on the Commission has been unavailable, so this discussion focuses on the Coalition for Women's Appointments.

20. "Bill Clinton's Pragmatists." *New York Times,* December 12, 1992, sec. A; "Looks Like America." *New York Times,* December 25, 1992, sec. A; and "U-Turn at Interior?" *Washington Post,* January 6, 1993, sec. A. Any "cautions" at this time were offered more emphatically by the *Washington Post* than the *New York Times,* although *Post* headlines were considerably more judgmental than were the associated articles. See Stephen Labaton. "Commerce Nominee's Lobbying Prompts Scrutiny." *Washington Post,* December 20, 1992, sec. A; Thomas W. Lippman. "Energy Nominee Unschooled in Nuclear Weapons Issues." *Washington Post,* December 22, 1992, sec. A; and Michael Isikoff. "Baird's Corporate Record Reveals Little on Justice Issues." *Washington Post,* December 25, 1992, sec. A.

21. See, for example, Steven Greenhouse. "Clinton's Choice of Reich Hints at a Stepped-Up Role for Labor Department." *New York Times,* December 12, 1992, sec. A; Robert Reinhold and Michael R. Gordon. "Pathfinders of the Middle Ground." *New York Times,* December 23, 1992, sec. A; Thomas L. Friedman. "Clinton's New Foreign-Policy Thinkers." *New York Times,* December 23, 1992, sec. A; and Clymer, "Insider for the Treasury."

22. Neil A. Lewis. "Compromiser Is Chosen to Run Commerce Dept." *New York Times,* December 13, 1992, sec. A.

23. "Clinton's Last Selections for the Cabinet Reflect His Quest for Diversity." *New York Times,* December 25, 1992, sec. A. The *Washington Post* spoke of Henry Cisneros in these terms, as did the *Los Angeles Times* in regard to Richard Riley. See David Maraniss. "Cisneros and Clinton Followed Parallel Paths to Power." *Washington Post,* December 18, 1992, sec. A; and Michael Ross. "Clinton, New Aide Have Career Parallels." *Los Angeles Times,* November 18, 1992, sec. A.

24. The December 1992 issue of the *Gallup Poll Monthly* reported that 67 percent of the public approved of the way Bill Clinton was handling his presidential transition, a slight increase over the 62 percent who awarded such a rating in November of that same year. Larry Hugick. 1992. "Clinton Transition Gains Favorable Reviews." *Gallup Poll Monthly* (December): 12.

25. "Looks Like America."

26. This treatment of Cisneros is particularly intriguing in light of his status as one of the most important Hispanic political figures in the country. Peña's links to the Latino community were later briefly noted in a factual biography that appeared in the *Washington Post* shortly before his confirmation hearing. Roberto Suro. "Cisneros Achieves Career Comeback with Nomination." *New York Times,* December 18, 1992, sec. A; Felicity Barringer. "Defender of the Rights of Veterans Masters Thickets of Regulations." *New York Times,* December 18, 1992, sec. A; "Clinton's Last Selections for the Cabinet Reflect His Quest for Diversity"; William Claiborne. "If Transportation Means Getting There, Peña May Be the Right Driver." *Washington Post,* January 7, 1993, sec. A; and Guy Gugliotta. "Legal Fees Are Strain for Cisneros." *Washington Post,* June 16, 1995, sec. A.

27. Gwen Ifill. "Three Women Are Said to Be Candidates for Cabinet Posts." *New York Times,* December 7, 1992, secs. A and B; Barnaby J. Feder. "New Energy Chief Has Seen Two Sides of Regulatory Fence." *New York Times,* December 22, 1992, sec. B; Gwen Ifill. "Clinton Planning to Name a Woman for Justice Dept." *New York Times,* December 24, 1992, sec. A. See also Devroy and Kamen, "Social Policy Posts Filled by Clinton"; Rudy Abramson. "O'Leary Surprised but Not Unaware." *Los Angeles Times,* December 22, 1992, sec. A; Dan Balz and Ruth Marcus. "Clinton Said to Fill Last Four Cabinet Jobs." *Washington Post,* December 24, 1992, sec. A; and Douglas Frantz. "O'Leary Wins Praise Amid Critical Views." *Los Angeles Times,* December 28, 1992, sec. A.

28. This expression is borrowed from Kay Lehman Scholzman. 1990. "Representing Women in Washington: Sisterhood and Pressure Politics." In *Women, Politics, and Change,* ed. Louise A. Tilly and Patricia Gurin. New York: Russell Sage Foundation. Donna Shalala was a long-standing board member of the Children's Defense Fund, an influential organization in the Washington "women's issues" network.

29. Friedman, "Clinton's New Foreign-Policy Thinkers"; U.S. Congress, Senate, Committee on Foreign Relations. *Hearing on the Nomination of Warren M. Christopher to Be Secretary of State.* 103rd Congress, 1st session; Elaine Sciolino. "Clinton's State Dept. Choice Backs 'Discrete' Force." *New York Times,* January 14, 1993, sec. A; Barbara Vobejda and Guy Gugliotta. "Shalala, Espy Received Warmly, Christopher Still Coasting on the Hill." *Washington Post,* January 15, 1993, sec. A; and Bernard Gwertzman. "State Department Under Vance Is Expected to Be Solid but Not So Colorful as Kissinger's." *New York Times,* January 9, 1977, sec. A.

30. Sara Fritz. "Brown and Kantor Stir Misgivings." *Los Angeles Times,* January 1, 1993, sec. D; "Breaking Bill Clinton's Promise." *New York Times,* January 8, 1993, sec. A; "More Questions for Ron Brown." *New York Times,* January 13, 1993, sec. A; Keith Bradsher. "Trade and Commerce Nominees Discuss Conflict of Interest Issues." *New York Times,* January 20, 1993, sec. A; Helen Dewar and Michael Weisskopf. "Senate Votes to Confirm All but Two of Clinton's Cabinet Nominees." *Washington Post,* January 22, 1993, sec. A; and U.S. Congress, Senate, Committee on Commerce, Science, and Transportation. *Hearing on the Nomination of Ronald Harmon Brown to Be Secretary of Commerce.* 103rd Congress, 1st session.

31. U.S. Congress, Senate, Committee on Labor and Human Relations. *Hearing on Robert Reich, of Massachusetts, to Be Secretary, Department of Labor.* 103rd Congress, 1st session.

32. U.S. Congress, Senate, Committee on Labor and Human Resources. *Hearing on Donna E. Shalala, of Wisconsin, to Be Secretary of Health and Human Services.* 103rd Congress, 1st session.

33. U.S. Congress, Senate, Committee on Energy and Natural Resources. *Hearing on the Nomination of Hazel R. O'Leary, to Be Secretary, Department of Energy.* 103rd Congress, 1st session. See especially the commentary by Senator Paul Wellstone (D, Minnesota) and Representative Bruce F. Vento (D, Minnesota), pages 22–25. For a substantive assessment of the O'Leary nomination—a notable exception to the coverage generally accorded this secretary-designate—see Keith Schneider. "Nominee Is a Veteran of Atomic-Waste Battles." *New York Times,* January 9, 1993, sec. A.

34. Drew, *On the Edge: The Clinton Presidency,* pp. 32–33, 37–41; Thomas L. Friedman. "Clinton Concedes He Erred on Baird Nomination." *New York Times,* January 23, 1993, sec. A; Ruth Marcus and David S. Broder. "President Takes Blame for Rushing Baird Selection." *Washington Post,* January 23, 1993, sec. A; and Ifill, "The Baird Appointment."

35. Neil A. Lewis. "Getting Things Done, Zoe Baird." *New York Times,*

December 25, 1992, sec. A; and Isikoff, "Baird's Corporate Record Reveals Little on Justice Issues."

36. Nelson W. Polsby. 1978. "Presidential Cabinet Making: Lessons for the Political System." *Political Science Quarterly* 93: 20. See also Ifill, "The Baird Appointment"; and Terrence Moran. "It's Not Just Zoe Baird." *New York Times,* January 23, 1993, sec. A.

37. Thomas L. Friedman. "Clinton's Cabinet Choices Put Him at Center, Balancing Competing Factions." *New York Times,* December 27, 1992, sec. A.

38. From 1990 to 1992, Baird and her husband, Yale law professor Paul Gewirtz, employed a Peruvian couple to provide household and child-care help. In doing so, Baird and Gewirtz violated two laws: hiring illegal immigrants and failing to pay social security taxes. This employment practice was voluntarily disclosed by Baird to the Senate and the FBI investigators, and Baird paid the taxes shortly after her nomination. Neither of the practices was initially considered a problem by the president-elect's administration. Drew, *On the Edge: The Clinton Presidency,* pp. 32–33, 37–41; Friedman, "Clinton's Cabinet Choices Put Him at Center, Balancing Competing Factions"; David Johnston. "Clinton's Choice for Justice Dept. Hired Illegal Aliens for Household." *New York Times,* January 14, 1993, sec. A; Michael Isikoff and Al Kamen. "Baird's Hiring Disclosure Not Seen as Major Block." *Washington Post,* January 15, 1993, sec. A; Clifford Krauss. "A Top G.O.P. Senator Backs Nominee in a Storm." *New York Times,* January 16, 1993, sec. A; Friedman, "Clinton Concedes He Erred on Baird Nomination"; Marcus and Broder, "President Takes Blame for Rushing Baird Selection"; Ifill, "The Baird Appointment"; and Moran, "It's Not Just Zoe Baird."

39. *Public Opinion Online: Roper Center, University of Connecticut.* Accession no. 0190955, Question no. 002.

40. *USA Today,* January 24, 1993, sec. A.

41. George Gallup Jr. and Frank Newport. 1993. "Baird Nomination Runs Up Against Wall of Public Disapproval." *Gallup Poll Monthly* (January): 29–30.

42. Robert Reinhold. "Fueled by Radio and TV, Outcry Became Uproar." *New York Times,* January 23, 1993, sec. A; Mary McGrory. "Why Zoe Got Zapped." *Washington Post,* January 24, 1993, sec. C; and Colman McCarthy. "When Baby Comes In Second to Career." *Washington Post,* February 2, 1993, sec. D.

43. Catherine S. Manegold. "Women Are Frustrated by Failed Nominations." *New York Times,* February 7, 1993, sec. A; and Mary Frances Berry. "The Father's Hour." *Washington Post,* February 10, 1993, sec. A. It would later be determined that Ron Brown, like Zoe Baird, had failed to pay social security taxes for his household workers. Karen Tumulty and John M. Broder. "Ron Brown Failed to Pay Employer Tax." *Los Angeles Times,* February 8, 1993, sec. A.

44. "Looks Like America."

45. Coalition for Women's Appointments, Initial List of Recommendations; and Ruth Marcus. "Clinton Berates Critics in Women's Groups." *Washington Post,* December 22, 1993, sec. A.

46. Previous women HHS secretaries are Oveta Culp Hobby (Eisenhower), Patricia Roberts Harris (Carter), and Margaret M. Heckler (Reagan).

47. Feder, "New Energy Chief Has Seen Two Sides of Regulatory Fence"; Lippman, "Energy Nominee Unschooled in Nuclear Weapons Issues"; Frantz, "O'Leary Wins Praise Amid Critical Views"; and U.S. Congress, Senate, Committee on Energy and Natural Resources. *Hearing on the Nomination of Hazel R. O'Leary, to Be Secretary, Department of Energy.*

48. Larry Rohter. "Tough 'Front-Line Warrior,' Janet Reno." *New York Times,* February 12, 1993, sec. A; Ruth Marcus. "Clinton Nominates Reno at Justice."

Washington Post, February 12, 1993, sec. A; Nancy Gibbs. "Truth, Justice, and the Reno Way." *Time,* July 12, 1993, pp. 20–27; "Unshakeable Janet Reno." *Vogue,* August 1993, pp. 258–263; U.S. Congress, Senate, Committee on the Judiciary. *Hearings on the Nomination of Janet Reno to Be Attorney General of the United States.* 103rd Congress, 1st session; and Mary McGrory. "Nanny with a Nightstick." *Washington Post,* March 11, 1993, sec. A.

49. Joe Davidson. "Miami Prosecutor Janet Reno Is Picked by President to Be Attorney General." *Wall Street Journal,* February 12, 1993, sec. A.

50. Ronald Smothers. "Choice for Justice Dept. Earns Hometown Praise." *New York Times,* February 15, 1993, sec. A; Max Boot. "Justice Nominee Reno Offers New Priorities." *Christian Science Monitor,* February 18, 1993, sec. A; Terry Eastland. "Attorney General and Social Worker." *Wall Street Journal,* March 10, 1993, sec. A; David Johnston. "Choice for Justice Is Treated Gently." *New York Times,* March 10, 1993, sec. A; and U.S. Congress, Senate, Committee on the Judiciary. *Hearings on the Nomination of Janet Reno to Be Attorney General of the United States.* For a contrasting perspective on Reno's Dade County record, see Larry Rohter. "Debate Arises on Record of Justice Dept. Nominee." *New York Times,* March 9, 1993, sec. A.

6

Women on the White House Staff: A Longitudinal Analysis, 1939–1994

Kathryn Dunn Tenpas

Of all the twentieth-century developments within the Office of the President, perhaps none has been more prominent than the radical growth of the president's staff.[1] The expansion of the staff was initially fueled by the Brownlow Committee's 1937 report, which recommended that "the president needs help."[2] Almost without exception, successive presidents have sought to expand the White House staff. A vivid example of this growth is provided by scholar John Hart:

> Before the publication of the Brownlow report, there were thirty-seven full-time staff officially working in the White House. . . . In the thirty years from 1944 to 1974, the number of people officially employed in the White House increased tenfold, from about 58 to approximately 560.[3]

And by 1993, Hart reported, there were 871 employees.[4]

An additional trend that is related to the Office of the President and that dates back to Franklin Roosevelt is the increasing centralization of policymaking. According to Sidney Milkis, "Many of the partisan efforts sought by the New Dealers were directed at legislating procedural reforms that would enhance the capacity and independence of the executive branch in the making of public policy."[5] And rather than delegate policy authority to executive agencies and departments, presidents since Franklin Roosevelt have internalized policy expertise so as to exercise greater control over the policymaking process.[6] Given the expansive role of the federal government in the post–New Deal era, White House staffers have performed integral and influential roles in both presidential policymaking and politics.

A parallel twentieth-century trend to the increasing size and policymaking role of the White House Office has been the expansion of women's opportunities in U.S. politics. Such advancements have come in the form of women obtaining elected positions at the local, state, and national levels, as well as in their greater political participation generally.[7] Currently, women register and vote at higher rates than men.[8] Thus, they represent an increasingly significant sector of the American electorate.

Along with women's increasingly influential role in the political sphere has been a concomitant surge in scholarship on the subject, particularly as it relates to women in elected office. Scholars have written numerous studies about women as both candidates and public officeholders.[9] Because women now hold more elected positions at the local, state, and national levels than ever before, it is equally important to recognize their contributions at the national executive level.[10] An assessment of women's roles on the White House staff is a natural outgrowth of studies of women in electoral politics and is this chapter's principal topic.

If one takes into account the simultaneous developments of White House staff enlargement and the staff's greater influence in matters of policy, as well as the expansion of women's political rights and participation, one might expect to find more women occupying White House positions. Given related trends concerning women's electoral success, there is no reason to expect otherwise.[11] Nevertheless, such assertions have not been documented. This chapter seeks to fill a void in the literature by examining the issue of women on the White House staff.

I proceed in three stages. In the first section I explain the study's methodology and display longitudinal data on women in the White House. I demonstrate the frequency with which women have served on the White House staff and the types of positions and level of seniority they have typically possessed. I then provide an analysis and interpretation of this data. Finally, I discuss the implications of these findings and the future of women in the White House.

In short, this chapter demonstrates that women have made substantial gains in terms of both sheer numbers and seniority (see Table 6.1). Despite such progress, there nevertheless appears to be a glass ceiling that prevents

Table 6.1 Milestones for Women in the White House

- From 1939 to 1957, women were employed as personal secretaries, social secretaries, administrative assistants, or secretaries to the first lady. It was not until 1957 that a woman, Anne W. Wheaton, assumed a nonclerical position as associate press secretary.
- It was not until 1967 that a woman assumed a policy-related position. Betty Furness served as a special assistant for consumer affairs to President Johnson.
- The next major breakthrough for women occurred in 1973 when Anne L. Armstrong was named counsellor to President Nixon.
- President Carter was the first to appoint a woman (Margaret ["Midge"] Costanza) to the position of assistant to the president, in 1977.
- In 1984 President Reagan was the first to appoint a woman to a foreign policy position. Karna Small was named deputy assistant to the president for national security affairs and senior director of public affairs to the National Security Council.
- In 1993 President Clinton appointed the first woman, Laura D'Andrea Tyson, to chair the Council of Economic Advisors.

women from obtaining access to the president's inner circle. Thus, although the gender gap within the White House has narrowed, at the most senior level women remain on the periphery, much as they do in the private sector.

Methodology and Findings

The longitudinal data presented in this section are based on information from the *U.S. Government Staff Manual,* an annual publication that lists White House staff members. This is the only publicly available and continuous (1939–present) source, and it has some shortcomings. The Government Printing Office (GPO) does not set specific guidelines as to who should be included but instead allows the White House staff to develop the listing. Whereas one administration may include the president's personal secretary and physician, another administration may exclude such positions. Generally, however, the listing typically includes those staff members in the most senior positions (e.g., heads of various White House offices, the chief of staff, the press secretary).

The GPO currently requests these lists by June of the year of publication. This timing may be both under- and overinclusive as it will neglect those whose employment or tenure was ill timed. Although the end measurement may be imperfect, the *U.S. Government Staff Manual* is nevertheless the best source for information on White House personnel.[12]

As can be seen in Figure 6.1 and Table 6.2, the percentage of women on the White House staff has increased. Since President Franklin Roosevelt, women have constituted from 6 percent (during the Eisenhower administration) to 39 percent (during the Clinton administration) of the staff. The climb has not always been steady, however, as Republican administrations have

Table 6.2   Average Percentage of Women on the White House Staff, by Administration

President	Women on White House Staff (%)
F. D. Roosevelt	10
Truman	15
Eisenhower	6
Kennedy	10
Johnson	13
Nixon	8
Ford	12
Carter	29
Reagan	18
Bush	25
Clinton	39

Source: Compiled by author based on listings in the *U.S. Government Staff Manual.*

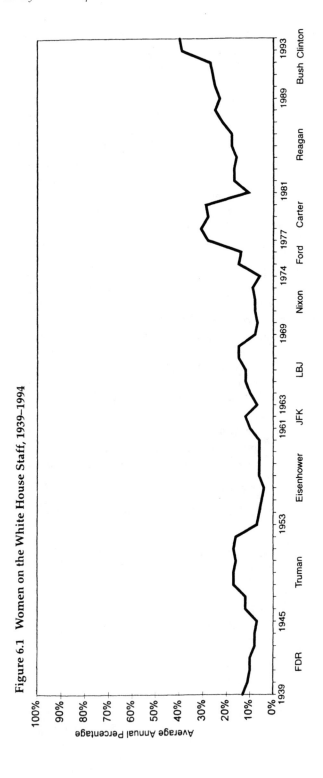

Figure 6.1 Women on the White House Staff, 1939–1994

been less inclined to appoint women than have Democratic administrations. On a percentage basis, from 1939 to 1995 Democratic presidents appointed more women to the White House staff than did their Republican counterparts of the same era. The explanation for this party variation is not entirely clear, although one can speculate that the parties' positions on women's issues may have influenced the appointment of women to the White House staff.

These figures alone do not tell the entire story. In addition to the raw numbers and percentages, it is equally, if not more, important to identify the types of jobs women obtained in the various administrations. Some administrations might provide more inclusive lists of White House staff than others, so it is necessary to clarify the seniority of female staff members.

To account for the nonstandardized means of reporting, I have developed a three-part categorization of White House staff positions, ranked in ascending order according to overall policy contribution: (1) nonpolicy positions, (2) mid-level positions, and (3) policy/managerial positions. Category 1 jobs include clerical, social, and first lady–related positions (e.g., personal secretary, social secretary, assistant to the first lady). Such traditional positions were once the only opportunities available to women seeking White House employment. Since the late 1960s and especially during the late 1970s, women have obtained more substantive positions. These Category 2 positions include those in which the occupant does not run a particular office but has a high level of substantive responsibility on a particular issue (e.g., special assistant to the president, associate counsel, or associate press secretary). Category 3 includes the most senior White House staff positions, such as assistant to the president for public liaison or counsellor to the president. Women have held these upper-echelon positions since 1973. Typically, the staff member in such positions directs a particular office, serving, for example, as chair of the Council of Economic Advisers. The figures in Tables 6.3, 6.4, and 6.5 represent the average number of female employees over the course of the president's term(s), except in the case of President Clinton, whose first two years only (1993–1994) are included.

As Table 6.4 indicates, since the Ford administration there has been a sharp increase in the number of women in mid-level positions. With increased opportunities, more education, and access to the common "apprenticeships" for White House employment (jobs on Capitol Hill, in state and local governments, and in campaigns), more women are seeking this type of employment.

Although the number of women in the most senior positions has increased (see Table 6.5), it is important to realize that *titles do not necessarily convey influence.* Whereas women may have obtained the most senior titles and a greater degree of access to the president, they are rarely as influential as their male counterparts who possess similar titles. As discussed later, women on the White House staff have never been members of

Table 6.3   Average Number of Women in Nonpolicy Positions (Category 1)[a]

President	Women in Nonpolicy Positions
F. D. Roosevelt	1
Truman	3
Eisenhower	2
Kennedy	3
Johnson	3
Nixon	3
Ford	6
Carter	11
Reagan	0[a]
Bush	2
Clinton	4[b]

Notes: a. Unlike previous staff listings, the Reagan administration did not list the clerical staff. Similarly, the Bush and Clinton administrations refrained from listing personal secretaries. b. During the Clinton administration, the position of chief of staff to the first lady was elevated to the status of assistant to the president and is included in Category 3 (see Chapter 10). The increased seniority may be a function of the first lady's interest in policymaking, professional work experience, and prior political activity. The same position existed during the Reagan administration, although it was not held by a woman.

Table 6.4   Average Number of Women in Mid-Level Positions (Category 2)

President	Women in Midlevel Positions
F. D. Roosevelt	0
Truman	0
Eisenhower	1[a]
Kennedy	0
Johnson	1[a]
Nixon	1
Ford	5
Carter	11
Reagan	14
Bush	18
Clinton	25

Note: a. This figure does not represent the exact average; note that Anne W. Wheaton was associate press secretary in the Eisenhower administration from 1957 through 1960, and Betty Furness was special assistant to the president for consumer affairs in the Johnson administration for the years 1967–1969.

the president's inner circle, and some have been marginalized despite their senior status.

Prior to 1977, women were limited primarily to clerical and social positions, and positions in support of the first lady with only four exceptions— two women served as special assistant to the president for consumer affairs

Table 6.5   Average Number of Women in Policy/Managerial Positions (Category 3)

President	Women in Policy/Managerial Positions
F. D. Roosevelt	0
Truman	0
Eisenhower	0
Kennedy	0
Johnson	0
Nixon	1[a]
Ford	0
Carter	2
Reagan	1
Bush	2
Clinton	8

Note: a. This figure does not represent the average number of positions because a woman joined the White House staff during the years 1973–1974. Anne L. Armstrong was counsellor to the president 1973–1974.

(Johnson and Nixon), one woman as counsellor to the president (Nixon), and another as associate press secretary (Eisenhower). Since then, women have moved into administrative and personnel positions, scheduling and advance positions, and jobs that require lobbying on behalf of the White House or general outreach (the Office of Political Affairs, the Office of Intergovernmental Relations, the Office of Congressional Liaison, the Office of Public Liaison). The least common positions for women include those in the areas of foreign, domestic, and economic policy; general policy development; and legal affairs, although women are making some headway in these offices.[13] Recent examples include these appointments from the first two years of the Clinton administration.

- Laura D'Andrea Tyson—chair, Council of Economic Advisors
- Carol Rasco—assistant to the president for domestic policy
- Kathleen A. McGinty—deputy assistant to the president and director, Office on Environmental Policy
- Sandra J. Kristoff—special assistant to the president and senior director for Asia-Pacific economic affairs
- Nancy E. Soderberg—special assistant to the president for national security affairs and staff director of the National Security Council
- Jenonne R. Walker—special assistant to the president and senior director for European affairs
- Cheryl Mills—associate counsel to the president
- Beth Nolan—associate counsel to the president

In addition to increased access to previously all-male offices, another indicator of women's advancement is the number of women who have held the most senior title, assistant to the president. Although the president's senior staff has often been characterized as a "men's club," in recent administrations women have been appointed to this most senior staff level.

As the number of women on the White House staff has increased, so has the number of senior-level female appointments (see Table 6.6). Whereas no women occupied the post of assistant to the president in the Nixon administration, seven women served as assistants to the president (39 percent) in the first year of the Clinton administration.

Table 6.6   Average Number of Female Assistants to the President[a]

President	Average Number of Female Assistants to the President
Nixon	0
Ford	0
Carter	2
Reagan	1
Bush	2
Clinton	7

Note: a. The existence of the title "assistant to the president" has not been constant. From 1939 to 1961 there was a single position called "the assistant to the president," and no woman was appointed to this position. From 1961 to 1969 the position did not exist; the most senior position was special assistant or special counsel. From 1971 to 1994 the title remained the same. Thus, the table begins with the Nixon administration.

Limited Progress and Cautious Optimism

From a more optimistic perspective, women have clearly made substantial gains in participation on the president's staff. A simple comparison of Roosevelt's administration with that of Clinton demonstrates this progress—more women than ever before are serving on the White House staff, more are serving in substantive policy capacities, and some are serving at the most senior levels. Additionally, it is important to note the increase in the number of women on the White House staff in recent administrations, both Democratic and Republican, suggesting that party is not the sole determinant of female participation. Instead, other socioeconomic factors, such as increased levels of education among women, may also be at work. And if one looks only at the two most recent administrations (Bush and Clinton), the findings are even more promising; women have increased not only in number but also in the frequency with which they hold senior positions on the White House staff. Future research will examine these trends in light of the proliferation of titles and offices in the Executive Office of the President.

But although gains have been made, the number of women in senior White House positions should be much higher, especially given the proportion of women in other elite positions in the executive branch. In the Bush administration, women represented, on average, 11 percent of high-level White House appointments (assistants to the president), far short of the percentage of women confirmed and appointed to positions in the executive branch (19.9 percent).[14] But during the first year of the Clinton administration, women held 39 percent of assistant to the president appointments and 31.5 percent of the confirmed and appointed positions in the executive branch.[15] If President Clinton's actions establish a precedent his successors seek to follow, the future for women holds some promise. If Clinton's successor follows the Bush benchmark, however, the hurdles and challenges for promotion to the highest White House level will remain intact.

Beyond the numbers and titles, there is one last major hurdle for women to clear—inclusion in the president's inner circle,[16] which, except for the first lady, has eluded women.[17] Barbara C. Burrell demonstrates the influence some first ladies have exerted in this context, but they have been the only female members of the inner circle. (See Chapter 10.) Whereas President Clinton expressed a commitment to increase the influence of female staff members, his inner circle has yet to include a woman.[18] This is particularly astonishing given his personal (he is married to a professional woman), generational (he grew up in an era when women made serious inroads into previously male-dominated professions), and partisan (Democratic presidents have tended to be more receptive than Republicans to women's issues and advancement) background. President Clinton, more than any recent president, has seemed inclined to appoint a woman to the inner circle, but he has yet to make this unprecedented staff appointment. Such an action will undoubtedly make major headlines when it occurs.[19]

Another difficulty, obfuscated by the numbers, is the failure some women in senior positions have experienced because they have not been granted access or influence equal to that of their male counterparts. As a result, their performance suffers by comparison. A recent example concerns President Clinton's first press secretary, Dee Dee Meyers. She was criticized for being uninformed and was forced to retract White House statements to the press largely because she was kept "out of the loop."[20] Her supporters suggest that if she had been "in the loop," as current press secretary Michael McCurry is reputed to be, she would have made fewer mistakes and would not have had to retire prematurely.[21]

Recall also that Meyers was initially appointed deputy assistant to the president and press secretary, and President Clinton appointed George Stephanopoulos to be the designated spokesperson. Meyers's predecessors, such as Marlin Fitzwater (Bush administration) and Jody Powell (Carter administration), were afforded much more discretion, responsibility, and access. And Meyers was named a deputy assistant, whereas Fitzwater was named an assistant to the president and Powell press secretary to the president. So although President Clinton can claim credit for appointing the first female press secretary, the dilution of responsibilities illustrates the status of women at the most senior levels of the White House staff. Presidents are choosing women but are not giving them the requisite access or influence.

On a related note, women are rarely found at the top of the pecking order among their fellow assistants to the president. Women tend to be placed in the political posts rather than in the policy positions. For example, although Elizabeth Dole served in a very senior position as assistant to the president for public liaison during the Reagan administration, based on staff memoirs it was apparent that she was not a "player" like Michael Deaver, Jim Baker, or Ed Meese.[22]

Another example concerns President Carter's groundbreaking appointment of a woman as an assistant to the president. In 1977 Carter appointed Margaret ("Midge") Costanza assistant to the president and director of the Office of Public Liaison. In retrospect, however, it appears this appointment was largely symbolic. Just four months after Costanza obtained this senior position, one press account stated that her appointment "is seen as a token gesture. Her non-policy duties largely entail public relations with interest groups of a hand-holding nature. Any meaningful action between the White House and outside organizations is handled by Hamilton Jordan."[23] Another press account, which lambasted President Carter for the excessive number of Georgians appointed to the White House staff, stated, "Surely, Margaret (Midge) Costanza, the former Rochester, NY, vice-mayor who is in charge of Carter's liaison with interest groups, hardly counts since she is the token woman and outsider within the White House hierarchy and makes only a meager contribution to policy."[24] Roughly six months later, Costanza lost her White House position and was demoted to running a new interagency task force on women.

So although titles are the most objective measurement of seniority and progress has clearly been made in this area, titles alone paint only a partial picture of the status of women. In fact, in some cases women who have obtained the most senior positions are worse off than they were before: Denied the necessary access and resources, they appear incompetent or irrelevant. When this occurs, it sends a mixed signal to other women working to achieve high-level positions on the White House staff. In the end, it is often difficult to determine whether such an achievement is tokenism, a president's transparent attempt to include women on his staff solely for political gain, or a well-deserved appointment.

Implications and the Future
for Women in the White House

The case for studying the role of women on the White House staff is rooted in studies of women in elected office. These studies are relevant in the electoral context, and they are also a vital component of examining women's status at the executive level. In short, such electoral studies have demonstrated that compared with their male counterparts, women possess different policy priorities, arrive in these institutions with different backgrounds, and provide different perspectives in policy debates. Thus, both presidency and gender studies scholars can learn from this study. Presidency scholars interested in the institutional developments within the White House will note women's unique policy priorities, particularly as increasingly more women obtain such positions. And gender studies scholars concerned with issues of discrimination and barriers to women's progress will also find this study revealing.

In the realm of electoral politics, political scientists generally speak of three types of barriers to greater female participation: socialization, situational, and structural barriers.[25] The socialization barrier refers to the process whereby young women were not brought up in environments that encouraged careers in politics. Situational barriers are those that exclude women because they lack the necessary resources (knowledge and opportunities) to obtain political careers. Finally, structural barriers refer to the institution itself and its inaccessibility to women—for example, the White House inner circle is drawn from the campaign staff, and women rarely play major roles in a presidential campaign. Whereas these "barriers" have long been cited as reasons for the lack of women in elected office, they can also be applied to a study of women at the national executive level.

In the case of women in the White House, two of the three barriers—situational and structural—may be at work. Although it is increasingly less likely that young women will be socialized to stay at home, situational variables might prevent them from working in the White House. Women tend to be the dominant child-care providers regardless of whether they are working, and working in the White House demands long hours under high-stress conditions. So although women may not necessarily be locked into the traditional homemaker role, many face dilemmas in balancing their commitments to their families and to their president.

The structural barrier also inhibits female participation. Based on a random sample of the biographies of various Bush staffers, most women and men arrive at the White House with similar career experiences: positions on Capitol Hill (staff or elected), employment with the president's campaign organization, positions in state and local government (staff or elected), employment with the party organization, and positions in the executive branch. Given the similarity between men's and women's career backgrounds, the disparity between the number of men and women on the White House staff may be a result of fewer women having worked in "White House–track" positions. Thus, as more and more women enter the so-called political workforce, we may see more women on the White House staff.[26] Just as women's numbers have increased in previously male-dominated professions such as medicine, law, and academia over the past several decades, a similar trend has been occurring in presidential politics. Thus, although the structural barrier continues to depress female participation, it is nevertheless eroding.

What does the future hold for women in the White House? This chapter began with a discussion of twentieth-century White House developments, notably the expansion of the president's staff and the staff's increasingly central role in policymaking. Although presidents and presidential candidates repeatedly pledge to decrease the size of their staff, they have not yet done so, and it is unlikely that future presidents will divest themselves of such a necessary resource.[27] Similarly, the White House role in policymaking is unlikely to decline as successive presidents continue to seek greater control over policy processes. In fact, now more than ever, as Congress and President Clinton spar over virtually every major policy issue, it would be extremely difficult to eliminate such vital expertise.

In light of these institutional developments, the outlook for women appears to be fairly bright. Assuming that White House staff size will remain relatively constant, there will be ample opportunity for women. And as women obtain more policy-oriented experience on Capitol Hill, in state legislatures, or in the executive branch, presidents are apt to employ them more frequently. The outlook for women grows dimmer, however, when one considers their role at the most senior level of the White House staff. Shattering the glass ceiling will likely prove formidable, since it will require far more influence and power than any job title or advanced degree can confer.

Notes

1. It is important to clarify the distinction between the Executive Office of the President (EOP) and the White House Office. The White House Office is a subset of the EOP. The EOP also includes such offices as the Office of Management and Budget, the Vice President's Office, and the Council of Economic Advisors. According to John Hart, "The White House Office became a division of the Executive Office of the President on the organization charts, but it has remained functionally distinct from the other units of the EOP as an intimate, immediate, and personal staff arm of the president." John Hart. 1995. *The Presidential Branch: From Washington to Clinton*, 2d ed. Chatham, N.J.: Chatham House, p. 4. This chapter refers solely to staffing patterns within the White House Office. Additionally, references to the "White House staff" include only those individuals who are formally

linked to the president through hierarchical reporting relationships and whose primary incentives (pay, title, tenure, and jurisdiction) are subject to direct presidential influence. For literature on the growth of the White House staff, see Samuel Kernell. 1989. "The Evolution of the White House Staff." In *Can the Government Govern?* ed. Paul E. Peterson and John Chubb. Washington, D.C.: Brookings Institution; and Thomas Cronin. 1986. "The Swelling of the Presidency." In *Classic Readings in American Politics,* ed. Pietro S. Nivola and David H. Rosenbloom. New York: St. Martin's Press, pp. 413–422.

2. The President's Committee on Administrative Management ("The Brownlow Committee"). 1937. "Administrative Management in the Government of the United States." (Washington, D.C.: U.S.G.P.O.), p. 5.

3. Hart, *The Presidential Branch,* p. 113. These numbers include staff members from the White House Office only. According to Hart, whereas some of these members serve from administration to administration (e.g., the executive clerk, some secretarial staff, switchboard operators), the figure does not include ushers or florists because those offices are not formally part of the White House Office—they are on the staff of what is formally known as the Executive Residence (which is under the jurisdiction of the National Park Service). It is also important to point out that calculating the White House staff size is extremely subjective as there are numerous sources and favored approaches. On pages 114–119, Hart demonstrates seven different measures of White House staff size.

4. Ibid., p. 119.

5. Sidney Milkis. 1993. *The President and the Parties.* New York: Oxford University Press, p. 4.

6. See Kernell, "The Evolution of the White House Staff"; Terry Moe. 1985. "The Politicized Presidency." In *The New Direction in American Politics,* ed. John Chubb and Paul Peterson. Washington, D.C.: Brookings Institution, p. 270; and Richard P. Nathan. 1986. *The Administrative Presidency.* New York: Macmillan.

7. In the aftermath of the 1992 elections, Susan Gluck Mezey noted, "The 1992 elections were especially notable for the marked increase of women elected at the federal level. The number of women elected to state and local office increased as well, but the results there were less dramatic as women had been making steady strides in filling state, county, and municipal offices over the years." Susan Gluck Mezey. 1994. "Increasing the Number of Women in Office: Does It Matter?" In *The Year of the Woman,* ed. Elizabeth Adell Cook, Sue Thomas, and Clyde Wilcox. Boulder, Colo.: Westview Press, p. 257.

8. According to the U.S. Department of Commerce report "Voting and Registration in the Election of November 1994," 63.2 percent of women were registered voters compared with 60.8 percent of men. In terms of percentage voting, women voted at a rate of 44.9 percent compared with 44.4 percent of men. Source (taken from an on-line computer service): Current Population Reports, Population Characteristics, U.S. Department of Commerce, Economics and Statistics Administration and Bureau of the Census, issued in 1995.

The results from the 1992 presidential election are even more decisive: 69.3 percent of women were registered to vote compared with 66.9 percent of men. In terms of percentage voting, women voted at a rate of 62.3 percent compared with men at 60.2 percent. This trend began in 1980; prior to 1980, a higher percentage of men were registered and also voted. Source: Jerry T. Jennings. 1993. "Voting and Registration in the Election of November 1992." Current Population Reports, Population Characteristics, P20-466, pp. v, vi.

9. See, for example, Sue Thomas. 1994. *How Women Legislate.* New York: Oxford University Press; R. Darcy, Susan Welch, and Janet Clark. 1994. *Women,*

Elections and Representation, 2d ed. Lincoln: University of Nebraska Press; Barbara C. Burrell. 1994. *A Woman's Place Is in the House: Campaigning for Congress in the Feminist Era.* Ann Arbor: University of Michigan Press; Susan J. Carroll. 1994. *Women as Candidates in American Politics,* 2d ed. Bloomington: Indiana University Press; and Linda Witt, Karen M. Paget, and Glenna Matthews. 1994. *Running as a Woman: Gender and Power in American Politics.* New York: Free Press.

10. See Janet M. Martin. 1991. "An Examination of Executive Branch Appointments in the Reagan Administration by Background and Gender." *Western Political Quarterly* 44: 173–184; and Janet M. Martin. 1989. "The Recruitment of Women to Cabinet and Subcabinet Posts." *Western Political Quarterly* 42: 161–172. See also Thomas J. Weko's book about the White House Personnel Office from 1948 to 1994 in which he makes several references to the marginalization of women in terms of executive branch appointments. Thomas J. Weko. 1995. *The Politicizing Presidency: The White House Personnel Office, 1948–1994.* Lawrence: University Press of Kansas, pp. 26, 28–29, 50, 84, 119.

11. Note, however, that an expansion in sheer numbers does not necessarily translate to greater power and influence, as this chapter demonstrates.

12. In my efforts to find the best possible source of White House personnel information, I spoke with White House Deputy Executive Clerk Sarah Emery. She indicated that such records were not available within the White House and that the *U.S. Government Staff Manual* was the best publicly available source for a longitudinal study.

13. This finding clearly begs the question of why women have differential rates of participation in constituency relations (outreach) and domestic and foreign policymaking. Perhaps more women than men served in public relations positions and are therefore predisposed toward outreach jobs; men, in turn, may possess more advanced degrees that have prepared them for policymaking and legal positions. The exact explanation of this variation is clearly beyond the scope of this chapter but is worthy of future research.

14. Figures on the percentage of women holding confirmed and appointed positions in the executive branch were obtained from the *CRS Report for Congress,* "Women Appointed to Full-Time Civilian Positions by President Clinton in 1993." March 16, 1994. Congressional Research Service, the Library of Congress, p. 2.

15. Ibid.

16. This term is somewhat vague, but it typically refers to a small group of the president's closest advisers who have a great deal of access to the president.

17. In *The Shadow Presidents: The Secret History of the Chief Executives and Their Top Aides.* (New York: Times Books, 1979), Michael Medved studied the presidents' closest aides. "The intimate portraits that make up this book begin in the year 1857, when Congress first appropriated government funds for the creation of a White House staff. For each administration from that time to the present, one Shadow President has been selected" (p. 6). Not surprisingly, given the time period, not a single woman is found in the group.

18. Note that the composition of this "inner circle" changes frequently. Advisers such as Thomas McLarty, James Carville, David Gergen, Paul Begala, and Stanley Greenberg were initially thought to hold this sacred position, but they lost hold over the course of the first term. See Bob Cohn and Bill Turque. "'The War Room' Stars Fade Out." *Newsweek,* August 7, 1995, pp. 30–31.

19. The same holds true for the president's reelection campaign staff—women are rarely, if ever, members of the inner circle. Whereas Mary Matalin, the Bush-Quayle political director, was a highly visible campaign figure, she notes that her inclusion in press conferences was purely symbolic:

It was unusual that the political director would be named at the same press conference as the chief of staff, the chairman, and the rest of the bigwigs. But if you look at that picture sans me you had five white boys up there. The reason I was announced in conjunction with the leadership was to have a woman in the picture. I had a very good and important job, but I was there to bring some legs into the photo op.

See Mary Matalin and James Carville, with Peter Knobler. 1995. *All's Fair: Love, War, and Running for President.* New York: Random House, p. 91.

20. See Lloyd Grove. "Dee Dee Meyers, In for a Spin; White House Aide Not on the Outs After All." *Washington Post,* September 24, 1994, sec. H; and Elizabeth Drew. "Boss Panetta; Forget Dee Dee, He's Taken Charge at the White House." *Washington Post,* October 2, 1994, sec. C.

21. Meyers's departure was not typical. Amid rumors of her imminent departure when the new chief of staff, Leon Panetta, came on board, Dee Dee Meyers refused to give in and eventually took her case to the president, who not only agreed to keep her on staff but also gave her a promotion. Not unexpectedly, however, the promotion was short-lived; she resigned less than four months later. For more details, see Grove, "Dee Dee Meyers, In for a Spin."

22. In Lou Cannon's book about the Reagan years, *President Reagan: The Role of a Lifetime* (New York: Simon and Schuster, 1991), Elizabeth Dole is not even mentioned. The same is true in Ronald Reagan's autobiography, *An American Life* (New York: Simon and Schuster, 1990), and Ed Meese's memoirs, *With Reagan: The Inside Story* (Washington, D.C.: Regnery Gateway, 1992).

23. Dom Bonafede. "Carter's First 100 Days—The Test Is Yet to Come." *National Journal,* April 30, 1977, p. 679.

24. Dom Bonafede. "The Cronying Touch." *National Journal,* December 10, 1977, p. 1934.

25. Alison Mitchell. 1995. "Assessing the Influence of the Women's Network on the Electoral and Legislative Processes: A Case Study of Women and Participation in the Massachusetts General Court." Honors Thesis in Government. Connecticut College, 1995. In Chapter One, "Contemporary Models and the Historical Patterns of Women's Political Participation," Mitchell provides an exhaustive literature review of the barriers that affect women's participation in electoral politics. See, for example, Irene Diamond. 1977. *Sex Roles in the State House.* New Haven: Yale University Press; Burrell, *A Woman's Place Is in the House;* Carroll, *Women as Candidates in American Politics;* R. Darcy and Sarah Slavin Schramm. 1977. "When Women Run Against Men." *Public Opinion Quarterly* 41: 1–12; Susan Welch. 1978. "Recruitment of Women to Public Office: A Discriminant Analysis," *Western Political Quarterly* 31: 372–380; Darcy, Welch, and Clark, *Women, Elections, and Representation;* Wilma Rule. 1981. "Why Women Don't Run: The Critical Contextual Factors in Women's Legislative Recruitment." *Western Political Quarterly* 34: 60–77.

26. It is important to note that in the case of the Clinton administration, many women who had served in prior administrations obtained more senior positions in the Clinton administration (e.g., Donna Shalala worked as an assistant secretary at HUD from 1977 to 1980 and became the secretary of HHS in 1993; Hazel O'Leary was a deputy administrator for the Energy Department from 1979 to 1981 and was appointed secretary of energy in 1993). One can argue that these women "earned their right" to serve at the most senior level of the Clinton administration because they had paid their dues by serving in less senior positions during the Carter administration. Scholars such as G. Calvin Mackenzie believe this movement "up the ladder" will

ultimately result in a greater number of women in these senior-level appointed positions. (Comment from discussant G. Calvin Mackenzie at the 1995 American Political Science Association Panel [Chicago], "Presidency Studies and Gender: Inclusive Research Strategies.")

27. Note that what often appears to be a "decrease" in staff size is merely creative accounting at its best, with executive branch employees detailed to the White House but not included in White House staff totals.

7

Style Does Matter:
The Impact of Presidential Leadership
on Women in Foreign Policy

Nancy E. McGlen & Meredith Reid Sarkees

Despite the overall male dominance of the field of foreign policy in the United States, in recent years women have made significant gains in terms of inclusion. Yet, the ability of women to have an impact on foreign policy is shaped by a number of factors. At the most general level, cultural stereotypes about the ability of women to conduct foreign policy have limited women's entrance into positions in the field. Relatedly, the historical practices of the two government departments assigned the primary responsibilities for managing the nation's foreign affairs, State and Defense, have further restricted the influence of women.[1]

In addition to these meta-characteristics of foreign affairs, we contend that presidential leadership can significantly influence the possibility of women assuming an equal role with men in shaping foreign policy. More specifically, we argue that three components of presidential leadership can either encourage or discourage the influence of women: (1) Presidential direction can set a tone or an environment that either encourages or discourages the inclusion of women and women's opinions; (2) presidential appointment practices in terms of the number of women, the agencies in which they function, their places in the hierarchy, and the types of positions they hold can shape the influence of women; and (3) presidential policy management style can structure a foreign policy decisionmaking process that includes (or excludes) positions held by women.

In this chapter we assess the impact of these three components of presidential leadership on women's ability to determine foreign policy, with a focus on Presidents Reagan, Bush, and Clinton. We contend that although the first two components are important, the last—management style—is perhaps the most crucial in determining women's influence in foreign policy. Interestingly, this relationship between management style and the influence of women has been virtually ignored in the research. We contend, however, that a president will not necessarily increase women's influence simply by appointing women to positions of authority; rather, those who have influential roles in the decisionmaking process are determined by the structure of the advising mechanism selected by the president. For this study, general personnel data have been augmented by interviews we conducted with women and men in the State and Defense Departments in 1988, 1991, and 1995.[2]

Women at State and Defense:
Cultural and Organizational Barriers

The State and Defense Departments are among the least hospitable environments for women in the federal government. Part of the reason for this situation can be traced to cultural stereotypes about women's abilities (or inabilities) to conduct the affairs of state and to go to war. As detailed by Jean Bethke Elshtain, in our society men have been assigned the role of citizen/warrior and women that of mother/peacemaker.[3] Hence, men have assumed the positions involved in conducting the affairs of state, whereas women have been relegated to domestic duties. Translated into modern politics, these stereotypes have made it particularly difficult for women to enter the field of foreign affairs. The ethos of the State and Defense Departments, which has been shaped by these stereotypes, has led to a history of practices that have added to the difficulties women face when seeking to enter and succeed in both departments.

For instance, before World War II the State Department openly discouraged women from joining the foreign service and utilized the foreign service exam to make the appointment of women difficult.[4] As late as the 1980s, lawsuits repeatedly found that the department continued to treat women unfairly in its examination, appointment, and promotion policies. As a result of this discrimination, women in State tend to be clustered in jobs seen as stereotypically female. For example, since 1960 women have constituted a majority of civil service employees—that is, those who manage the less glamorous secretarial, communications, logistics, and domestic tasks of foreign relations, largely from Washington, D.C. Not only is the percentage of women in these posts high, but approximately 66 percent of the women in the civil service are in nonpolicymaking positions, grades GS-12 and below. In contrast, the most influential positions within the civil service—the Senior Executive Service (SES)—include few women, with the percentage of women increasing slightly from 8 percent in 1987 to 12 percent in 1991 and to 14.2 percent in 1993.[5]

The more prestigious sector of the State Department, the foreign service, which represents the United States around the world, has been even slower to hire and promote women. In 1957 there were 306 women, which constituted 8.9 percent of the foreign service officers (FSOs). The percentage of women FSOs actually declined to 4.8 percent in 1970, then rebounded in 1977 to 9.6 percent.[6] In 1987 women finally passed token status (defined as 15 percent) when they attained 22.7 percent. In 1993 women constituted 26.1 percent of the 5,071 FSOs. Moreover, the senior foreign service (SFS) has been overwhelmingly male-dominated. Between 1970 and 1981, the percentage of SFS personnel who were women edged up just slightly from 2 percent to 3 percent. Although the 1993 figure reflects a tripling to 10.7 percent, women still have token status.[7]

The situation is even worse in the other major institution charged with foreign policy responsibilities, the Department of Defense (DOD), where women have faced discrimination in both the military and civilian sectors. Indeed, women were initially treated as a temporary force until the Women's Armed Services Integration Act of 1948 established the principle of a permanent presence of women in the military, although with fairly restricted roles.

Similarly, in part because of the attitudes concerning women's military abilities, civilian women's participation within the DOD has also been limited. Clustered in jobs in lower grades, women have generally been excluded from the policymaking ranks. Thus, in 1986 women made up 75.1 percent of all employees in ranks GS-1 to GS-6. Conversely, women constituted just 2.6 percent of all DOD SES in 1990. In 1994, when 13 percent of SES positions in the federal government were held by women, only a dismal 7 percent of the Defense Department's SES ranks were occupied by women.[8] This would seem to indicate that the DOD, like State, has not been a particularly welcome place for women's advancement. It is these departmental cultures that a president may address.

Presidential Direction

Although limited by the cultural and institutional contexts of the foreign policy arena, presidents can still have an important role in setting the tone of their administration with respect to the inclusion of women and women's voices. Favorable actions can range from presidential pronouncements on the need to place women in positions of authority to issuing executive orders or sponsoring legislation that would force government departments to recruit or promote women. Alternatively, presidents can adopt positions that oppose or disparage the need to hire women or the abilities of women to contribute to foreign policy.

With respect to the State Department, not all presidents have been equally committed to correcting past discriminatory practices, although some presidential actions have been important in improving opportunities for women. For instance, a major policy shift took place in 1946 at the initiative of President Truman with the Foreign Service Act, which established the goal of a foreign service broadly representative of the American people.

As a result, during the 1950s and 1960s more women were admitted to the State Department. Subsequently, Secretary Cyrus Vance, Jimmy Carter's appointee, urged the department to make a special effort to hire women and minorities so that the service could become truly representative of American diversity. Yet, the cultural milieu in the department resisted, and the administration was forced to bring in women political appointees for senior-level jobs rather than promote women employees from within.

If progress was agonizingly slow under relatively supportive leadership, it was restricted even further during the less hospitable Reagan administration. Many of our interviewees in 1988 cited comments by Donald Regan, Ronald Reagan's chief of staff, that women would rather read the "human interest stuff" about Nancy and Raisa and would not "understand throw weights or what is happening in Afghanistan or what is happening in human rights" as reflective of the administration's dismissive attitude toward women.[9] Indeed, two 1989 studies (one by a congressional agency,[10] the other by the department[11]) both concluded that State was still failing to recruit sufficient numbers of women and minorities.

The response of recent presidents to this environment of discrimination can best be seen in the reaction of the various administrations to the lawsuits brought by women against State. The most important of these was a class action suit filed in 1976 by Alison Palmer and the Women's Action Organization. In the ensuing years the department, under the tacit authority of several presidents and their secretaries of state, disputed the claims of discrimination. The attitude of many within the State Department hierarchy was reflected in the comments of the under secretary for administration in the Ford years, whose response to the lawsuit was one not of conciliation but of retribution: "I don't care what it takes, we are going to *get* Alison."[12] Alison Palmer persisted, however, and in 1987 the Court of Appeals ruled that the department had engaged in a number of serious discriminatory practices, including in the administration of the foreign service exam, assignments, evaluations, and awards.

Neither the Reagan nor the Bush administrations moved to seriously resolve the issues raised by the lawsuit. In fact, during this period many women refused to avail themselves of court-ordered remedies for past discrimination because they feared retaliation.

The Clinton administration took a different approach; it decided to enter global settlement negotiations in an attempt to resolve all of the remaining concerns. The settlement requires changes in the department's evaluation process to make it more equitable and to provide specific relief for individually affected women. Thus, a case that went unresolved through five presidential administrations may at last be settled. Although most of the credit must go to Alison Palmer's resolve in continuing her fight in the face of departmental and, by implication, presidential opposition, the Clinton administration's action indicates the important role a president can have in

affecting the status and power of women in the department and, by extension, in the realm of foreign policy.

The Defense Department also evidences ways in which individual presidents can set a tone that encourages or discourages women's participation,
particularly in terms of women in the military. For example, Presidents
Kennedy and Johnson both spoke about advancing the progress of women in
the military by decrying the "underutilization of the American women . . . as
the most tragic and most senseless waste of this century."[13] Yet, neither president took action to expand the role of women in the military. The adoption
of the All Volunteer Force in 1973 under the initiative of President Nixon,
although not directly concerned with improving women's position, also did
much to move women's progress by requiring that the military recruit
women when too few men volunteered.

A period of backsliding for women came during the Reagan administration, when a report by Assistant Secretary of Defense Lawrence Korb
argued that women were poor substitutes for men in many military
roles. The branches quickly interpreted the report as an opening to roll
back the progress of women by imposing new restrictions on their
recruitment and roles.[14] There was, however, an apparent difference of opinion on this issue within the administration. Secretary of Defense
Weinberger, motivated by the administration's desire to build up the military, issued a memo to the secretaries of the branches reminding them of the
need to break down barriers that prevented the department from making the
fullest use of women. In 1984 Weinberger also established the DOD Task
Force on Equity for Women to examine opportunities for women in the military.[15] Women we interviewed in the Defense Department during the last
year of the Reagan administration generally reported that it was the secretaries of defense, Weinberger and Carlucci, not the president, who had been
the impetus for what progress had occurred for women during the Reagan
era.

From the perspective of many women in DOD, however, the exclusion
of women from combat and direct combat support positions has had a very
detrimental effect on women in the military and in civilian policymaking
positions as well, particularly in terms of establishing their credibility. As
retired Brigadier General Evelyn P. Foote noted, "As long as women are
operationally excluded, they will never acquire the experience that leads to
their acquiring rank of more than one star. Unless they get the operational
experience, they will never be in a position to have a significant impact on
national defense policy."[16]

In spite of the prominent role played by women in the Gulf and Panama
conflicts, President Bush generally resisted expanding the combat role of
women. Under President Clinton, however, policy began to change.
Secretary of Defense Les Aspin, following a general administration plan to
open the military to gays and women, removed the ban on women flying

combat planes and was instrumental in allowing women to serve on combat ships.

The increased number of women recruited into the military and the elimination of some of the combat restrictions on women will have a doubly positive effect throughout the Defense Department. First, more women will be available for selection to military branch–related Pentagon slots. Second, the stereotype that because women do not and cannot have combat experience they lack expertise in military-related issues and, by implication, foreign policy issues, will be weakened. The eventual result should be an increase in the credibility and influence of women in the Pentagon.

Presidential Appointments

A president can dramatically change the numbers and authority of women in the foreign policy establishment through the appointment of senior officials in the two major departments. Recent research on the appointment process found it has changed considerably over the years. One of the important changes has been the increased number of positions open to presidential appointment, which has grown from 71 political appointees in 1933 to more than 600 positions today. In addition, as a result of the Civil Service Reform Act of 1978, presidents now have the power to appoint and to shift the placement of persons in the SES and SFS.[17] Presidents, thus, now have more latitude to increase the number of women appointees and their authority.

Whereas some presidents have wanted diversity[18] (see Chapters 4 and 5), others have been more concerned with picking cabinet and subcabinet officials to use "as a mechanism of policy control."[19] This has meant that these presidents have emphasized "loyalty, ideology, or program support" in their selections.[20]

For Reagan, the key objective was to select appointees who could control a bureaucracy that was perceived as too liberal to effectively implement the president's reforms. "Personnel is policy" became the administration's credo.[21] Reagan's appointment staff, however, found it had to bend to the influence of the campaign team. The result was a gauntlet all appointees had to run, which checked their loyalty to Reagan, their ideological credentials, and their work on the campaign.[22] This situation may have been particularly daunting for women, many of whom may have been at odds with the Reagan administration over social issues such as abortion and few of whom had been active in the presidential campaign.

A counterforce to the lack of interest in appointing women during the Reagan administration may have been the cabinet secretaries. Reports are that both Secretary of Defense Weinberger and Secretary of State Shultz exerted considerable influence in the selection of their under and assistant secretaries, much to the dismay of the White House.[23] The pressure from these two secretaries, both of whom were more open to the participation of women than others in the administration, may have caused women to be more prominent in foreign policy than they would have been otherwise.

The Bush appointment process was less focused than Reagan's. Without a clear policy agenda, Bush was less concerned with emphasizing the appointee's ideology, although loyalty to him was important.[24] With respect to diversity, the Bush appointment team seemed more concerned than Reagan's about nominating women, although this may have been the case mainly to prevent criticism by the press that women were being passed over.[25]

More than those of his predecessors, the Clinton appointment process put a high premium on diversity. In fact, "He was determined to equal George Bush, or go him one better, in naming a diverse Cabinet."[26] Having pledged to make the cabinet "look like America," the Presidential Personnel Office organized itself to achieve that goal. Although Clinton's overall record was relatively good, like his predecessors he appointed considerably fewer women to the Defense and State Departments than his first-year record would suggest. Among the cabinet departments, State was tied for twelfth, with 22 percent women appointees, and Defense ranked thirteenth, with 18.5 percent women appointees among those that required Senate approval during the first year.[27] Furthermore, among the top foreign policy advisers, Clinton selected only one woman, Madeleine Albright, U.S. ambassador to the United Nations.

Although his overall record has been somewhat disappointing, Clinton's appointments in the State and Defense Departments have included more women than his predecessors. Table 7.1 gives the number of women selected by Reagan, Bush, and Clinton for positions that required Senate confirmation in each of the years for which we have data. Clinton not only appointed more women to both departments in his first year than either Bush or Reagan, but Clinton's total number of women appointees in his first two years exceeded the numbers nominated by Reagan in eight years and Bush in four years.

Clinton's first two years of appointments also included more women in higher-ranking positions in both departments than Reagan or Bush appointed in their entire presidencies. Whereas all of the Reagan and Bush women appointees to State and Defense positions were level 4 or below (with the exception of Jeane Kirkpatrick, who was a level 2), Clinton nominated one woman at State for a level-2 position (Madeleine Albright to the United Nations), two women at State for level-3 positions, and one woman, Sheila Widnall, to a level-2 position as secretary of the Air Force at Defense.[28] With this appointment, Clinton became the first president to name a woman to head a branch of the military.

Clinton's support for women is also evident with respect to SES and SFS appointments. Analysis of the State Department's 1995 *Organizational*

Table 7.1   **Number of Women Appointed to State and Defense Policy Positions That Required Consent of the Senate, 1981–1994**

	First-Year Appointments, State	First-Year Appointments, Defense	Total Appointments, State	Total Appointments, Defense	Total Appointments, State and Defense[a]
Reagan	2	0	8	4	12
Bush	4	4	8	7	15
Clinton	7	5	10	12	22

Source: Numbers are calculated from Rogelio Garcia, 1989, "Women Nominated and Appointed to Full-Time Civilian Positions By President Reagan," Washington, D.C.: Congressional Research Service; Rogelio Garcia, 1993, "Women Nominated and Appointed to Full-Time Civilian Positions by President George Bush, 1989–1992," Washington, D.C.: Congressional Research Service; Rogelio Garcia, 1994, "Women Appointed to Full-Time Civilian Positions by President Clinton in 1993," Washington, D.C.: Congressional Research Service; Rogelio Garcia, 1995, "Presidential Appointments to Full-Time Positions in Executive Departments During the 103d Congress," Washington, D.C.: Congressional Research Service.

Note: a. Totals do not include any ambassadors, except for representatives to the United Nations and the United Nations Educational, Scientific, and Cultural Organization. The total figures for Reagan are for eight years, those for Bush for four years, and those for Clinton for two years.

Directory found that women made up half of the noncareer (political) SES appointments, although they represented only 22 percent of the career SES appointments. A similar analysis of the spring 1995 *Federal Yellow Book* for the Office of the Secretary of Defense in the DOD revealed much the same picture. Whereas 33 percent of the noncareer SES appointments went to women, only 12 percent of the career SES positions were held by women. This inequality reflects the dearth of women in the lower ranks of the civil service at Defense and the historical discrimination against women, which is only partially correctable by any single president.

In addition to the leadership positions in the State and Defense Departments, another important set of appointments is ambassadorships. The number of women ambassadors is important, but also key in evaluating a president's record is the specific country assignments of women ambassadors and whether the president relies on career foreign service officers or noncareer political appointees for ambassadorships.

Looking first at the numbers, we find that historically the ranks of ambassador have contained few women. For the time period from 1933 until the mid-1970s, only twenty women received presidential ambassadorial appointments. As recently as 1989, only 7 percent of ambassadors were women.[29] President Clinton has significantly increased the number of women ambassadors, as seen in Table 7.2. As of June 30, 1995, the State Department's *List of Chief of Mission* included twenty-two women ambassadors, which represented 14.7 percent of all filled positions. Only one woman, Pamela Harriman, however, is ambassador to a major power state.

Table 7.2 Women Ambassadors, 1995

Name of Ambassador	Nation/Organization	Status
Swanee Hunt	Austria	Noncareer
Jeanette Hyde	Barbados/Grenada	Noncareer
Jennone Walker	Czech Republic	Noncareer
Pamela Harriman	France	Noncareer
Jean Kennedy Smith	Ireland	Noncareer
March Fong Eu	Micronesia	Noncareer
Elizabeth Frawley Bagley	Portugal	Noncareer
Madeleine Albright	United Nations	Noncareer
Harriet Babbitt	Organization of American States	Noncareer
Ruth Davis	Benin	Career
Theresa Tull	Brunei	Career
Harriet Isom	Cameroon	Career
Donna Hrinak	Dominican Republic	Career
Marilyn McAfee	Guatemala	Career
Aurelia Brazeal	Kenya	Career
Eileen Malloy	Kyrgyz Republic	Career
Dorothy Myers Sampas	Mauritania	Career
Leslie Alexander	Mauritius/Comoros	Career
Mary Pendleton	Moldova	Career
Sandra Vogelgesang	Nepal	Career
Teresita Schaffer	Sri Lanka/Maldives	Career
Mary Ann Casey	Tunisia	Career

As the table also makes clear, some of the best assignments have been given to the noncareerists, including Swanee Hunt and Pamela Harriman—both major players in, and contributors to, Bill Clinton's campaign. Under Clinton, 41 percent of the women ambassadors are noncareerists (compared with 32 percent of male ambassadors who are noncareerists), which may reflect an attempt to utilize noncareer appointees to overcome a bureaucratic culture that has been hostile to women.

Management Style

The third component of presidential leadership relates to the process by which a president makes policy. Specifically, management style concerns the way in which the president structures and utilizes the foreign policy team. We argue that the management style a president adopts shapes the role women can play in foreign policy by either utilizing or marginalizing the positions they hold.

Variations in presidential management style have been conceptualized in a number of ways.[30] The variation utilized here is a tripartite categorization that consists of differences in: (1) the president's valuation of the foreign policy bureaucracy; (2) the competing degrees of influence of the various agencies, specifically the balance between the Executive Office of the

President (EOP) and the Departments of State and Defense; and (3) the types of people upon whom the president relies, whether civil servants or noncareer political appointees.

Turning to the first area, there have been two general views concerning the relationship between the president and the bureaucracy. The first view has emphasized the power of the bureaucracy because it possesses important resources (such as expertise and tenure). Attempts by presidents to control the bureaucracy's influence are seen as ineffectual because of their transience and lower level of expertise.[31] This perspective has come under attack by observers of the policy process who, articulating a second and alternative interpretation of presidential power in bureaucratic relations, have noted the increasing power of the presidency and the declining influence of other government forces in major foreign policy decisions. Particularly in national security policy matters, presidents have placed a priority on gaining control of the foreign policy bureaucracy.[32]

This conflict is further played out in the second component, the relationship between the EOP and the departments. Presidents, with varying degrees of success, have attempted not only to take power away from the departments but also to center that power within the White House or the EOP (including the National Security Council [NSC]). The State Department in particular has suffered a general decline in its influence relative to the White House. Decisions to place greater emphasis on the White House or the EOP reflect presidential management strategies for policymaking. Scholars have also described staff management in terms of hierarchical structures, spokes-in-a-wheel organization, or collegial approaches.[33] In a hierarchical system, the president is at the apex with the advisory system and authority patterns well-defined, generally with someone designated chief of staff to insulate the president from policy conflicts. The multiple channels structure, often called the spokes-in-a-wheel model, pictures the president at the hub or focal point of the advisers who can then produce differing policy recommendations. In the collegial model, the president relies on advice provided by a limited number of people, each of whom has access.

Finally, management style is also reflected in the types of people upon whom the president relies—career government officials or political appointees. Centering decisionmaking in the White House has often been coupled with maneuvers to politicize the bureaucracy by placing political appointees in many top leadership positions. (This transfer of influence in the direction of political appointees has challenged the view of bureaucratic influence discussed earlier.) For presidents, promoting political appointees can have two major benefits: It places confidantes in leadership positions and isolates the civil service by creating multiple layers of political appointees between it and the top levels of its departments.[34] In terms of the influence of women, to the extent that the president restricts the group of advisers to an inner circle of close (generally male) advisers, women careerists may find themselves without a voice.

The next issue involves the ways in which management-style decisions in these three areas during the past three administrations have affected women.

Reagan's Style

Ronald Reagan came to power with relatively little interest in, or specific knowledge of, foreign policy, yet he did have a simple, ideologically driven agenda. This lack of presidential knowledge or concern would seem to provide more opportunities for bureaucratic influence.[35] Indeed, Reagan initially promised to restore leadership in U.S. foreign policy by organizing policymaking more coherently and more frequently involving the State Department and the cabinet in decisionmaking.[36] Yet, Reagan's lack of interest and his delegation of authority in what he called "cabinet government" contributed to a perhaps unprecedented fragmentation of policy.[37] Moreover, fearful that granting too much autonomy to the bureaucracy might sabotage its policy efforts, the Reagan administration pursued the well-publicized intent of curtailing bureaucrats' access to sources of leverage and influence.[38]

In evaluating Reagan's organizational style in regard to the EOP, Richard Rose has argued that there were three distinct phases of Reagan's presidency. During his first term he utilized a hybrid version of spokes-of-the-wheel and collaborative models to develop a collegial organization under the troika of Edwin Meese, James Baker III, and Michael Deaver.[39] This structure delegated a great deal of authority to the threesome and thus reduced the workload for Reagan, which served him well. Not surprisingly, Jeane Kirkpatrick (U.S. ambassador to the United Nations, 1981–1985) was not one of Reagan's close advisers. She claimed that because of her sex her views were seldom heeded.[40]

The second phase, 1985–1987, took place with Donald Regan as chief of staff; he headed a closed, hierarchically structured White House. During this phase the flow of command was unidirectional: Reagan would set policy goals and expect subordinates to implement them. The president increasingly relied on his personal staff and the EOP. In terms of foreign policy, the National Security Planning Group, which consisted of the president's closest personal advisers, emerged as a kind of "executive committee" of the NSC.[41] This reliance on a small group was moderated (in part as a result of the Iran contra scandal) during the third phase, 1987–1988, in which Reagan adopted a relatively nonhierarchical management style.[42]

Finally, Reagan's ideological agenda exacerbated the conflict between career civil servants and political appointees. In addition to the Reagan administration's general distrust of the career executives, the administration's goal was to increase the influence of the political appointees by increasing their numbers and promoting increased contact between them and the White House.[43] Reagan wanted to place partisans deep within the bureaucracy, even if expertise was lacking.[44] This policy further undermined the opportunity for the bureaucracy to provide professional input.[45] The Reagan appointees were successful in reducing the discretion or policy power of the top bureaucrats.[46] The tension between these two groups was further exacerbated by the impression among the careerists that the Reagan appointees were not overly qualified for their positions. One of our interviewees, a careerist at Defense, commented in 1988:

> Generally, I think political appointees, male or female, tend not to be of the caliber of the career civil servants in terms of brains, experience, dedication. . . . One reason is that the Reagan administration brought in a lot more political appointees than we [had] ever had into lower levels of the organization. Another reason is that to get cleared for the White House, to get nominated as a political appointee . . . you had to be ideologically pure.

There were numerous consequences for women of Reagan's management style. His distrust of the bureaucracy and his reliance on a policy formulation style that emphasized, first, a troika of men and, later, the hierarchical control of Don Regan contributed to the further marginalization of all career employees. The high ideological profile of the Reagan appointees, few of whom at State and Defense were women, increased conflict between career officials and political appointees. Thus, the elements of the Reagan management style combined to give latitude to mostly male political appointees, with women playing a very minor role.

Bush's Style

The tensions between the bureaucracy and the careerists continued in the Bush administration, although in a slightly different form. President Bush, the consummate insider, seemed more likely than his predecessor to use the bureaucracy, thereby allowing the careerists an avenue for security policy input. In contrast to Reagan, Bush appointed a relatively large number of career public servants to high-level executive posts and treated the mission of the civil service with respect.[47] "What Bush added was a supportive public rhetoric about the bureaucracy. This lent an aura of comity to what, in many respects, still involved a great deal of top-down discipline."[48]

Bush's leadership style also reflected contradictory components. On one hand, he demonstrated a penchant for a very "hands-on" style of leadership, in which he engaged in congenial consultations and collaborative decisionmaking.[49] On the other hand, he adopted a more restricted, hierarchical policymaking model that concentrated foreign policy making within the hands of a few close personal advisers and tended to exclude the bureaucracy (the State Department in particular).

Consequently, the relationship between the president and the departments was very poor, the use of consultative mechanisms declined, and teamwork within the administration became spasmodic—for example, the NSC rarely met at the principals' level. This propensity was fueled by "Bush's dark side"—his tendency to be secretive, to "personalize conflict, and to couch his reasoning in harsh and vindictive terms."[50]

In terms of the foreign policy bureaucracy, the Bush administration was essentially devoid of officials who had their own strong political agendas; instead, it was characterized by insider politics. In general, Bush wanted loyal team players around him; particularly in difficult situations, only advisers who shared Bush's vision became part of the inner circle.[51] Bush relied on a small group of personal friends—including James Baker, Brent Scowcroft, and Dick Cheney—without bringing career officials into deliberations. Moreover, this propensity was also common among the secretaries; Secretary Baker was particularly known for ignoring the foreign service.[52]

Thus, whereas Bush appeared more supportive of the bureaucracy and placed more women in positions of authority within State and Defense than Reagan had, his management style relied heavily on old friends who were male and were not career government employees. Thus, women, particularly women careerists, tended to be excluded from influence in setting foreign policy in the Bush administration.

Clinton's Style

In contrast to Bush, President Clinton's primary interest has not been foreign policy. Overall, Clinton's policy style reflects the fact that he likes thinking about policy, which sometimes means he gets caught up in the details.[53] Foreign policy is not President Clinton's forte, and he does not "like this stuff because he is not a master of it."[54] This situation can lead to ambiguity in his relationship with the bureaucracy. Whereas Clinton has avoided antibureaucratic rhetoric and allows foreign policy decisionmakers a great deal of latitude in specific areas of expertise or regions of the world, this strategy can often seem like neglect. A recent political appointee in the State Department (interviewed in summer 1995) noted that the by-product of Clinton's lack of interest can particularly be seen at State: "Generally, the president has some issues on which he feels strongly. However, on a majority of foreign policy issues, [Warren] Christopher has taken the lead." This latitude can benefit the bureaucracy only if the appointees are seen as strong personalities, which is not generally perceived to be the case at State. As an appointee explained to us:

> Christopher is lawyerly—steady—doesn't have the flair Baker had. . . . His problem is that he is not a "stump" person, not an effective speaker. The United States has been just as involved in foreign affairs as [it was] in the last two administrations, but we just don't trumpet our successes enough, like Haiti, North Korea, and Russia. Nobody is out there saying it. . . . Baker was good that way. He could make nothing into something, and so could Bush.

In terms of the relationship between the president and his advisers, Clinton's weakness is his unwillingness to think about organizational structure or dividing the labor. Clinton wants to be involved in everything, envisioning a spokes-in-the-wheel model; yet, he has neglected the staffing that could make that model function well. For example, there has been no one to serve as surrogate to a president who has wanted to focus his major efforts on domestic policy.[55] Specifically, Clinton has not used cabinet-level structures and has neglected the NSC,[56] which shifted to more of a coordinating role under Anthony Lake. A Defense careerist whom we interviewed complained: "Under Clinton, NSC has not played the role it should. It should be the disciplinarian and the honest broker, but it isn't. It is not playing its role, it is not bringing questions to closure." Despite this indecision and inefficiency, "President Clinton has not attempted to create a counterbureaucracy in the White House with a staff that gets involved in the administrative details."[57]

This structural chaos is abetted by Clinton's personal hands-on way of formulating policy in which he confers widely and is willing to compromise.[58] This style has sometimes been referred to as Clinton's "let's deal" presidency.[59] Such a team-building approach works well only when the president has experts on whom he can rely to provide a variety of policy options.[60] This is not seen as the case in foreign policy.

> The president revealed an especially unimaginative approach toward staffing his national security team. Christopher; Anthony Lake, assistant to the president for national security; Samuel Berger, Lake's deputy; James Woolsey, the CIA director; Madeleine Albright, ambassador to the United Nations, all had served in the Carter administration. They struck many observers as retreads. Indeed, Lake speculated nine months into the administration that Clinton perhaps had stressed too much building a national security team consisting of collegial, like-minded advisers.[61]

Such reliance on previous government officials (mostly male) also limits the opportunities for women to break into the process.

Thus, Clinton's style has had a major impact on the role of women in foreign policy formulation. Although Clinton has clearly promoted women, they have often not been placed in positions of authority. As one State Department appointee reported to us: "Christopher has more top-ranked women than ever. I would give them a B+. Yet, there are still some problems. Women are struggling in positions that are not as influential [except for Albright]." Moreover, Clinton's management style by default often results in reliance for major policy positions on a few trusted advisers who are almost exclusively white males, with peripheral advisers calculated to meet diversity quotas.[62]

Conclusion

Those who desire the inclusion of more women in the foreign policy establishment have rarely focused on the role of the presidency in bringing about equity. The analysis in this chapter suggests this may be an important oversight. Individual presidents have taken actions that have improved the climate for women in foreign policy and have increased the numbers, status, and influence of women in foreign affairs positions. Of the three presidents we examined, Clinton has taken the most dramatic steps to expand the representation of women. Even in an administration committed to eliminating discrimination and promoting diversity, however, the desire to include the views of women often falls by the wayside—a victim of a management style that, although it includes many women (although few in the inner circle), lacks direction and leadership. The result is that women are the most represented in the foreign policy establishment during the presidency that is most criticized for its poor management of foreign affairs.

We should not, moreover, be lulled into thinking that because women have a more visible presence in the foreign policy establishment their status will continue to improve. Some trends do suggest that progress will continue. The increased number of women in the bureaucracy at the State and Defense Departments is not likely to subside soon, but the agonizingly slow gains of 1 to 2 percent a year suggests that equity may not come before the end of the twenty-first century—especially at the highest bureaucratic echelons in both departments, the SES and SFS, where few women are in the pipeline for promotion. Because promotions to these ranks require the internal evaluation of supervisors who are generally male, a recent study by the U.S. Merit Systems Protection Board indicated that women may be at a disadvantage.[63] Presidents have the power to do something about such situations, as Clinton's decision to resolve the lawsuit at State indicates, but changes in cultural values and entrenched practices are often difficult to achieve no matter how committed the president may be.

Chief executives, of course, need not rely on bureaucratic channels to move women into positions of authority. They can appoint women to influential posts as political appointees and in the foreign and executive service. We should not expect all presidents to follow these strategies, however. The best example may be Reagan, who felt little obligation to choose women and perhaps even resisted selecting them and whose appointments of women declined from the previous administration. Even Clinton, who has appointed many more women than his predecessors to key slots in his administration (such as Madeleine Albright and Sheila Widnall), has no women among his inner circle of foreign policy advisers. In the current era of backlash against affirmative action, the next president will likely feel less obligation to make the administration "look like America."

Most important, as our review of presidential management styles indicates, placing more women in positions within the foreign policy establishment is not sufficient to increase their influence. The management styles of all three of the presidents reviewed here reflect a tendency, at least in the foreign policy sector, of relying ultimately on a small group of mostly male political advisers to make decisions.

The overall practice of presidential leadership in terms of direction, appointments, and management style has a major impact on the extent to which women are included in (or excluded from) the foreign policy process. Women may be in the anteroom more so today than in the past, but they are still rarely at the table when the crucial decisions about foreign policy are made.

Notes

1. Nancy E. McGlen and Meredith Reid Sarkees. 1993. *Women in Foreign Policy: The Insiders.* New York: Routledge.
2. This research was done with the assistance of research grants from Niagara University and the Center for the American Woman and Politics at the Eagleton Institute of Politics, Rutgers University.
3. Jean Bethke Elshtain. 1987. *Women and War.* New York: Basic Books.
4. McGlen and Sarkees, *Women in Foreign Policy: The Insiders,* pp. 62–66.
5. Data from Department of State. 1993. *Multi-Year Affirmative Action Plan: FY 1990–1992.* Washington, D.C.: Department of State.
6. Homer Calkin. 1978. *Women in the Department of State: Their Role in American Foreign Affairs.* Washington, D.C.: Department of State, p. 151.
7. Office of Equal Employment and Civil Rights. 1987. *Update of the Affirmative Action Plan and Annual Accomplishment Report of Equal Employment Activities for Fiscal Year 1987.* Washington, D.C.: Office of Equal Employment and Civil Rights; Department of State, *Multi-Year Affirmative Action Plan: FY 1990–1992;* and Department of State. 1994. *Affirmative Employment Program Accomplishment Report.* Washington, D.C.: Department of State.
8. Office of Personnel Management. 1994. *The Status of the Senior Executive Service.* Washington, D.C.: Office of Personnel Management.
9. Joanne Edgar. 1986. "Women Who Went to the Summit." *Ms.* (February): 84; and McGlen and Sarkees, *Women in Foreign Policy: The Insiders,* p. 101.
10. *State Department: Minorities and Women Are Underrepresented in the Foreign Service* (Washington, D.C.: General Accounting Office, 1989).
11. Department of State, Office of Equal Employment and Civil Rights. 1989. *Update of the Affirmative Action Plan and Annual Accomplishment Report of Equal*

Employment Activities for Fiscal Year 1988 (Washington D.C.: Department of State).

12. McGlen and Sarkees, *Women in Foreign Policy: The Insiders,* p. 121.

13. Major General Jeanne Holm, USAF (ret.). 1982. *Women in the Military: An Unfinished Revolution.* Novato, Calif.: Presidio, p. 178.

14. Judith Hicks Stiehm. 1989. *Arms and the Enlisted Women.* Philadelphia: Temple University Press.

15. Department of Defense. 1987. *Selected Manpower Statistics.* Washington, D.C.: Department of Defense.

16. Quoted in McGlen and Sarkees, *Women in Foreign Policy: The Insiders,* p. 126.

17. See Richard M. Pious. 1996. *The Presidency.* Boston: Allyn and Bacon, pp. 279–280; and James P. Pfiffner. 1988. *The Strategic Presidency: Hitting the Ground Running.* Pacific Grove, Calif.: Brooks/Cole Publishing Company.

18. Constance Horner. 1993. "The Politics of Presidential Appointment." *American Enterprise* 4 (September–October): 20.

19. Terry M. Moe. 1993. "Presidents, Institutions, and Theory." In *Researching the Presidency: Vital Questions, New Approaches,* ed. George C. Edwards III, John H. Kessel, and Bert A. Rockman. Pittsburgh: University of Pittsburgh Press, p. 254. Quoted in Thomas J. Weko. 1995. *The Politicizing Presidency: The White House Personnel Office, 1948–1994.* Lawrence: University Press of Kansas, p. 5.

20. Weko, *The Politicizing Presidency,* p. 5.

21. Ibid., p. 90.

22. Charles O. Jones. 1994. *The Presidency in a Separated System.* Washington, D.C.: Brookings Institution, pp. 98–99.

23. Weko, *The Politicizing Presidency,* p. 5.

24. Ibid., pp. 108–109; and Horner, "The Politics of Presidential Appointment," p. 22.

25. Weko, *The Politicizing Presidency,* p. 189.

26. Elizabeth Drew. 1994. *On the Edge: The Clinton Presidency.* New York: Simon and Schuster, p. 25.

27. Rogelio Garcia. 1994. "Women Appointed to Full-Time Civilian Positions by President Clinton in 1993." Washington, D.C.: Congressional Research Service.

28. Executive level 1 positions are some high-level EOP positions and all cabinet positions; Executive level 2 positions are deputy secretaries of departments, secretaries of military departments, and heads of major agencies; Executive level 3 positions are under secretaries of departments and heads of middle-level agencies.

29. *Joint Hearing Before the Subcommittee on International Operations of the Committee on Foreign Affairs and Subcommittee on the Civil Service of the Committee on Post Office and Civil Service.* 1990. Washington, D.C.: U.S. Government Printing Office.

30. Colin Campbell. 1996. "Management in a Sandbox: Why the Clinton White House Failed to Cope with Gridlock." In *The Clinton Presidency: First Appraisals,* ed. Colin Campbell and Bert A. Rockman. Chatham, N.J.: Chatham House Publishers, p. 58.

31. John T. Rourke, Ralph G. Carter, and Mark A. Boyer. 1994. *Making American Foreign Policy.* Guilford, Conn.: Dushkin Publishing Group, p. 269; and Pfiffner, *The Strategic Presidency: Hitting the Ground Running,* p. 90.

32. Samuel Kernell. 1989. "The Evolution of the White House Staff." In *Can the Government Govern?* ed. Paul E. Peterson and John E. Chubb. Washington, D.C.: Brookings Institution.

33. Campbell, "Management in a Sandbox," p. 69; Margaret G. Hermann.

1995. "Advice and Advisers in the Clinton Presidency." In *The Clinton Presidency: Campaigning, Governing, and the Psychology of Leadership,* ed. Stanley A. Renshon. Boulder, Colo.: Westview Press, p. 150.

34. Joel D. Aberbach and Bert A. Rockman. 1990. "What Has Happened to the U.S. Senior Civil Service?" *Brookings Review* 8 (4): 38.

35. See Stephen Hess. 1988. *Organizing the Presidency.* Washington, D.C.: Brookings Institution.

36. Charles W. Kegley and Eugene R. Wittkopf. 1987. *American Foreign Policy: Pattern and Process,* 3rd ed. New York: St. Martin's Press, pp. 341–342.

37. Duncan L. Clarke. 1989. *American Defense and Foreign Policy Institutions.* New York: Harper and Row, p. 7.

38. Aberbach and Rockman, "What Has Happened to the U.S. Senior Civil Service?" p. 40.

39. Richard Rose. 1991. *The Postmodern President: George Bush Meets the World,* 2d ed. Chatham, N.J.: Chatham House Publishers, p. 159.

40. Edward P. Crapol, ed. 1987. *Women and American Foreign Policy: Lobbyists, Critics, and Insiders.* New York: Greenwood Press, p. 167.

41. Kegley and Wittkopf, *American Foreign Policy: Pattern and Process,* p. 359.

42. Lance Blakesley. 1995. *Presidential Leadership from Eisenhower to Clinton.* Chicago: Nelson-Hall Publishers, pp. 177–178; and Kernell, "The Evolution of the White House Staff."

43. Aberbach and Rockman, "What Has Happened to the U.S. Senior Civil Service?" p. 39.

44. Terry M. Moe. 1985. "The Politicized Presidency." In *The New Direction in American Politics,* ed. John E. Chubb and Paul E. Peterson. Washington, D.C.: Brookings Institution, p. 260.

45. Lester M. Salamon and Alan J. Abramson. 1984. "Governance: The Politics of Retrenchment." In *The Reagan Record: An Assessment of America's Changing Domestic Priorities,* ed. John L. Palmer and Isabel V. Sawhill. Cambridge, Mass.: Ballinger Publishing Company, p. 64.

46. Steven D. Stehr. 1989. "Top Bureaucrats and the Distribution of Influence in Reagan's Executive Branch." Presented at the Annual Meeting of the American Political Science Association, Atlanta, Georgia, p. 2.

47. James P. Pfiffner, cited in Blakesley, *Presidential Leadership from Eisenhower to Clinton,* p. 205.

48. Campbell, "Management in a Sandbox," p. 60.

49. Blakesley, *Presidential Leadership from Eisenhower to Clinton,* p. 58.

50. Campbell, "Management in a Sandbox," p. 63.

51. Hermann, "Advice and Advisers in the Clinton Presidency," p. 155.

52. Roxanne Roberts. "The Silence of the Diplomat." *Washington Post,* March 15, 1991, sec. C.

53. Drew, *On the Edge: The Clinton Presidency,* pp. 79, 232. Cited in Bert A. Rockman. 1996. "Leadership Style and the Clinton Presidency." In *The Clinton Presidency: First Appraisals,* ed. Campbell and Rockman, p. 349.

54. Campbell, "Management in a Sandbox," p. 67.

55. Ibid., p. 79.

56. Ibid., p. 76.

57. Blakesley, *Presidential Leadership from Eisenhower to Clinton,* p. 249.

58. Ibid., p. 51.

59. Campbell, "Management in a Sandbox," p. 62.

60. Hermann, "Advice and Advisers in the Clinton Presidency," p. 157.

61. Campbell, "Management in a Sandbox," p. 67.

62. Ted Van Dyk. 1993. "Clinton Team: Loyal, Politically Correct." *Financial World* (February 2): 88.

63. U.S. Merit Systems Protection Board. 1993. *A Question of Equity: Women and the Glass Ceiling in the Federal Government.* Washington, D.C.: U.S. Merit Systems Protection Board.

PART 3

Institutional Perspectives: The President, Congress, and the Courts

8

Diversity and the Politicization of Presidential Appointments: A Case Study of the Achtenberg Nomination

Jean Reith Schroedel, Sharon Spray & Bruce D. Snyder

> No other nation relies so heavily on non-career personnel for the management of its government. In its breadth and importance, the in-and-outer system of leadership selection is uniquely American.[1]

The Constitution requires that the president nominate and the Senate confirm the appointment of federal executive officers. The Senate is often criticized for its passivity in this process; indeed, statistically it seemingly rubber-stamps nominations.[2] For key administrative and judicial positions, however, the president's extensive nomination apparatus consults important senators—party leaders, chairs of committees, and home-state senators—during the selection process. Poorly received potential nominees are unlikely to be nominated in the first place. Those who survive the preliminary process then face a security review. The comprehensive vetting process enhances the Senate's traditional deference to presidential selection.

Until the early 1970s, nearly all nominations that reached the floor were confirmed by the full Senate, usually with perfunctory voice votes—often as part of a slate of nominations and treaties.[3] Whereas the number of nominations targeted for full Senate debate and roll call vote has increased since the 1970s, such contestations remain rare.[4] Most nominations contested on the Senate floor encounter little controversy in committee and are opposed by only a handful of senators when the actual floor vote occurs.[5] These senators increasingly use the debates that precede roll calls to challenge the president's judgment, draw attention to the administration's political agenda, and, in some cases, garner publicity for individual political gain.[6]

Whereas President Clinton's commitment to make his administration "look more like America" surpassed that of his predecessors, it also made his nominations more vulnerable to attack by members of an increasingly partisan, yet highly individualistic, Senate. In addition to expanding dramatically the numbers of women and racial minorities appointed to high federal office and the courts, Clinton appointed thirty-five open homosexuals to government positions.[7] The first and most prominent of these was Roberta

129

Achtenberg as assistant secretary of fair housing and equal opportunity at the Department of Housing and Urban Development (HUD). We believe her nomination is particularly appropriate for an analysis of the growing politicization of the confirmation process.

The Achtenberg nomination is typical because the nominee was highly qualified and received little objection within committee and because the nomination rewarded an important constituency group. But it is atypical in that the group being rewarded was homosexuals. In a system dominated by white male elites,[8] this nomination stood out not only because Achtenberg was the first open lesbian to be nominated for high federal office but also because she was a gay rights activist. The nomination is also unusual because of the hundreds of subcabinet appointments made by Clinton in 1993, fewer than a half dozen were subjected to roll call votes. As with most other recent disputed nominations, Achtenberg's qualifications were never in serious question, but her personal life and political beliefs were the subject of extensive debate.

We begin by examining the reasons Senate challenges to presidential nominations have increased and then show how these factors affected the Achtenberg nomination. We note how changes in Senate norms and the rise of groups outside the Senate created a climate in which the nomination could be politicized. To illustrate these trends, we analyze the themes raised in the committee hearing and the content of the floor debate and examine the subsequent roll call vote. Finally, we compare Achtenberg's and other nominees' treatment by the Senate to ascertain whether her homosexuality made her confirmation more difficult.

Changing Patterns of Behavior

Achtenberg's confirmation came only after protracted debate and, atypically, a roll call vote. The Senate's behavior in the Achtenberg nomination, although unusual, was consistent with recent changes in its institutional character. The Senate was transformed from an "encapsulated men's club" to a "publicity machine operated for the purpose of linking senators with national interest groups and factions,"[9] an assessment probably even more accurate today than it was over a decade ago. The contemporary Senate is dramatically different from the Senate of the 1950s, when it was governed by a set of institutional "folkways" and senators focused on legislative activities and respected de facto systems of apprenticeship, reciprocity, courtesy, and organizational patriotism. Emphasizing stability and conformity, the Senate then resembled a "small town."[10]

The Senate changed into "a more open, more fluid, more decentralized, and more democratic chamber."[11] Pressure for change from within came with the election in the late 1950s and early 1960s of a large group of liberal northern Democrats whose policy aims were frustrated by entrenched conservative Democratic committee chairs. Additional pressure came from changes in the broader political environment outside the Senate. As previously unrepresented groups became mobilized, senators confronted issues that transcended the boundaries of their old "small town."[12]

In the "change from a dominantly communitarian Senate in the 1950s to the dominantly individualistic Senate of the 1980s,"[13] the old folkways and rules were recast to enable individual senators, regardless of seniority, to respond to the increased demands of these newly mobilized constituencies.[14] Nowhere has the change in senators' behavior been more dramatic than on the Senate floor. Roll call votes that previously required the support of the party leadership are now granted at the request of individual senators regardless of the degree of overall support.[15] The debate that precedes voting increases opportunities for media attention and credit taking. Not only are almost all senators floor activists, but "media savvy" senators—those who receive unusually large amounts of media attention—are now respected by their peers.[16]

Although liberal groups were the first to become politically active, Christian fundamentalists and social conservatives, organized under the penumbra of the "New Right," found allies on Capitol Hill. The more prominent conservative religious groups—Christian Voice, the Christian Action Network, the Traditional Values Coalition, the Christian Coalition, and the Family Research Council—are less than twenty years old, avowedly oppose gay rights,[17] and collectively have become an important Republican constituency group, providing money and committed activists.[18]

A coterie of conservative senators typify the Senate's "new individualism" and are closely associated with right-wing groups outside Congress.[19] They are also among the most outspoken opponents of homosexuality. As one of the most senior senators, the aggressively conservative Jesse Helms (R-NC) has seen his previously unmatched bombastic style embraced if not emulated by some colleagues, who remember his hard-fought 1990 reelection in which he galvanized national New Right support through repeated attacks on affirmative action and homosexuality. Helms's prominence among the anti-Achtenberg forces and in the arguments propounded against her can be linked to the growing influence of individualism in the Senate and religious conservatism in the Republican Party.

Whereas Helms's and the other conservative senators' objections to Achtenberg's nomination were not surprising, her qualifications and support from her home-state senatorial delegation made their disregard of senatorial norms and the request for debate and roll call unusual.

The Achtenberg Nomination

Roberta Achtenberg had been a law school professor and dean, a civil rights attorney, executive director of the National Center for Lesbian Rights, and

San Francisco supervisor. She was an early supporter of Bill Clinton's 1992 presidential campaign in electoral vote–rich California, where exit polls indicated that he garnered 72 percent of the gay vote.[20]

In one sense, Clinton's nomination of Achtenberg was a typical presidential appointment, rewarding an early and important contributor to his campaign with an administration position. The nomination also symbolically rewarded the gay community for its 1992 electoral and financial—$3.2 million—support of Clinton.[21] The nomination also symbolized the increased legitimacy of gays and lesbians as political actors and represented a political breakthrough for gay rights organizations.[22]

Other groups interpreted the nomination's symbolism very differently.[23] The depth of disagreement with political advances of gays and lesbians can be understood through the language used by opponents to describe them. An anonymous lobbyist said, "There is a spirit of fear and intimidation that comes with homosexuality. Homosexuals are very spiritual—spiritual in the dark sense—[representing] the devil."[24] Among the public, opinion is almost evenly divided between those who accept homosexuality and those who believe it should be discouraged.[25]

On March 30, 1993, the White House sent the Achtenberg nomination to the Senate, where it was referred to the Senate Banking, Housing and Urban Affairs Committee. It attracted very little early media attention. Among selected major newspapers (*New York Times, Los Angeles Times, Washington Post,* and *Wall Street Journal*), only one significant article—a favorable profile—appeared prior to the nomination hearing.[26] Simultaneously, however, Clinton's relations with the gay community were severely scrutinized because of his efforts to lift the ban on gays in the military. Thus, the nomination was played out at a time of unusual political salience for homosexuality.[27]

The Committee Hearings

Committee Chair Senator Donald Riegle (D-MI) scheduled hearings for April 29, 1993. Achtenberg was introduced to the committee by traditional sponsors, namely, home-state senators and representatives. Senators Barbara Boxer and Dianne Feinstein and Representative Nancy Pelosi praised her public service and civil rights career,[28] only obliquely referring to her sexual orientation. For example, Feinstein said the appointment was "important . . . to a community that has often felt excluded from the decisionmaking process." Achtenberg, however, addressed her homosexuality directly in her opening statement: "I'd like to begin by introducing my family to the committee. My beloved partner, Judge Mary Morgan, my rabbi and friend, Yoel Kahn."[29] Thus, what Achtenberg made explicit her senatorial allies felt they could, at most, treat only implicitly. The "new" Senate is not an institution that openly supports lesbian family values.

The strategy among supporters of the nomination was to portray Achtenberg as an advocate of civil rights for all, a public official with big-city experience in housing issues, an aggressive lawyer, and a law school academic who—incidentally but not insignificantly—also happened to be a lesbian. The moderate Republican position was staked out by Senator Christopher Bond (R-MO), whose questioning of Achtenberg seemed designed to distinguish between her past gay rights activism and the practical and legal limitations of HUD's Office of Fair Housing and Equal Opportunity that would subsequently preclude such activism. Her answers provided Bond and other moderates with the requisite political "cover" needed to assure themselves (and their constituents) that existing law would protect against lesbian activism and the promotion of the "homosexual lifestyle."

Sparks came from first-term Senator Lauch Faircloth (R-NC), a Helms protégé. In his opening comments, Faircloth referred to "some people [who] are only for diversity when it fits their special agenda and comes out the way they want it by the results." He later asked a series of questions that related exclusively to gay rights, ranging from the federal government's role in "discouraging" anti-gay state constitutional amendments to Achtenberg's opposition to public funding for the Boy Scouts because they refused to allow gays to serve as scouts or scout leaders. The latter issue involved then-Supervisor Achtenberg's support in 1992 of various San Francisco resolutions that criticized the local Boy Scouts for discriminating against gays in violation of a long-standing local policy of nondiscrimination. Faircloth also read into the record a statement opposing Achtenberg's actions against the Boy Scouts. Under questioning from Riegle, Faircloth acknowledged that the statement had been prepared by the Family Research Council, which maintains that the dissemination of information to Congress is one of its most important activities and devotes about a quarter of its resources to opposing the "homosexual agenda."[30]

The only other hostile questioner was Senator Phil Gramm (R-TX), who submitted his one-query, self-titled "Boy Scout Vendetta" in writing.[31] Faircloth and Gramm raised themes that would reappear in the floor debates, which followed the committee's May 5 recommendation to confirm the nomination.[32]

The Senate Debate

Floor debates for subcabinet appointments are rare. Since 1900, only eight assistant secretary positions—and none at HUD—have gone to a roll call vote for confirmation. Achtenberg's confirmation was a foregone conclusion when the debate began on May 19, but her opponents used procedural rules to extend deliberation over several days.[33] The floor provides individualists and entrepreneurs with optimal exposure.[34] It is also a place from which nominees are excluded; it renders them personally defenseless and makes them easy targets for stereotypical and objectifying portrayals. Thus, it is not surprising that the floor debate rather than the committee hearing was the forum at which Achtenberg's opponents unleashed their attack.

Nineteen senators spoke on her behalf, and sixteen spoke against her. Four pro-Achtenberg senators spoke more than once, led by Boxer, her chief home-state sponsor (seven speeches), and Riegle, chair of the reporting committee (six speeches). Only two opponents spoke more than once: Helms (five speeches) and Trent Lott (two speeches), both conservative white males from the southern Bible Belt. The tone of the speeches was marked by exchanges that were often personal with respect to both Achtenberg and the senators themselves.   ·

Riegle first presented the nomination, describing the duties of the office, and detailing Achtenberg's accomplishments and a litany of endorsements but also foreshadowing the ensuing controversy: "During the course of the debate on this nomination, I suspect that many issues [other than her qualifications] will be raised."[35] Initially, Achtenberg's supporters tried to defend her nomination through traditional means—that is, citing her qualifications and urging deference to the president. Like Riegle, Boxer ended her presentation with an indirect allusion to the nominee's sexual orientation: "As we confirm Roberta Achtenberg . . . we will be taking a real step forward because we will be saying that discrimination is unacceptable, and we will be saying that the promise of equal opportunity is alive and well in the Senate Chamber."[36]

The tone of the opposition was set by the next speaker, Senator Trent Lott (R-MS), who described Achtenberg's record as "one of intolerance, discrimination and vendetta against those who do not share her values or beliefs." Lott quickly "reemphasized" that his criticism was based not on "sexual preference or orientation" but on his belief that Achtenberg was a "militant extremist promoting a special-interest agenda." He concluded by introducing into the record her hearing testimony and excerpts from various newspapers regarding the San Francisco Boy Scouts issue, arguing that Achtenberg's "intolerance" and her advocacy of radical gay and lesbian rights placed her outside mainstream political behavior—anyone who "opposes" the Boy Scouts "does not represent the tradition of tolerance upon which this Nation was founded."[37]

Unlike Lott, who assiduously avoided any overtly homophobic comments, Senator Helms[38] bluntly stated, "Any senator who assumes that this is not a national issue should be advised that it is . . . because we are cross-

ing the threshold into the first time in the history of America that a homosexual, a lesbian, has been nominated by a President of the United States for
a top job in the U.S. Government."[39]

The parameters of the debate, which continued over parts of the next
four days, were set. To determine what arguments were made and the extent
to which they recurred, we analyzed the thematic content of all fifty-four
speeches on the nomination. Because some senators spoke more than once,
we also analyzed the principal theme raised by each senator.

Each speech (defined as a distinct presentation rather than a dialogue or
colloquy with another senator) was read several times and coded according
to its primary message. The speeches fell into discrete topical categories.
Supporters stressed Achtenberg's qualifications ("nominee qualifications");
rebutted attacks against her ("defend against attacks"); emphasized that the
Senate's role was deferential or that it should decide policy and not waste
time on a foregone conclusion ("limited Senate role"); urged that their colleagues be tolerant and inclusive ("urge tolerance"); or, after criticizing her
character or qualifications, voiced lukewarm support ("qualified but . . .").

Opponents' speeches stressed fewer points: They overtly criticized
Achtenberg for her sexual orientation ("anti-homosexuality"); accentuated
her ideological rigidity, militancy, and dogmatism ("nominee intolerance");
or voiced support for the Boy Scouts over Achtenberg ("support Boy
Scouts"). Only one speech, by Hank Brown (R-CO), emphasized her lack of
substantive housing policy experience ("unqualified").[40]

For example, Riegle's introduction focused on Achtenberg's qualifications, as did both Boxer's and Feinstein's initial speeches ("nominee qualifications"). Lott's first oppositional speech emphasized her overall intolerance, employing the Boy Scout controversy as a brief example (coded
"nominee intolerance" rather than "support Boy Scouts"). Table 8.1 depicts
the number of speeches in each of the thematic categories.

Table 8.1   Thematic Content of Speeches

Supporting Speeches		Opposing Speeches	
Defend against attacks	10	Anti-homosexuality	8
Nominee qualifications	8	Nominee intolerance	6
Limited Senate role	7	Support Boy Scouts	6
Urge tolerance	4	Unqualified	1
Qualified but . . .	4	—	—
Total	33	Total	21

Several trends are apparent. Achtenberg's opponents were successful in employing a cohesive strategy with a single theme—the Boy Scouts. The "Boy Scouts" and "intolerance" groupings are related; the former is the alleged manifestation of the latter. The Boy Scouts theme was repeatedly characterized as symptomatic of the nominee's "blatant intolerance and hostility," of "discrimination," and of "abuse of power."[41] The continual linkage of opposition to funding the Boy Scouts with intolerance created powerful rhetorical opportunities, allowing Senator Bob Dole (R-KS), then minority leader, to simply base his opposition on Achtenberg's criticism of the Boy Scouts.[42]

Thirty-five senators made speeches during the debate. Table 8.2 depicts the principal themes raised in these speeches. For senators who spoke more than once, the table shows only the principal theme they discussed. Three such senators—Feinstein, Carol Moseley-Braun, and Lott—gave different thematic speeches; thus, the "mixed themes" category refers to them. For example, Boxer spoke seven times, once about Achtenberg's qualifications and six times defending attacks. All are included in Table 8.1, but only her main theme ("Defend against attacks") is included in Table 8.2, which shows that Boxer was the only senator whose speeches primarily defended the nominee.

Table 8.2   Themes Raised by Senators

Supporting Senators		Opposing Senators	
Limited Senate role	6	Nominee intolerance	5
Nominee qualifications	4	Support Boy Scouts	5
Qualified but . . .	4	Antihomosexuality	4
Urge tolerance	2	Unqualified	1
Mixed themes	2	Mixed themes	1
Defend against attacks	1	—	—
Total	19	Total	16

In contrast to other senators' use of rhetorical symbols, four of Helms's five speeches dealt directly with Achtenberg's sexual orientation ("antihomosexuality"). His criticism was often personal and, by his own description, bigoted. On the first day of the debate, Riegle asked Helms if a newspaper article that quoted him was accurate:

Riegle: Mr. Helms said he would try to block the nomination when the full Senate brings it up . . . "because she's a damn lesbian. I am not going to

put a lesbian in a position like that. If you want to call me bigot, fine."
Helms: That is largely correct. I'm not sure about the "damn" but everything else I know is accurate.[43]

Helms also threatened to request a rare closed session of the Senate to show
a film of the 1992 San Francisco Gay Pride Parade in which Achtenberg and
her "lesbian partner, whatever she calls her" participated, and he repeatedly
mentioned her efforts to keep gay bathhouses open in San Francisco.

Helms's aggressiveness forced many of Achtenberg's supporters to
react defensively (precisely what makes contemporary roll call confirmation
fights damaging affairs regardless of outcome). A plurality (ten of thirty-
three) of the pro-Achtenberg speeches primarily defended her against
charges of intolerance and explained the Boy Scout situation (see Table 8.1).
Supporters were compelled to present what Achtenberg was not rather than
emphasize her accomplishments and qualifications.

A few senators spoke and acted in ways consistent with the old Senate
folkways and norms, voicing restrained displeasure with the president's
nomination but ultimately voting to confirm. This group (four of nineteen
senators who spoke on Achtenberg's behalf [see Table 8.2]) gave speeches
(four of thirty-three [see Table 8.1]) that somewhat tentatively supported
her. Senator William Cohen (R-ME) said his doubts were based not on her
sexual orientation but on her evasion concerning the Boy Scouts. Cohen
voted to confirm, however, because he believed Achtenberg would not "promote" gay rights at HUD and, if she does, "we will hold the President fully
accountable."[44] Other moderate Republicans voiced similar criticisms but
argued that Achtenberg was constrained by law from pushing her "personal
agenda" at HUD.

Few senators supported Achtenberg enthusiastically on the floor, perhaps because the vote was a fait accompli, thereby obviating their need to
traverse a political limb. They emphasized the Senate's limited advice-
and-consent function and its traditional deference to the president's preferences on subcabinet appointments or simply urged the Senate to stop wast-
ing time.

Although the president, Senate Democrats, and Achtenberg "won," the
nomination's opponents did not really "lose" the debate because the issue
and their perspective were presented to the public. Whereas the rhetoric was
dominated by New Right ideas and issues, the effect of the floor debate on
senators' roll call votes cannot be measured.

The Confirmation Vote

After "one of the most bitter and emotionally intense floor debates in recent
memory," Achtenberg was confirmed by a vote of fifty-eight to thirty-one on
May 24.[45] Republicans opposed the nomination thirteen to twenty-six;

Democrats supported it forty-five to five (with all five dissenting votes from senators representing the South or border states).

An unusually large number of senators were absent from the floor during the vote. Usually, 97 percent to 99 percent of senators are present for roll calls, and 99 percent voted on Clinton's other controversial subcabinet nominees.[46] Four Republicans (three conservatives and one moderate) and seven Democrats (five relative conservatives) missed the Achtenberg vote. The unusually high absentee rate, especially among conservative Democrats, illustrates the difficulty in casting a "pro-gay" vote. This finding is consistent with previous studies of votes on gay-related issues, which found that few senators cast visible pro-gay votes unless their constituents were unlikely to discover them.[47]

Conservative groups opposed three of Clinton's other 1993 nominees to subcabinet positions, but none garnered as much opposition as Achtenberg. The groups fought Thomas Payzant's nomination to be assistant secretary of education for elementary and secondary education because, as the San Diego superintendent of schools, he had banned the Boy Scouts from conducting programs on school property during school hours. Payzant was confirmed seventy-two to twenty-seven. Sheldon Hackney, the nominee to chair the National Endowment for the Humanities, was confirmed seventy-six to twenty-three despite accusations that he was an advocate of "political correctness." Although Dr. Joycelyn Elders's nomination to be surgeon general was delayed because of her support for abortion rights and for making birth control available to high school students, she was confirmed sixty-five to thirty-four.

Each of these nominees received more favorable votes than Achtenberg; only Elders encountered a proportion of opposition approaching Achtenberg's. Of the eighty-seven senators who voted on all four nominations, sixty-three voted identically on each. Among senators whose votes on Achtenberg differed from their votes on any of the other nominees, 68 percent voted against Achtenberg and in favor of the other nominee, further indicating the perceived liability of a "pro-gay" vote.

We explored the dynamics of the Achtenberg roll call. Because her homosexuality was prominent in the debates, we expected the determinants of voting on her nomination to differ from those of the other three nominees. We constructed a model of the Achtenberg vote to assess its prediction of the Payzant, Hackney, and Elders votes. Since the model's dependent variable is dichotomous (i.e., aye or nay votes) rather than continuous, we used logit instead of regression analysis.[48]

Statistical analyses of congressional roll call votes disagree about which variables have the greatest utility. Currently, the major debate is between political scientists who employ unidimensional models and economists who favor multidimensional models. The former believe roll call votes are best explained by a single left-right (liberal-conservative) ideological measure;[49]

the latter argue that various constituency (i.e., economic) characteristics are the most salient.[50]

We first used both ideological and constituency-related variables and a series of gay-related variables unique to roll call analysis. This approach is justified on two grounds. First, because the voting on Achtenberg differed from the voting on the other controversial nominees, votes on gay-related issues may be distinctive. Second, the only previous study of votes on gay-related issues found they were best explained by a combination of ideological, constituency, and gay variables.[51]

The ideological measures were, first, American Conservative Union (ACU) scores and, second, partisanship. Since the ideological orientations and voting patterns of southern and northern Democrats differ significantly,[52] we created a political party variable in which northern Democratic senators scored 0, southern Democrats 1, and Republicans 2.[53]

Traditional constituency variables performed poorly, confirming our belief that votes on social and moral issues cannot be explained by economic criteria. We therefore developed constituency variables that measured social liberalism or conservatism. Because many people's views about social issues, including homosexuality, are rooted in religious faith,[54] we used each state's percentage of people who belonged to major conservative Protestant churches to measure the religious right's strength.[55]

For more than two decades, scholars have utilized Ira Sharkansky's adaptation of Daniel Elazar's typology of political culture to categorize states as moralistic, individualistic, or traditionalistic. In states with moralistic political cultures (e.g., New England, the northern Plains, and the Pacific Northwest), government is viewed as a positive force for the enhancement of citizens' well-being. In individualistic states (e.g., the Mid-Atlantic and Great Plains), politics is seen as a marketplace in which groups and individuals pursue their self-interest. In states with traditionalistic cultures (e.g., the South and border states), the primary role of government is to uphold the social order and established values.

Sharkansky uses a 1–9 additive scale, in which 1 indicates a pure moralistic political culture and 9 a pure traditionalistic political culture; midrange scores denote an individualistic political culture.[56] Critics have argued that the scale fails to measure three distinct political cultures.[57] David Morgan and Sheilah Watson instead use a range of political, institutional, and policy variables to derive moralistic, individualistic, and traditionalistic scores for each state.[58] Although we utilized Sharkansky's overall assessment of political culture and Morgan and Watson's measures of all three typologies, we expected traditionalistic culture to be the most powerful because homosexuality is viewed by many as a threat to traditional values.

We also developed two variables that more directly measure attitudes toward gays; one indicated whether each state had enacted legislation to punish hate crimes, and the other revealed the level of each state's antidiscrimination legislation to protect gays. Because there are no generally accepted means to measure the number of gays within states, we used a proxy developed by the National Organization of Gay and Lesbian Scientific and Technical Professionals—the number of nonfamily members sharing a household was highly correlated with the number of homosexuals.

These gay-related variables poorly predicted the Achtenberg vote, and the relationship between a state's percentage of conservative Protestants and voting on Achtenberg was weak. Despite our intuition and evidence from the floor debate, no gay-related variables were independently predictive, possibly because Clinton's support for Achtenberg and the traditional deference to the president diminished their effect. Some normally anti-gay senators either were absent or voted for the nomination.

We compared voting on the Achtenberg nomination to Boxer's amendment to the fiscal 1994 Defense authorization to overturn the "don't ask, don't tell" compromise on gays in the military, leaving to presidential discretion whether open gays could serve (a pro-gay proposal without presidential support). Twenty-five pro-Achtenberg senators voted against the Boxer amendment; no senators switched from an anti-gay (i.e., opposed Achtenberg) to a pro-gay position (supported the Boxer amendment). This finding suggests that presidential influence and patterns of deference decreased opposition to Achtenberg and limited the explanatory power of the gay-related variables.

Voting on Achtenberg was best explained by a model that combined ideological and constituency variables that, in varying degrees, measure social conservatism. The model is expressed as:

$$\text{Log } \frac{1}{1-P} (\text{VOTE}) = a + b_1\text{ACU} + b_2\text{PARTY} + b_3\text{TRAD} + e$$

where VOTE is the roll call vote on Achtenberg's nomination, ACU the senator's American Conservative Union score, PARTY the conservatism of the senator's party affiliation, and TRAD the degree of traditionalistic culture within the state (see Table 8.3).

Although all of the variables in this model are significant, ideology (ACU score) most powerfully predicts a senator's vote. As expected, the relationship between the ACU score and support for Achtenberg is inverse, and senators from more traditionalistic states were less likely to vote for Achtenberg. Surprisingly, when ideology and traditionalistic culture are controlled for, Republicans were more likely than Democrats to support her.

Logit has no direct equivalent to the R-square statistic, so other goodness-of-fit measures, including a pseudo R-square, evaluate the model's overall performance.[59] The 0.64 pseudo R-square for this model is fairly high, and the chi square has less than a 0.00005 probability of random occurrence. Prediction of individual votes on the nomination, a stronger

Table 8.3   Determinants of Achtenberg Vote

Variable	Estimated coefficient	Standard error	*t*-score	Probability
Constant (a)	4.85	1.11	4.34	0.000
ACU score	−0.12	0.03	−3.51	0.000
Political party	1.98	1.11	1.79	0.078
Traditionalism	−4.37	2.49	−1.76	0.083

Notes: Number of observations: eighty (senators serving in the 102nd Congress who voted on the Achtenberg nomination in the 103rd Congress)
Chi-square: 66.61
Chi-square probability: 0.00005
Pseudo R-square: 0.64
Correct predictions: 90%

performance indicator, is based on the probability of each senator's vote being greater or less than 0.5. The model correctly predicts 90 percent of all actual votes.

The model does nearly as well in predicting the voting on the other three controversial Clinton nominations; it explains 89 percent of the votes on Payzant's nomination and 85 percent on both the Hackney and Elders nominations. Again, the strongest predictor is each senator's ideological orientation as measured by ACU score.

Conclusion

The confirmation of Roberta Achtenberg provides insight into the politicization of the confirmation process and into comparisons of the Senate's treatment of homosexuals and other controversial nominees. The appointment was not only a political payback to an early supporter in a pivotal electoral state; it also more broadly rewarded an important bloc within Clinton's electoral coalition and showed that homosexuals, although still highly stigmatized, had come out of the political closet.

In one sense, the controversy over Achtenberg was unusual. She was one of only four subcabinet nominees targeted by the New Right in 1993. The challenge to her nomination was consistent with the assertiveness and independence of the modern Senate. Individual senators, even some who voted in favor of the nominee, saw an opportunity to embarrass a president from the opposing party. Well-organized socially conservative groups worked closely with their Senate allies in spearheading the opposition to the other three nominations, but their opposition to Achtenberg was different. Achtenberg was the first open lesbian to be appointed to high federal office, and, notwithstanding other issues raised in the Senate about her fitness for office, the threshold "issue" was whether an openly gay person could hold a high public office in this country. In the committee hearings and on the Senate floor, her supporters deemphasized her homosexuality through indirect and infrequent references followed by extended discussions of her qualifications or traditional deference to the president on appointments. Her opponents were much more straightforward and, in some cases, openly homophobic, linking her homosexuality to radicalism, intolerance, and—through the Boy Scouts—anti-Americanism.

To what extent did Achtenberg's homosexuality distinguish her confirmation from that of the other nominees? Was the Senate's political perception and treatment of her fundamentally different from that of a mere "social liberal"? Or was the debate about "damn lesbians" merely a lot of sound and fury on Capitol Hill? Many more senators, especially conservative Democrats, were absent from the floor when the Achtenberg vote was taken, and she received fewer favorable votes than any of the other nominees. But the variables that measured constituents' attitudes toward gays were not significantly related to votes on Achtenberg. Instead, the measures designed to reflect the general (not uniquely antihomosexual) social conservatism of senators and their constituents strongly predicted the votes on Achtenberg and the other nominees. Whereas anti-gay feelings are closely linked to other socially conservative views, the effect on the *intensity* of opposition to gay issues remains to be explored.

It remains axiomatic that most highly controversial appointments will not get beyond the committee stage and that nearly all nominations will survive a roll call vote. Yet, as the Achtenberg nomination illustrates, nomination floor votes are often valuable for opponents. Floor debate provides a stage for the orchestration of political drama and a means for showcasing both traditional and extremist views. We can only assume that the threat of controversy, whether real or manufactured, plays a role in the selection process and may ultimately affect the willingness of unconventional individuals to accept presidential appointments. In either case, the power exercised by minority factions within the Senate cannot be ignored.

Notes

1. G. Calvin Mackenzie, ed. 1987. *The In-and-Outers: Presidential Appointees and Transient Government in Washington.* Baltimore: Johns Hopkins University Press, p. xiii.

2. The greatest number of nominations actually rejected by any single Senate was 27 (out of 15,330 nominations received) in the 75th Congress (1937–1938). Since then, the number of nominations has grown exponentially, whereas the number of formal rejections has dropped—often to zero. Of course, the Senate can use and has used other, less direct ways of communicating its displeasure with nominees to the president. See Harold W. Stanley and Richard G. Niemi. 1994. *Vital Statistics on American Politics,* 4th ed. Washington, D.C.: Congressional Quarterly Press, p. 279.

3. Christopher J. Deering. 1987. "Damned if You Do and Damned if You Don't: The Senate's Role in the Appointment Process." In *The In-and-Outers: Presidential Appointees and Transient Government in Washington,* ed. Mackenzie.

4. From the 57th through the 91st Congresses, roll calls averaged 4.38 per Congress. Roll calls averaged 12.16 for the 92nd through the 103rd Congresses, with the largest number (37) in the 97th; Sharon Spray. Forthcoming. "The Politics of Confirmations: A Study of Senate Roll Call Confirmation Voting." Ph.D. dissertation. Claremont Graduate School.

5. In the 1940s and 1950s, the Senate leaders determined which nominations would be subject to a roll call. Although the rules required that only a fifth of those present support a motion for a roll call, it was difficult to muster that support without the backing of the leadership. Most senators would not even second a request for a roll call unless the majority leader indicated support for it. But as Sinclair noted, "In the 1960s, under the extremely permissive leadership of Mike Mansfield, it became a courtesy and then a right of any senator to get a roll call at will." See Barbara Sinclair. 1989. *The Transformation of the U.S. Senate.* Baltimore: Johns Hopkins University Press, p. 133.

6. Ibid., p. 113.

7. Sources within the administration and a representative from one of the major gay and lesbian rights groups both placed the number of "open" gay men and lesbians appointed by the Clinton administration at thirty-five. They also pointed out that Achtenberg was the highest ranking of the appointees (anonymous spokesperson at the Gay and Lesbian Victory Fund, December 13, 1995). It is difficult to determine the exact number of open homosexuals in the administration, however, because "openness" may be limited to particular contexts (i.e., a person may be open to family and friends but not on the job, or vice versa). The number of homosexual men and women who are open to some degree may in fact be higher than the thirty-five typically mentioned for gay and lesbian appointees of the Clinton administration.

8. Linda L. Fisher. 1987. "Fifty Years of Presidential Appointments." In *The In-and-Outers: Presidential Appointees and Transient Government in Washington,* ed. Mackenzie.

9. Nelson W. Polsby. 1981. "Transformation of the American Political System, 1950–1980." Paper delivered at the Annual Meeting of the American Political Science Association in New York, p. 22.

10. Donald R. Matthews. 1960. *U.S. Senators and Their World.* New York: Vintage Books.

11. Norman J. Ornstein, Robert L. Peabody, and David W. Rohde. 1993. "The U.S. Senate in an Era of Change." In *Congress Reconsidered,* 5th ed., ed. Lawrence C. Dodd and Bruce I. Oppenheimer. Washington, D.C.: Congressional Quarterly Press, p. 38.

12. Sinclair, *The Transformation of the U.S. Senate.*

13. Richard F. Fenno. 1989. "The Senate Through a Looking Glass: The Debate over Television." *Legislative Studies Quarterly* 14: 314.

14. Steven S. Smith and Christopher J. Deering. 1990. *Committees in Congress,* 2d ed. Washington, D.C.: Congressional Quarterly Press.

15. Sinclair, *The Transformation of the U.S. Senate,* p. 133.

16. John R. Hibbing and Sue Thomas. 1990. "The Modern United States Senate: What Is Accorded Respect." *Journal of Politics* 52: 126–145.

17. Paul J. Weber and W. Landis Jones. 1994. *U.S. Religious Interest Groups: Institutional Profiles.* Westport, Conn.: Greenwood Press.

18. Kenneth Jost. 1994. "Religion and Politics." *Congressional Quarterly Researcher* 4: 891–911.

19. Christopher J. Bailey. 1986. "The United States Senate: The New

Individualism and the New Right." *Parliamentary Affairs: A Journal of Comparative Politics.* 39(3): 362.

20. Beth Donovan. 1993. "Gay Activists' Cash, Votes Ride on Ban Decision." *Congressional Quarterly Weekly Report,* July 10: 1814–1816.

21. Tim McFeeley. January 1993. "Holding President Bill Clinton to His Gay, Lesbian, and AIDS Campaign Promises." Washington, D.C.: Human Rights Campaign Fund.

22. Each of the four major national gay rights organizations has a somewhat different focus. The 20,000-member National Gay and Lesbian Task Force, the oldest national civil rights group working on behalf of gay rights, seeks to influence the legislative and executive branches of government and to organize activists (Peri Rude Radecic, deputy director of public policy, interview, May 21, 1992). The Human Rights Campaign Fund (HRCF), with 80,000 members, is primarily a federal lobbying organization. Since its founding in 1980, the HRCF has endorsed and given political action committee contributions to roughly 200 gay and nongay congressional candidates in each electoral cycle (Eric Rosenthal, political director, interview, May 22, 1992). The Gay and Lesbian Victory Fund, founded in 1991, supports only openly gay and lesbian candidates for office. (See Christine Kehoe. 1994. "Gay and Lesbian Victory Fund." In *Out for Office,* ed. Kathleen Debold. Washington, D.C.: Gay and Lesbian Victory Fund, pp. 54–55.) The Lambda Legal Defense Fund, founded in 1973, supports impact litigation to combat antihomosexual discrimination. (See Lambda Legal Defense and Education Fund. 1992. "Lambda's Critical National Work on Behalf of Lesbians Benefits You." Los Angeles: Lambda Legal Defense and Education Fund.)

23. Several organizations lead the political opposition to gay rights. The Free Congress Research and Education Foundation (FCREF), founded in 1982, was created to promote research and training in "cultural conservatism." The FCREF provides its congressional allies with research, lobbies undecided members, testifies before committees, and endorses candidates who are running for office (Michael Schwartz, director of child and family policy division, interview, May 19, 1992). The Family Research Council devotes much more of its research and lobbying efforts than does the FCREF to opposing gay civil rights laws, which it considers to be "pernicious" and "a great threat, not only because they sanctify homosexuality, but they open the legal door to all those behaviors" (Robert Knight, director of Cultural Studies Project, interview, May 19, 1992). Since its founding in the early 1970s, the Traditional Values Coalition (TVC), which operates through a network of 25,000 churches, has considered homosexuality to be a threat to Christianity. One of the TVC's major adjuncts is SHAPE (Stop Homosexual Advocacy in Public Education), which publishes an antihomosexual newsletter and other educational materials. See *SHAPE* 6(2) (June 1989). Anaheim: California Coalition for Traditional Values. The Concerned Women for America also views itself as a grassroots education and lobbying organization that supports traditional family and Judeo-Christian values. (Peter LeBarbara and Trudy Hutchens. July 1992. "The Homosexualization of U.S. Culture." *Family Voice* 14(7): 4–15.) The group's 535 Program, a volunteer lobbying effort, brings women from every congressional district to Washington, D.C., to lobby Congress. (See Concerned Women for America. 1992. "535 Program: Holding Congress Accountable." Washington, D.C.: Concerned Women for America.)

24. Anonymous. 1992. Interview, May 20.

25. Times Mirror Center for the People and the Press. 1994. *The People, the Press and Politics: The New Political Landscape.* Los Angeles: Times Mirror Center for the People and the Press, p. 150.

26. Richard C. Paddock. "Likely Nominee: A Strong Voice for Gays." *Los Angeles Times,* January 29, 1993, sec. A.

27. During the campaign, Clinton often spoke of his intention to end the ban on gays serving in the military, but few outside the gay community noticed. Shortly after the election, two events focused attention on the proposal. Clinton's discussion of the issue in his first postelection press conference raised its salience. Media attention was also triggered by an exogenous event—a U.S. district court decision a few days after the election ordering the Navy to reinstate Keith Meinhold, who had been discharged when he admitted his homosexuality. Public conflicts over the issue among the Clinton administration, senior military officers, and Senate Armed Forces Chair Sam Nunn (D-GA) dragged on throughout spring and summer 1993.

28. Achtenberg's civil rights record notwithstanding, the San Francisco black firefighters group was one of the few African American organizations to endorse her nomination.

29. The hearing transcript can be found at U.S. Congress, Senate, Committee on Banking, Housing and Urban Development. 1993. *Nomination of Roberta Achtenberg to Be Assistant Secretary of Housing and Urban Development and Fair Housing and Equal Opportunity.* 103rd Congress, 1st session, April 29.

30. Robert Knight. 1992. Interview, May 19.

31. U.S. Congress, Senate, Committee on Banking, Housing and Urban Development, *Nomination of Roberta Achtenberg to Be Assistant Secretary of Housing and Urban Development and Fair Housing and Equal Opportunity,* p. 79.

32. *Congressional Record.* 1993. 103rd Congress, 1st session, vol. 139, part 61, S5517.

33. The Senate's tradition of unlimited debate allows a handful of senators to use floor speeches to extend the confirmation process. There are very few formal restrictions on debate. See Walter J. Oleszek. 1996. *Congressional Procedures and the Policy Process,* 4th ed. Washington, D.C.: Congressional Quarterly Press, p. 232.

34. Deering, "Damned if You Do and Damned if You Don't: The Senate's Role in the Appointment Process."

35. *Congressional Record,* part 71, S6091.

36. Ibid., S6092.

37. See generally ibid., S6093–6096.

38. An official with the Family Research Council described Helms as the "point man . . . who advanced the arguments against the enemy" on gay rights issues (Robert Knight interview, May 19, 1992).

39. *Congressional Record,* part 71, S6099.

40. Ibid., part 72, S6217.

41. Ibid., part 74, S6217 and S6348–9.

42. Ibid., part 74, S6348–6349.

43. Ibid., part 71, S6101.

44. Ibid., part 72, S6210–6212.

45. Michael Ross. "Gay Activist Okayed for Fair Housing Post." *Los Angeles Times,* May 25, 1993, sec. A.

46. The number of absentee senators on the Achtenberg vote was higher than that on *any* of Clinton's other nominations, for which the average turnout was 98.3 percent of Republicans and 97.5 percent of Democrats. Only 90.6 percent of Republicans and 87.7 percent of Democrats cast votes on Achtenberg.

47. Jean Reith Schroedel, Jennifer Liu, and Paul Peretz. Forthcoming. "Gay Politics in the Legislative Arena: The Politics of Concealment." In *Lesbian and Gay Political Behavior in the United States,* ed. Sarah Slavin. New York: Routledge Press.

48. Robert S. Pindyck and Daniel L. Rubinfeld. 1981. *Econometric Models and Economic Forecasts,* 2d ed. New York: McGraw Hill, pp. 275–300.

49. See Keith T. Poole and Howard Rosenthal. 1985. "A Spatial Model for

Legislative Roll Call Analysis." *American Journal of Political Science* 29: 357–384; and Keith T. Poole and Howard Rosenthal. 1991. "Patterns of Congressional Voting." *American Journal of Political Science* 35: 228–278.

50. See, for example, Joseph P. Kalt and Mark A. Zupan. 1984. "Capture and Ideology in the Economic Theory of Politics." *American Economic Review* 74: 279–300; and James M. Snyder. 1992. "Committee Power, Structure-Induced Equilibria, and Roll Call Votes." *American Journal of Political Science* 36: 1–30.

51. Schroedel, Liu, and Peretz, "Gay Politics in the Legislative Arena."

52. Christopher J. Deering. 1989. *Congressional Politics.* Pacific Grove, Calif.: Brooks/Cole, pp. 126–128.

53. Our political party variable uses *Congressional Quarterly's* distinction between northern Democrats and southern Democrats. Southern Democrats are from the Old South and the border states (i.e., Alabama, Arkansas, Florida, Georgia, Kentucky, Louisiana, Mississippi, North Carolina, Oklahoma, South Carolina, Tennessee, Texas, and Virginia); all others are northern Democrats.

54. Paul Chalfant, Robert E. Beckley, and C. Eddie Palmer. 1981. *Religion in Contemporary Society.* Sherman Oaks, Calif.: Alfred Publishing Company.

55. Members of the following churches and groupings were included: white Southern Baptist, Church of Christ, Evangelical/Fundamentalist, Nazarene, Pentecostal/Holiness, Assemblies of God, and Adventists. See Wade Clark Roof and William McKinney. 1987. *American Mainline Religion: Its Changing Shape and Future.* New Brunswick, N.J.: Rutgers University Press, pp. 195, 214.

56. For a complete state-by-state listing, see Ira Sharkansky. 1969. "The Utility of Elazar's Political Culture: A Research Note." *Polity* 2: 66–83; and Daniel J. Elazar. 1966. *American Federalism: A View from the States.* New York: Thomas Y. Crowell Company.

57. See Charles A. Johnson. 1976. "Political Cultures in American States: Elazar's Formulation Examined." *American Journal of Political Science* 20: 491–509.

58. David R. Morgan and Sheilah S. Watson. 1991. "Political Culture, Political System Characteristics, and Public Policies Among the States." *Publius* 21(2): 31–48.

59. William H. Greene. 1983. *Econometric Analysis,* 2d ed. New York: Macmillan, pp. 651–653.

9

A President's Legacy: Gender and Appointment to the Federal Courts

Richard L. Pacelle, Jr.

The legal and judicial systems are male institutions, basically derived by men, for male behavioral standards. It was never anticipated initially that women would play a role in those systems and, in fact, it was not until the mid-1970s that the last state finally agreed that women could serve as jurors let alone be lawyers or judges.

Federal District Judge Fern Smith[1]

When nominees are confirmed as federal judges, they receive an engraved commission from the president. Until the 1970s, the plates used to print the commissions referred to the nominees as "he" and "him." On the rare occasions when a woman was appointed to a federal court, the personal pronouns had to be erased, and "she" and "her" had to be hand lettered.[2] Although this can be understood as a reflection of attitudes toward the appointment of women, it was also a clear indication of empirical reality.

This chapter analyzes the appointment of female judges to the federal courts. I examine the formal and informal barriers that kept women off the bench for many years and institutional devices used to raze those barriers. Ultimately, I examine the role of presidents in increasing or limiting the diversification of the federal bench.

The Importance of the Federal Courts

Long after presidents leave office, their judicial appointments influence the course of public policy. When Justice William Douglas resigned from the U.S. Supreme Court in 1975, that move officially ended Franklin Roosevelt's direct influence over the Court. Given normal actuarial expectations, the president who will nominate Clarence Thomas's successor is probably now a high school student. Because of the small size of the Court and the lifetime tenure of justices, the stakes of the selection process are very high.

The selection of Supreme Court justices is the most visible manifestation of a president's judicial policy, but it is far from the only one. Increasingly, analysts recognize the importance of district courts and courts of appeals. The increase in caseloads, changes in the nature of business before the federal courts, and the expansion of the role of the courts in implementing policy make judicial appointments a critical tool for presidents.[3] Federal courts now decide most of the controversial issues of the day, and some issues do not attract the attention of the Supreme Court. In those areas, lower federal courts make policy in a vacuum. For example, issues concerning the rights of lesbians and gays and the right to die have largely been ignored by the Supreme Court, leaving lower courts with the last effective word.

The Importance of Diversity: Representation and Beyond

Diversity is important on philosophical and practical grounds. Descriptive representation has long played a role in Supreme Court appointments.[4] Factors such as religion and geography have been considered in making nominations. Justices have been selected to fill the Catholic or Jewish seat. Region has been involved, as in Richard Nixon's "Southern strategy."[5] When Thurgood Marshall resigned, George Bush's short list was made up almost exclusively of African Americans and Hispanic Americans. Since Sandra Day O'Connor's confirmation, analysts have believed there will always be a woman's seat.[6]

Descriptive representation also has implications for decisionmaking. Analysts consider the background of judges to be a critical determinant of judicial behavior.[7] The party of the judge or appointing president, religion, prior experience, region, socioeconomic status, and race are among the factors associated with variations in decisionmaking. Some dismiss the direct influence of background in favor of the values and attitudes of judges.[8] Even if values and attitudes are the most important determinants, however, they stem from one's background.

Gender has found its way into a few studies now that enough women have judicial appointments to make analysis meaningful.[9] Studies demonstrate that women follow different career paths to the judiciary than men; thus, gender differences reinforce other differences analysts consider important.[10]

Research suggests that gender differences are magnified in a number of issues. Studies of Congress and state legislatures suggest that increasing diversity has helped to place women's issues on the agenda and has introduced liberalism into policy debates and substantive outputs.[11] With the number of women in legislatures and Congress increasing, it is expected that the existing gender gap will continue to grow. Newer female legislators are not only less deferential to traditions, but many were raised in the first cohort to embrace feminism.

Another central concern with the composition of the bench is the policy implications. Cultural feminists argue that the presence of women in the legal system will have a profound impact because female lawyers and judges bring different perspectives to the law, employ different methods, and reach different conclusions.[12] In a study of courts of appeals judges, Sue Davis, Susan Haire, and Donald Songer found significant gender differences in employment discrimination cases.[13] Female judges supported employment discrimination claims 63.5 percent of the time, compared with 46.1 percent support among male judges. Studies of district judges found similar results: Women were more liberal in race and sex discrimination cases. In other issue areas, differences were less pronounced or nonexistent.[14]

More specifically, diversity is important because the federal judiciary has been arguably the most important actor in women's rights. The constitutional and statutory bases of women's rights are limited, which leaves the protection of such rights to the federal courts. The issues that most directly affect women—reproductive rights and gender equality—are judicially created rights. Representation increases the credibility of the judiciary, particularly for victims of discrimination.[15]

Gender doctrine was the result of a legal analogy with race litigation under the Fourteenth Amendment. The problem for women was that the issues that were analogies for gender equality and reproductive rights were constructed by males.[16] A diversified judiciary might permit female judges to reconstruct existing doctrine to reflect the unique situations women face. Unlike other areas of law, litigation in gender equality and reproductive rights has been directed by women.[17] It is reasonable to inquire whether individuals are present in the courts who have had the same life experiences as the women who argued the cases or as the women they represented.

There are apparent limits to the changes that diversity in the legal system can bring. Beverly Cook has argued that "acceptance of a woman judge depends upon her adherence to the inherited norms. . . . Women judges probably can not make major changes in policy outputs."[18] Judges have been socialized to the norms and rules of the legal system and are expected to follow precedent. In lower federal courts, there are informal norms that lead to consensus in decisionmaking. In addition, selection processes reflect the priorities of the appointing executive. If presidents have a defined agenda, they will select candidates who reflect their views. On the broadest level, the construction of law and of precedents has been male-dominated. Thus, women seeking to make a difference must overcome significant hurdles.

Still, increasing the representation of women on the bench could have profound effects. First, women who have climbed through the male-dominated legal profession might be more sympathetic to gender-related issues. Feminists argue that women who have "shared the cultural place of the sex are more likely to be sensitive to the problems and give higher priority to the issues than men who have followed the prototypical male social script."[19] Second, the presence of women on these panels would expose men to different perspectives.[20] Federal appellate courts typically decide cases in panels that range in size from three (on courts of appeals) to nine (on the Supreme Court) members. Thus, one or a few women can have an impact on a divided court. Selecting women to the federal courts will have long-term effects as well. Visible nominations serve as role models for other women in the profession and for young women as they consider a career in law.

The Judicial Appointment Process: Theory Versus Practice

There are three levels to the federal judiciary: district courts, courts of appeals, and the Supreme Court. Article II, section 2 of the U.S. Constitution holds that the president appoints judges by and with the advice and consent of the Senate. In practice, the selection process and the relative influence of the major actors vary by level. The influence of the executive rises with the level of the judiciary. Typically, tensions exist between the White House, which has political designs for the appointments, and the Justice Department, which is interested more in appointees' legal qualifications and objective excellence.

Although the process varies by the level of court, each level has traditionally been closed to women. Donald Jackson has argued that the participants are constant—senators, the president, the Justice Department, candidates campaigning for vacancies, and the American Bar Association (ABA)—but their relative strength varies in individual cases. Thus, "each selection is a fresh spin of the wheel."[21] Unfortunately for women, the wheel has not been calibrated fairly, and the process by which candidates are appointed and confirmed has not been neutral. To diversify the composition of the federal bench, institutional arrangements had to be altered.[22]

The District Court Level

Joe Dolan, a former assistant attorney general, has argued, "The Constitution is backwards. Article II, section 2 should read: 'The senators shall nominate, and by and with the consent of the President, shall appoint.'"[23] Almost from the outset, lower court judges became objects of patronage for senators. Presidents were willing to trade district judgeships for legislation they wanted passed and for good relations with the Senate. Under the process known as senatorial courtesy, when a vacancy occurred on a district court the senator from that state (if he or she was from the same party as the president) would get to "name" the new district judge. If a president had the temerity to appoint someone else, the senator might submit a "blue slip" stating that the president's candidate was "personally obnoxious" to that senator. Given the reciprocity that exists in the institution, the rest of the Senate would oppose the nomination. The blue slip is seldom invoked, but senators are able to use the threat as a bargaining tool.[24]

Senatorial courtesy emerged because presidents believed district judgeships were relatively insignificant positions that could be bartered for other purposes. When presidents finally realized the district court was an important venue for policymaking, it was too late to reclaim the appointment power from senators who thought nominations were their privilege. Jimmy Carter made a formal attempt to shift the locus of power away from individual senators by advocating the creation of voluntary district panels. Carter urged senators to construct commissions in their states and to delegate their authority to choose judges to the panels.[25]

The Circuit Court of Appeals

Whereas district courts are contained within a state, which makes them easy targets for individual senators, each court of appeals (except for the D.C. Circuit) contains at least three states, which reduces the claims of individual senators. Senators still suggest names, and there is a tradition of rotating the nominations among the states that make up the circuit or replacing the judge who leaves with a nominee from the same state, but the constraints on the president are reduced.[26]

Presidents do not normally personally select nominees for the courts of appeals. The president's advisers and the Justice Department compile a list of potential nominees. The Senate Judiciary Committee plays a greater role than is the case at the district level but still generally accepts nominees.[27]

The Supreme Court

At the Supreme Court level, power shifts decidedly toward the president. The Senate's role is more reactive. When a vacancy occurs, the president contacts advisers and the Justice Department to consider potential nominees. Presidents have long understood the importance of a Supreme Court nominee, but they have not been consistent in their use of the appointment power.

Because the American Bar Association considers the judicial temperament of nominees, presidents normally seek candidates who have judicial experience, incorruptible character, and intellectual capacity. Presidents may be motivated by more "political" concerns, such as appointing someone who fits demographic qualifications. The president may seek a candidate who is a certain religion, race, or gender or who will balance regional representation on the Court. The president may pay a debt by appointing a supporter or the favorite candidate of a supporter. Recently, presidents seem to have taken greater pains to find nominees who are ideologically consistent with their own views.[28]

The Senate Judiciary Committee plays an active role in evaluating the nominee. The Senate is expected to investigate the fitness and qualifications of the nominee. Partisan evaluation is expected, but questions remain about the legitimacy of asking prospective justices about their views or using a litmus test to determine whether to approve the nominee.[29]

Barriers to Full Participation

Until recently, the eligible pool of women judicial candidates was shallow, and formal and informal processes were exclusionary. For generations, women did not or could not attend law school. In 1977 women constituted less than 6 percent of the membership of the bar. Within five years, however, the percentage had doubled. By the year 2000, the percentage of women lawyers is expected to exceed one-third of the profession.[30] Women have also been excluded from the major law firms, judicial clerkships, and governmental, political, and state court positions—all of which provide a springboard into the federal judiciary for men.

The Senate has traditionally been an exclusive men's club. At the district level, senators make the ultimate decision on appointments. At the court of appeals level, senators are consulted on nominees. Thus, an "old boy" network has dominated selection processes and disenfranchised women. The Justice Department and the president's key advisers have also overwhelmingly been male. Thus, there have been few, if any, female voices to suggest specific women for the federal bench or to even mention the positive implications of diversity.[31]

Until recently, the ABA committees that review the qualifications of nominees had no female representation. The ABA standards did not recognize the pathways women followed to the bench. The ABA rigorously adhered to its requirement of twelve to fifteen years' experience for judges, which excluded most women.[32] The ABA has long been charged with favoring older, affluent corporate attorneys. Because there were few female attorneys, there were even fewer female judges.

Women judges and lawyers have attributed male domination of the judiciary to the exclusion of women from the networks that influence appointments. New institutional arrangements had to be created to recruit qualified minorities and women to ensure their inclusion. The use of merit commissions to recommend names for judicial vacancies expanded the number of participants in the judicial selection process.[33] It took a president committed to opening the process to nontraditional nominees to modify the rules and thereby reduce existing barriers.

Presidential Selections to the Federal Courts

The number of women appointed to federal courts prior to the Carter presidency speaks volumes about the obstacles women faced. In 1934 Florence Allen became the first woman confirmed to a federal court. Attorney General Homer Cummings remarked that "Florence Allen was not appointed because she was a woman. All we did was to see that she was not rejected because she was a woman."[34] No other woman was appointed to a court of appeals for thirty-four years. A woman was not appointed to a district court until 1949.[35] Richard Nixon and Gerald Ford selected no female judges to circuit courts and chose just one each to a district court. Table 9.1 shows the numbers and percentages of women appointed to the federal courts since 1969.

Table 9.1   Women Appointed to the Federal Courts as a Percentage of Total Appointments, 1969–May 1996

Administration	Women Appointed to District Courts		Women Appointed to Courts of Appeals	
	Number	Percentage	Number	Percentage
Nixon	1	0.6	0	—
Ford	1	1.9	0	—
Carter	29	14.4	11	19.6
Reagan	24	8.3	4	5.1
Bush	29	19.6	7	18.9
Clinton	45	24.3	6	18.8

Sources: Sheldon Goldman, 1993, "Bush's Judicial Legacy: The Final Imprint," *Judicature* 76: 287, 293; and Matthew P. Sarago, assistant manager of information services, and Peter A. Wonders, assistant historian, Federal Judicial Center, Washington, D.C., provided appointment statistics.

Judge Allen also had the distinction of being the first woman considered for the Supreme Court. She was recommended to presidents Hoover, Roosevelt, and Truman as the only woman qualified to join the Court, but it is difficult to tell how seriously they treated her candidacy. There was little motivation to name a woman: Male justices opposed her nomination, there was little demand from the legal community, and the general public was opposed to selecting a woman for the Supreme Court.[36]

Nixon paid lip service to the idea of selecting women and even put state Judge Mildred Lillie and Sylvia Bacon, a local judge with seven months' experience, on his short list of candidates for the Court. The ABA evaluated Lillie and pronounced her "unqualified." Nixon complained that few women were judicially qualified and ideologically and philosophically compatible with his strict constructionist views.[37]

When William Douglas resigned, Ford instructed advisers to include women in the search for Douglas's replacement. The first list contained no women. Several days later, a second list was issued with the names of two women—Judge Cornelia Kennedy (nominated to the district court by Nixon and later elevated to the circuit court by Carter) and Judge Shirley Hufstedler (a Johnson nominee and the first woman appointed to a circuit court since Allen). Judge Kennedy even received a qualified rating from the ABA. The name of Carla Hills, secretary of housing and urban development, also surfaced as a possible nominee. Despite the counsel of First Lady Betty Ford, who publicly urged her husband to select a woman and who favored Hills, Ford selected John Paul Stevens.[38]

The consideration of these women was a signal that public and elite opinion was changing. Although Chief Justice Warren Burger felt there were no women with impressive qualifications during the Stevens nomination, a number of justices advocated the selection of a woman. For the first time in history, some justices selected female law clerks.[39] Following a visit by the National Association of Women Judges, Burger recanted his negative statement. A year before Sandra Day O'Connor was nominated, the Court dispensed with the designation "Mr. Justice" and replaced it with "Justice."[40]

The Carter Revolution

Jimmy Carter had both the interest and the opportunity to diversify the federal courts. Carter announced an affirmative action program for the bench and instructed the Justice Department to look for qualified African Americans and women he could nominate to the federal courts. A window of opportunity was opened when Congress passed the 1978 Omnibus Judgeship Act, which created 152 new federal judgeships.[41] Carter also had the normal number of vacancies, which had been enhanced by the stalling tactics of Democratic senators late in President Ford's term.

Carter set out to limit the institutional mechanisms that might block his affirmative action plans. The first obstacle was to convince the Justice Department to consider women for judicial vacancies. Carter also had to modify the role of the ABA, whose participants and standards were predominantly white and male. Although it was a private organization, the ABA had created a semigovernmental role for itself. To open the process and diversify participation, Carter included the National Bar Association (an African American bar association) and women's groups in screening candidates and assessing qualifications.[42]

Carter had another formidable barrier to negotiate: the role of the Senate. At the district level, senators were used to the prerogative of selecting lower-court judges, which was a perk and a long-standing source of patronage. Carter did have allies on the Judiciary Committee. Senator Edward Kennedy, the new chair of the committee, was also committed to diversifying the bench. Kennedy modified the selection process by weakening the force of the blue slip, which senators could no longer quietly use as an absolute veto.[43]

Because there was less resistance, Carter aimed at the courts of appeals first. He used an executive order to create nominating commissions for circuit court judges that were to be the federal equivalent of the merit plans for choosing state judges. The most notable feature of Carter's plan was the diversity and expansion of involvement in the selection process.[44] Over 40 percent of the nominating commissioners were women. Many of these women were not attorneys, which limited their influence on the commissions, but for the first time they were participating.[45]

Carter charged the commissions with making "special efforts" to find and nominate well-qualified women and minorities.[46] Attorney General Griffin Bell held up nominations if he was not convinced the commissions or senators had considered women and minorities.[47] The plan had the additional effect of expanding presidential power over the appointment of judges at the expense of senatorial patronage.

Another executive order did not compel but instead encouraged senators to set up district court commissions. Such a plan struck at the heart of senatorial courtesy, and initially nominating commissions were instituted in fewer than half the states. Some senators set up pro forma commissions that became a facade for nominating their choices.

The nominating commissions were widely criticized. The ABA and senators, who felt the locus of power over nominations shifting away from them, were quick to criticize the new methods. Critics argued that the commissions were a means of packing the courts with ideologues under a veneer of merit. Some claimed the reliance on affirmative action came at the cost of merit. Certainly, the commissions did not eliminate politics from the process or ensure merit. The real question was whose definition of merit would prevail.[48] Many nontraditional candidates were qualified, although not from the perspective of the ABA.

The new process succeeded in opening nomination activity to fuller participation and also expanded the pool of potential nominees. Carter was able to redefine the eligible pool of candidates to emphasize group representation. Carter fulfilled his pledge by selecting eleven women to the courts of appeals—almost 20 percent of his appellate appointments—and twenty-nine women to the district courts, 14.4 percent of the total district court appointments (see Table 9.1). The forty women judges represented more than the total number of women from all previous administrations combined.[49]

The paths for women appointed to the federal courts were a departure from the routes white males followed. White male judges have tended to come from high socioeconomic backgrounds, elite law schools, high-status legal careers, and activity in politics. These factors created access to the patronage-oriented federal judgeships for men but limited opportunities for women. Whereas 20 percent of the males appointed by Carter had less than twenty years' experience in the legal profession, almost 60 percent of the women had under twenty years' experience.[50] According to ABA ratings, almost 60 percent of Carter's male appointees were judged to be well qualified or exceptionally well qualified, whereas less than 20 percent of the women achieved the same ratings.[51]

Yet, as Sheldon Goldman showed in a study of these appointees, the rankings were actually an indictment of the ABA system. By other indicators, the women were as qualified as or more qualified than the men selected. Just under half the females Carter appointed graduated from elite law schools, and just under half attained law school honors. Less than 40 percent of the men appointed went to elite law schools, and under 30 percent of the male Carter appointees earned honors in law school.[52]

Most of the women Carter appointed felt the commissions gave them opportunities the old system would have denied them. States with district court commissions had the largest numbers of women appointed. States without commissions had the lowest percentage of nontraditional candidates considered.[53]

Elliot Slotnick has argued that the commissions were not responsible for the rise in the number of women appointed. Rather, the increase occurred because Carter made affirmative action a priority. Still, the commissions were institutional devices by which to loosen the grip of senators and strengthen the position of the executive branch, meaning a president who was committed to diversifying the federal courts had a better chance to do so. The commissions broadened participation and brought formerly excluded groups into the process.[54]

Ronald Reagan: The Revolution of the New Right

Ronald Reagan was critical of using affirmative action to diversify the courts. He vowed to select the best judges and ignore factors such as gender and race. Reagan abolished the circuit nominating commissions, thereby reducing the number of participants in the process. The administration did not encourage the use of district court commissions, but many senators retained them. Termination of the commissions was opposed by women's groups, which felt the commissions were their sole avenue to the bench. Reagan removed the National Bar Association, which represented black attorneys, and women's groups from those consulted about appointments.[55] The administration also had a damaged relationship with the ABA.

Reagan increased the role of the Senate but modified senatorial courtesy. In the past, senators of the president's party had been asked to submit a name when a district court vacancy occurred in their state. Under the modified version of senatorial courtesy, senators would be asked to submit three to five names, and the administration would select the ultimate nominee.[56]

Analysts argue that the Reagan administration was more systematic and ideological than any previous administration in recruiting and screening judicial candidates.[57] According to Attorney General Ed Meese, "Through the appointment of federal judges the administration may institutionalize the Reagan revolution so that it can't be set aside no matter what happens in future presidential elections."[58] The administration centralized the process in the Federal Judicial Selection Committee, which was composed of officials from the White House and the Justice Department.[59] The White House Office of Legal Policy was responsible for screening candidates and sending evaluations to the committee. The plan was to give the president greater control over the process. By enhancing the role of the White House, the administration was positioned to limit senatorial patronage. The process was closed to the diversity that had marked the Carter plan.

The process consisted of an ideological screening of possible nominees. Despite claims that there was no litmus test for nominees, Reagan promised to appoint only those who supported "traditional family values" and opposed judicial activism.[60] His judicial philosophy included resistance to both abortion rights and equal rights for women, which he viewed as threats to traditional family values. The result, as Nina Totenberg has pointed out, was that "given their ideological bias, there are not many women and minorities available to them."[61]

Reagan sought appointees who were active Republicans, had judicial experience, and had published judicial or academic work. The administration sought candidates with proven track records that could be examined to reveal their judicial philosophies.[62] Whether deliberate or not, this selectively excluded women and minorities from consideration. Women were less likely than men to be party activists or to have the judicial experience that would create the prerequisite paper trail.

Some Republican senators complained about the process. A candidate supported by moderate senators Arlen Specter and John Heinz was held up until Democrats took control of the Senate. Judith Whittaker, a respected judge from Kansas, was "Borked,"[63] despite the support of Republicans Nancy Kassebaum and Robert Dole, because she had supported the Equal Rights Amendment and was not considered a strong enough opponent of abortion.[64] Law school dean Lizabeth Moody was recommended by Ohio Republicans for a district judgeship, but conservatives flagged her nomination for additional attention. One state judge remarked, "We're not going to get these judgeships unless we're willing to commit to a particular position, which would be improper."[65] Women were particularly suspect because of the administration's concern with traditional family values and its stance on abortion.

By removing institutional devices that had helped women and reconstructing the barriers that had excluded them, the Reagan administration made the judicial process less inclusionary. Reagan successfully nominated four women to the circuit courts, about 5 percent of his successful appointments. The twenty-four women confirmed to the district courts during his two terms represented 8.3 percent of those appointments (see Table 9.1).[66] His record was better than any previous president except Carter. Whether causal or coincidental, the number of women appointed increased after Reagan's first two years when two women were brought into the circle of advisers who screened potential nominees.

Still, the overall numbers represented a retreat, given that Carter had paved the way by opening the federal courts to women; the environment was increasingly favorable to gender equality; and the pool of women in the legal profession was growing. Reagan's record on district appointments appears even worse because senators influence district nominations. In fact, senators suggested women such as Judge Whittaker who were blocked by the administration. At the circuit level, where the president's advisers had more influence, the record was not impressive.

Yet, it was Ronald Reagan who blazed the trail for women on the Supreme Court. During the 1980 campaign, Reagan pledged to appoint a woman to the Court. When Potter Stewart retired, Reagan's list of candidates included a dozen women, among them Judge Kennedy, Chief Justice Mary Coleman of the Michigan Supreme Court, and Carter appointee court of appeals Judge Amalya Kearse.[67] The fact that Judge Kearse, a black liberal, showed up on Reagan's lists reflected the dearth of women at the top of the legal profession. The final list had the names of two women, O'Connor and Kennedy, and three men.

O'Connor, the first woman to survive the selection process, symbolized the barriers women faced. Despite having finished third in her class at Stanford Law School (classmate William Rehnquist finished first), O'Connor found doors closed to her at law firms; rather, she was offered secretarial positions. Attorney General William French Smith, whose law firm had denied O'Connor a position because she was a woman, was among those who now urged her appointment.[68]

There were rumors O'Connor would be elevated to chief justice when Warren Burger resigned. White House and Justice Department advisers, however, derisively referred to her as an "80 percenter" because she had cast occasional votes for affirmative action and against school prayer and was not solidly antiabortion—which ended her chances of becoming the first woman chief justice.[69] O'Connor is basically a conservative, but on gender issues she is significantly more liberal. Most analysts claim O'Connor does not "speak in a distinctively different [read feminist] voice."[70]

George Bush: A Kinder, Gentler Ronald Reagan?

George Bush largely continued Reagan's policies regarding the judiciary, but he did make some practical and symbolic modifications. The Bush administration prodded the ABA to change its procedures and eventually again began to submit the names of nominees. After the White House Office of Legal Policy was abolished, Attorney General Richard Thornburgh created the Office of Policy Development in the Justice Department.[71] Like his predecessor, Bush retained the systematic screening process in the form of the centralizing Federal Judicial Selection Committee and asked senators to submit three names for district court vacancies. All of this continued to move the locus of power over judicial selections to the White House (to the White House counsel's office in particular) and to the attorney general and away from the institutional Justice Department.

Bush stressed a desire for highly qualified persons who were philosophically conservative and were proponents of judicial restraint. He wanted to expand recruitment to provide access for those excluded under the old boy network, particularly qualified women and minorities. Bush did not reinstitute the nominating commissions that had expanded participation in the process and led to the selection of more women and minorities.[72] For the first time, though, women (Lee Lieberman in the White House and Barbara Drake in the Department of Justice) assumed major roles in the judicial selection process in the executive branch.

Like Carter, Bush had an unusual opportunity to appoint judges. The Federal Judgeships Act of 1990 created eighty-five new positions. In his single term in office, Bush appointed seven women to the circuit courts (18.9 percent of his 37 appointments) and twenty-nine to the district courts (almost 20 percent of his 148 district appointments).[73] Bush therefore equaled Carter's record of appointing a larger number of women to the district courts. And, in fact, a higher percentage of the Bush district court appointees were women, and there was less than a percentage point difference in regard to their appointments of women to the appellate courts. The numbers of women were limited somewhat because Bush elevated several district judges to courts of appeals.[74]

In some ways, the controversy surrounding the Clarence Thomas nomination may have helped women. Carl Tobias has argued that many women were chosen for purely political reasons after the Thomas debacle as Bush sought reelection. The appointments were said to have been a politically expedient means of damage control.[75] Ultimately, almost a quarter of Bush's nominations in his last two years in office were women.[76]

Bush almost nominated a woman to the Supreme Court. When William Brennan resigned, Carla Hills (again) and circuit Judge Pamela Rymer—the first woman Bush had appointed to a lower court—were on Bush's short list. Ultimately, David Souter was nominated to fill the vacancy, but the other finalist was Edith Jones, a Reagan circuit court appointee with very strong conservative credentials.[77] It was thought Jones would be next in line when another vacancy occurred. But when Thurgood Marshall resigned, Jones was displaced by the perceived need to choose a racial minority.

Bill Clinton and the Second Revolution

When Bill Clinton was elected, the pool of qualified Democrats for the judiciary was deep. Democratic senators had also waited for the opportunity to exercise influence. But under Carter's reforms, senators had surrendered some of their prerogatives, and the president had acquired additional power over the process. A different climate prevailed, in part because of the Thomas nomination. The 1992 campaign, dubbed "the year of the woman," had energized women's groups. As a result, more women ran for office, the policy environment had been altered, and women sought additional representation on the federal courts.[78]

Clinton had more initial appointments than most presidents, with over a hundred vacancies when he took office. A rift between Bush and the Judiciary Committee following the Thomas nomination had slowed the process of filling vacancies. Bush then had to spend more time on his reelection campaign, and he let vacancies accumulate and never filled all of the newly created judgeships. Because Bush was trailing in the polls, Democrats had incentive to block or delay his late appointments.[79]

Clinton encouraged district nominating commissions but did not require them. Senatorial courtesy and patronage played a role at the district level, but they were not unchecked.[80] Clinton did not reinstitute the circuit nominating commissions that had been credited with the increase in the number of women appointed to the federal courts. Whereas Clinton kept the centralizing mechanisms that had been used by Reagan and Bush (although he shortened the name to the Judicial Selection Group), like Carter he vowed to open participation to women and minorities.

The selection process within the Clinton administration has been divided by level. The Justice Department handles district court appointments. The critical screening for district court vacancies was returned to the Office of Policy Development, headed by Eleanor Acheson. At the court of appeals level, the initiatives come from the Office of the White House Counsel. The top deputy on the office's judicial selection committee is Victoria Radd, and women are well represented on the panel.[81]

Clinton's appointments have created "a revolutionary change in the composition of the federal judiciary."[82] Through his first two-and-a-half years in office, Clinton appointed 6 women to the courts of appeals and 45 women to district courts.[83] Those figures represent about 20 percent of his courts of appeals appointments and approximately a quarter of his district court selections. These percentages are approximately equal to the percentages of women in the profession. Clinton also appointed a higher percentage of African Americans to the bench.[84]

The political clock has slowed Clinton's progress in filling all of the court vacancies.[85] The 1994 election delivered a Republican majority to the Senate. As the 1996 presidential campaign season began, Republicans had little reason to act on Clinton's nominees, hoping a victory in 1996 would make them Republican appointments instead.

Clinton did appoint the second woman to the Supreme Court. It had been assumed that Ruth Bader Ginsburg's time had passed. Ginsburg was a Carter selection to the appeals court for the D.C. Circuit. She received the highest marks from the ABA, and she was confirmed despite being nominated in an election year. With Reagan and Bush in the White House for twelve years, Ginsburg passed the age generally considered in selecting a justice. Her name was not prominent on the short list for Byron White's vacated seat, the first selection by a Democrat in a generation. After a protracted process, in 1993 Clinton surprised everyone by selecting Ginsburg. Clinton had been criticized for the meandering process and the vacillation that seemed to mark his administration, but he was praised for the ultimate selection.[86]

The indignities that confronted Justice Ginsburg in her early career may have been less overt than those that faced O'Connor, but Ginsburg's commitment to gender equality is unquestioned, and she served as lead counsel for the Women's Rights Project.[87] As with Thurgood Marshall a generation before, she has the opportunity to protect the precedents she helped to establish as an advocate.

Conclusion

The legal system represents a history of exclusion.[88] To lower existing barriers and begin the process of making the judiciary more representative, institutional rules, elite behavior, and public opinion had to change. The contribution of Jimmy Carter cannot be minimized. As students of policy and politics increasingly recognize, structure and process matter. The process has evolved since Carter's reforms opened a window for presidents to exert more influence over the judicial selection process. As a result, Carter, Reagan, Bush, and Clinton have been able to stamp an ideological imprint on the federal courts.

Ronald Reagan continued the process Carter began by placing more authority in the White House, although the Justice Department was still a major player. The Bush administration refined the process, locating even more power in the White House. The Clinton process has been a cooperative effort between the Justice Department and the White House, with the president exercising more influence as the court level rises.

The legacy presidents bequeath through their judicial appointments can be measured by the qualifications of appointees, their ability to achieve policy goals, and their ability to diversify the bench. These categories are not mutually exclusive, despite attempts by some presidents and their advisers to cast them as competing alternatives. Studies have demonstrated that female judges have not diminished the overall quality of the bench. Certainly, the influence of the first women appointed to the Supreme Court cannot be underestimated. O'Connor represents a crucial vote in the center of the Court. In fact, many litigants aim their arguments specifically at her.[89] Ginsburg has not established a clear ideological position. Clinton chose her to be a coalition builder. By adopting a moderate position, Ginsburg has the potential to play an important role in the construction of doctrine.[90]

As of January 1996, women made up 16.6 percent of the courts of appeals positions, 17.7 percent of the district court judgeships, and two of the nine Supreme Court seats.[91] Thus, much of the business of the federal courts can occur with no women present. Still, as the number of women on the bench grows and female judges author precedents that percolate through the judicial system, the influence of women will grow.

Notes

1. Symposium. 1990. "Different Voices, Different Choices? The Impact of More Women Lawyers and Judges on the Legal System." *Judicature* 74: 145.

2. Elaine Martin. 1982. "Women on the Federal Bench: A Comparative Profile." *Judicature* 65: 306–313.

3. David O'Brien. 1988. *Judicial Roulette: Report of the Twentieth Century Fund Task Force on Judicial Selection.* New York: Priority Press.

4. Barbara Perry. 1991. *A "Representative" Supreme Court?: The Impact of Race, Religion, and Gender on Appointments.* New York: Greenwood Press. p. 10.

5. Although the South had traditionally been Democratic, Republicans had made inroads. Nixon hoped to attract disaffected Democrats and make his party viable in the South. He tried to use judicial appointments to provide southern representation on the Court and to encourage the electoral tides that were flowing in his party's direction. David O'Brien. 1996. *Storm Center: The Supreme Court in American Politics,* 4th ed. New York: Norton, p. 72.

6. Perry, *A "Representative" Supreme Court?*

7. C. Neal Tate. 1981. "Personal Attribute Models of the Voting Behavior of the U.S. Supreme Court Justices: Liberalism in Civil Liberties and Economic Decisions, 1946–1978." *American Political Science Review* 75: 355–367; Donald Songer, Jeffrey Segal, and Charles Cameron. 1994. "The Hierarchy of Justice: Testing a Principal-Agent Model of Supreme Court–Circuit Court Interactions." *American Journal of Political Science* 38: 673–696; and Robert Carp and C. K. Rowland. 1983. *Policymaking and Politics in the Federal District Courts.* Knoxville: University of Tennessee Press.

8. Jeffrey Segal and Harold Spaeth. 1993. *The Supreme Court and the Attitudinal Model.* New York: Cambridge University Press.

9. Thomas Walker and Deborah Barrow. 1985. "The Diversification of the Federal Bench: Policy and Process Ramifications." *Journal of Politics* 47: 596–617; Elaine Martin. 1987. "Gender and Judicial Selection: A Comparison of the Reagan and Carter Administrations." *Judicature* 71: 136–142; and Sue Davis, Susan Haire, and Donald Songer. 1993. "Voting Behavior and Gender on the U.S. Courts of Appeals: The Votes of Women Circuit Court Judges in Employment Discrimination and Search and Seizure Cases Differ from Those of Their Male Counterparts." *Judicature* 77 (November–December): 129–133.

10. Elliot E. Slotnick. 1984. "Gender, Affirmative Action, and Recruitment to the Federal Bench." *Golden Gate University Law Review* 14: 536–561.

11. Barbara C. Burrell. 1994. *A Woman's Place Is in the House: Campaigning*

for Congress in the Feminist Era. Ann Arbor: University of Michigan Press, p. 154; and Sue Thomas. 1994. *How Women Legislate.* New York: Oxford University Press.

12. Gayle Binion. 1993. "The Nature of Feminist Jurisprudence." *Judicature* 77 (November–December): 140–143.

13. Davis, Haire, and Songer, "Voting Behavior and Gender on the U.S. Courts of Appeals," pp. 129–133. The findings are consistent with analyses of state supreme court judges. David Allen and Diane Wall. 1993. "Role Orientations and Women State Supreme Court Justices." *Judicature* 77: 156–165.

14. Elaine Martin. 1990. "Men and Women on the Bench: Vive la Difference?" *Judicature* 73: 204–208; and Jon Gottschall. 1983. "Carter's Judicial Appointments: The Influence of Affirmative Action and Merit Selection on Voting on the U.S. Courts of Appeals." *Judicature* 67: 164–173.

15. Sheldon Goldman. 1979. "Should There Be Affirmative Action for the Judiciary?" *Judicature* 62: 490–494.

16. For a further discussion of the legal analogies that affected gender doctrine, see Chapter 11 in this volume.

17. Karen O'Connor. 1980. *Women's Organizations' Use of the Courts.* Lexington: Lexington Books.

18. Beverly Cook. 1978. "Political Culture and Selection of Women Judges in Trial Courts." Paper presented at the Annual Meeting of the Law and Society Association. As quoted in Elliot E. Slotnick. 1984. "The Paths to the Federal Bench: Gender, Race and Judicial Recruitment Variation." *Judicature* 67: 373.

19. Beverly Cook. 1988. "Women as Judges." In *Women in the Judicial Process,* Beverly Cook, Leslie Friedman Goldstein, Karen O'Connor, and Susette Talarico. Washington, D.C.: American Political Science Association, p. 9.

20. Martin, "Men and Women on the Bench: Vive la Difference," p. 204.

21. Donald Jackson. 1974. *Judges.* New York: Atheneum, p. 255.

22. Martin, "Gender and Judicial Selection: A Comparison of the Reagan and Carter Administrations," p. 140.

23. As quoted in Howard Ball. 1987. *Courts and Politics: The Federal Judicial System,* 2d ed. Engelwood Cliffs, N.J.: Prentice-Hall, p. 192.

24. Elliot E. Slotnick. 1980. "Reforms in Judicial Selection: Will They Affect the Senate's Role?" *Judicature* 64: 70.

25. Alan Neff. 1981. *The United States District Judge Nominating Commissions: Their Members, Procedures and Candidates.* Chicago: American Judicature Society, p. 27.

26. Robert Carp and Ronald Stidham. 1991. *The Federal Courts,* 2d ed. Washington, D.C.: Congressional Quarterly, p. 101.

27. Larry Berkson and Susan Carbon. 1980. *The United States Circuit Judge Nominating Commission: Its Members, Procedures and Candidates.* Chicago: American Judicature Society, pp. 13–25.

28. Richard Pacelle and Patricia Pauly. 1996. "The Freshman Effect Revisited: An Individual Based Analysis." *American Review of Politics* 17: 1–22.

29. Mark Silverstein. 1994. *Judicious Choices: The New Politics of Supreme Court Confirmations.* New York: Norton, pp. 152–155.

30. Cook, "Women as Judges," p. 10.

31. Carl Tobias. 1993. "Closing the Gender Gap on the Federal Courts." *University of Cincinnati Law Review* 61: 1248.

32. Berkson and Carbon, *The United States Circuit Judge Nominating Commission,* p. 2.

33. Martin, "Gender and Judicial Selection: A Comparison of the Reagan and Carter Administrations," p. 140.

34. Florence E. Allen. 1965. *To Do Justly*. As quoted in Miriam Goldman Cederbaum. 1993. "Women on the Federal Bench." *Boston University Law Review* 73: 45.

35. Slotnick, "Gender, Affirmative Action, and Recruitment to the Federal Bench," p. 525.

36. Beverly Cook. 1982. "Women as Supreme Court Candidates: From Florence Allen to Sandra O'Connor." *Judicature* 65: 314–326.

37. Nixon's reported response to the ABA's evaluation of Lillie and Bacon was "fuck the ABA" and a vow to exclude the ABA from the judicial process. Henry Abraham. 1992. *Justices and Presidents: A Political History of Appointments to the Supreme Court*. 3rd ed. New York: Oxford University Press, p. 20.

38. Ibid., p. 323.

39. Cook, "Women as Supreme Court Candidates: From Florence Allen to Sandra O'Connor," p. 325. Clerkships are considered a path to the Supreme Court and the lower federal courts. This path had been blocked to women until the 1970s.

40. Ibid.

41. Gottschall, "Carter's Judicial Appointments," p. 166. The creation of new judgeships had been stalled by Democrats since 1970 in hopes that the party would win the presidency. Neff, *The United States District Judge Nominating Commissions*, p. 32.

42. W. Gary Fowler. 1984. "Judicial Selection Under Reagan and Carter: A Comparison of Their Initial Recommendation Procedures." *Judicature* 67: 268.

43. Elliot E. Slotnick. 1979. "The Changing Role of the Senate Judiciary Committee in Judicial Selection." *Judicature* 62: 503.

44. Larry Berkson. 1979. "The U.S. Circuit Judge Nominating Commission: The Candidate's Perspective." *Judicature* 62: 466–467.

45. Berkson and Carbon, *The United States Circuit Judge Nominating Commission*, pp. 45–49.

46. Martin, "Women on the Federal Bench: A Comparative Profile," p. 308.

47. Slotnick, "The Changing Role of the Senate Judiciary Committee in Judicial Selection," p. 503.

48. Slotnick, "Reforms in Judicial Selection: Will They Affect the Senate's Role?" pp. 60–73; and Elliot E. Slotnick. 1980. "Reforms in the Judicial Selection: Will They Affect the Senate's Role? Part II." *Judicature* 64: 114–129.

49. Sheldon Goldman. 1981. "Carter's Judicial Appointments: A Lasting Legacy." *Judicature* 64: 347–350.

50. Slotnick, "Gender, Affirmative Action, and Recruitment to the Federal Bench," pp. 519–571.

51. Slotnick, "The Paths to the Federal Bench," p. 381.

52. Sheldon Goldman. 1978. "A Profile of Carter's Judicial Nominees." *Judicature* 62: 246–254; and Goldman, "Carter's Judicial Appointments: A Lasting Legacy," pp. 344–355.

53. Neff, *The United States District Judge Nominating Commissions*, pp. 124–136.

54. Elliot E. Slotnick. 1981. "Federal Appellate Judges' Selection During the Carter Administration: Recruitment Changes and Unanswered Questions." *Justice Systems Journal* 6: 301–302.

55. Martin, "Gender and Judicial Selection: A Comparison of the Reagan and Carter Administrations," pp. 140–142; and Sheldon Goldman. 1985. "Reaganizing the Judiciary: The First Term Appointments." *Judicature* 68: 316.

56. Fowler, "Judicial Selection Under Reagan and Carter," pp. 266–268.

57. Sheldon Goldman. 1983. "Reagan's Judicial Appointments at Mid-Term: Shaping the Bench in His Own Image." *Judicature* 66: 346; and Sheldon Goldman. 1987. "Reagan's Second Term Judicial Appointments: The Battle at Midway." *Judicature* 70: 325.

58. O'Brien, *Judicial Roulette,* pp. 21–24.

59. Jon Gottschall. 1986. "Reagan's Appointments to the U.S. Courts of Appeals: The Continuation of a Judicial Revolution." *Judicature* 70: 49.

60. Goldman, "Reaganizing the Judiciary: The First Term Appointments," pp. 319–321.

61. Nina Totenberg. 1986. "Women on the Bench, the Constitution and the Reagan Administration." Address to the National Association of Women Judges, Key Biscayne, Florida. As quoted in Martin, "Gender and Judicial Selection: A Comparison of the Reagan and Carter Administrations," p. 141.

62. Sheldon Goldman. 1989. "Reagan's Judicial Legacy: Completing the Puzzle and Summing Up." *Judicature* 72: 321–328.

63. The verb "Borked" found its way into the political lexicon during the nomination of Robert Bork to the Supreme Court. The term refers to ideological opposition to a nominee, using past writings and decisions to construct a case against the putative justice. In Whittaker's case, before the Bork nomination, her writings and views were used to disqualify her. The process appeared to be repeated for a number of women.

64. Herman Schwartz. 1988. *Packing the Court: The Conservative Campaign to Rewrite the Constitution.* New York: Scribners, p. 66.

65. Ibid., p. 87. During interviews with the Justice Department, Moody refused to answer direct questions about abortion and was not nominated.

66. Reagan also nominated two women to the courts of appeals toward the end of his second term, but the Senate did not act on the nominations. Goldman, "Reagan's Judicial Legacy: Completing the Puzzle and Summing Up," p. 325.

67. Abraham, *Justices and Presidents,* pp. 338–339.

68. Elder Witt. 1986. *A Different Justice: Reagan and the Supreme Court.* Washington, D.C.: Congressional Quarterly, p. 29.

69. David Savage. 1992. *Turning Right: The Making of the Rehnquist Supreme Court.* New York: John Wiley & Sons, p. 5.

70. Jilda Aliotta. 1995. "Justice O'Connor and the Equal Protection Clause: A Feminine Voice?" *Judicature* 78: 232–235; and Sue Davis. 1993. "The Voice of Sandra Day O'Connor." *Judicature* 77: 134–139.

71. This new Office of Policy Development no longer had the authority over judicial selection, however, Sheldon Goldman. 1991. "The Bush Imprint on the Judiciary: Carrying on a Tradition." *Judicature* 74: 296–300.

72. Ibid., pp. 294–306.

73. Sheldon Goldman. 1993. "Bush's Judicial Legacy: The Final Imprint." *Judicature* 76: 286–292.

74. The numbers mask the fact that presidents choose some women for more than one position. Thus, presidents may choose a district court judge and later promote her to the circuit court. Reagan promoted two of his district appointees to the court of appeals. Bush promoted two of Reagan's appointees to the circuit court, as well as one of Carter's appointees and one of his own. In Chapter 4, Janet M. Martin found a similar phenomenon for other appointments.

75. Carl Tobias. 1994. "Keeping the Covenant on the Federal Courts." *SMU Law Review* 47: 1866.

76. Tobias, "Closing the Gender Gap on the Federal Courts," p. 1241.

77. Abraham, *Justices and Presidents,* p. 366.

78. Savage, *Turning Right: The Making of the Rehnquist Supreme Court*, p. 424.

79. Sheldon Goldman. 1995. "Judicial Selection Under Clinton: A Midterm Examination." *Judicature* 78: 278.

80. Tobias, "Keeping the Covenant on the Federal Courts," p. 1870.

81. Goldman, "Judicial Selection Under Clinton: A Midterm Examination," pp. 278–279.

82. Sheldon Goldman and Matthew Saronson. 1994. "Clinton's Nontraditional Judges: Creating a More Representative Bench." *Judicature* 78: 68.

83. Matthew P. Sarago, assistant manager of information services, and Peter A. Wonders, assistant historian, of the Federal Judicial Center provided me with information concerning federal appointments.

84. In his first two years, over a quarter of Clinton's district appointees were African Americans. By comparison, 14 percent of Carter's, 7 percent of Bush's, and 2 percent of Reagan's appointees were African Americans. At the circuit level, about 17 percent of Clinton's appointees were black, which is almost identical to the percentage for Jimmy Carter; the percentage is higher than the figures for Bush (5 percent) and Reagan (1 percent). Goldman, "Judicial Selection Under Clinton: A Midterm Examination," pp. 276–291.

85. As of June 1, 1996, there were seven pending nominations of women (six to district courts). Given the politics of an election year, their confirmation was unlikely.

86. James Simon. 1995. *The Center Holds: The Power Struggle Inside the Rehnquist Court.* New York: Simon and Schuster, p. 29.

87. David O'Brien. 1995. *The Supreme Court: The 1995 Term.* New York: Norton, p. 5.

88. Symposium, "Different Voices, Different Choices? The Impact of More Women Lawyers and Judges on the Legal System," p. 141.

89. Lee Epstein and Joseph Kobylka. 1992. *The Supreme Court and the Legal Change: Abortion and the Death Penalty.* Chapel Hill: University of North Carolina Press.

90. Joyce Ann Baugh, Christopher E. Smith, Thomas R. Hensley, and Scott Patrick Johnson. 1994. "Justice Ruth Bader Ginsburg: A Preliminary Assessment." *University of Toledo Law Review* 26: 1–34.

91. Through 1992, there were fifty-nine women on state supreme courts, although forty-one had been sitting on the courts only since 1992. Allen and Wall, "Role Orientations and Women State Supreme Court Justices," pp. 156–158.

PART 4

Policy and Participation: Women as Executive Activists and as Citizens

10

The Office of the First Lady and Public Policymaking

Barbara C. Burrell

When we think about women in the executive branch we tend to focus on women in the bureaucracy, women as presidential appointees in the departments and agencies and in the Executive Office of the President, and perhaps a woman being elected to the Oval Office. We seldom include the first lady in such analyses and with good reason, as this position has not been obtained through achievement, professional credentials, or election by the people. The role has been essentially a private one with public duties. First ladies, however, have served their husbands as policy advisers and political assistants—some privately, some more publicly. This participation in the presidential advisory system makes them appropriate subjects for this book.

Edith Mayo, creator of the Smithsonian Institution exhibit "First Ladies: Political Role and Public Image," has written that "it is sad and telling that the press and public alike are unaware that Presidential wives since Abigail Adams have been wielding political influence. Further, it is disheartening to find that virtually every First Lady who has used her influence has been either ridiculed or vilified as deviating from women's proper role or has been feared as emasculating."[1] Karen O'Connor, Bernadette Nye, and Laura van Assendelft have concluded that at least twenty-six first ladies could be considered confidants or advisers and that "those who have done so go back to the early period."[2]

But first ladies have served primarily as "the nation's hostess," performing ceremonial duties as the helpmate to the president.[3] Their public role has been mainly social, in keeping with the traditional role of women as performing in the private rather than the public sector of society. First ladies have become an icon, symbolizing ideal womanhood for Americans.

The first ladyship is virtually distinctive to the United States. In no other country is the spouse of the elected head of the government given a title and a quasi-official role to play. At the same time, cultural notions of women's place in society constrain the activities of the person who holds this position. But the first lady's policy advisory role deserves reassessment, particularly given Hillary Rodham Clinton's attempt to redefine the first ladyship into a public advisory role and contemporary efforts to achieve equality for women in this nation's social, economic, and political life. This focus on the public policy advisory role of the first lady requires a conceptualization of her and her office as part of the president's staff.

In 1937 the President's Committee on Administrative Management, the Brownlow Committee, issued a report calling for a reorganization of the executive branch and an increase in the size of the president's staff. In what has become a well-known conclusion, the committee stated that "the President needs help." This report set in motion the development of a more institutionalized staffing system around the president. In their quest to implement and organize an advisory system within the White House since the 1937 report, how have presidents used the first lady and her office as a source of assistance and advice and with what consequences?

The involvement of the first lady and her office in the presidential advisory system depends upon what both the president and the first lady want, their interaction, and the organizational structure available to implement these desires. Further, whereas the first lady's office has become institutionalized, her role is still dependent on personal preferences. Thus, whereas Jimmy and Rosalynn Carter viewed his presidency as more or less a partnership, Barbara Bush distinctly stayed away from policymaking in the Bush White House, and Bess Truman and Mamie Eisenhower presented a public persona of noninvolvement in presidential decisionmaking while in private being important advisers to the president.[4]

Office of the First Lady

The Office of the First Lady as part of the organizational structure of the Office of the President is a contemporary phenomenon.[5] The Carter White House organizational chart had three tiers flowing from the president. The "first lady's staff" appears at the bottom rung—along with the chief usher, the visitors' office, chief speechwriter, appointments secretary, and personnel office—but it flows in a direct line to the president.[6] In the Reagan White House, organizational responsibility flowed from the president to the director of the First Lady's Office through the chief of staff to the assistant to the president and the deputy chief of staff.[7] For the Bush administration, the deputy assistant to the president and chief of staff to the first lady were placed under the chief of staff to the president.[8] [No chart is available for the Clinton White House.] (It should be kept in mind that formal positions in the White House as listed on an organizational chart may not reflect actual influence and power within an administration.)

Interestingly, George Edwards and Stephen Wayne, in the second and third editions of their book *Presidential Leadership*, illustrate what they call the principal structural units of the contemporary White House by placing a triumvirate at the top that consists of the president, first lady, and the vice president, with the president at the center. In their depiction, the first lady was part of this triumvirate in both the Bush and Clinton presidencies.[9]

Recognition of the distaff side of the White House as an official part of the president's staff within the executive branch organization began with the Eisenhower administration, when the 1953 *Congressional Directory* listed Mary McCaffree as acting secretary to the president's wife.[10] (*The Congressional Directory* did not mention the first lady herself until the March 1965 edition.) During the Eisenhower administration a need for an organized staff for the first lady began to emerge because Mamie Eisenhower received thousands of letters a month—all of which she wanted answered—and because the Eisenhowers entertained a record number of foreign heads of state, which required organization and staff.[11]

Contemporary first ladies have established a staff that includes, in addition to those responsible for carrying out the social and symbolic duties of the office, press personnel and policy experts for whatever problem becomes their "issue." Hillary Rodham Clinton's staff consists of between fourteen and sixteen people in the Office of the First Lady, a number that is not out of proportion to the staffs of her predecessors.[12] (Rosalynn Carter had approximately twenty-three on her staff and complained that she needed more staff.[13])

In 1978, during the Carter administration, Congress passed the White House Personnel Authorization-Employment Act (Public Law 95-570), which provided legal authority for an office to fund the administration of the White House. Prior to this law's passage, federal law had authorized the president to have only fourteen staff members, whereas in actuality the White House staff had grown to over three hundred. Although Congress had approved annual appropriations for the larger staff, the money had been challenged on the floor several times because it had not been authorized.[14] The new law aimed to rectify this situation. What is important for our purposes is that the law included authorization for "assistance and services . . . to be provided to the spouse of the President in connection with assistance provided by such spouse to the President in discharge of the President's duties and responsibilities." Prior to enactment of this legislation, funds for the first lady's staff and travel were appropriated on an as-needed basis from the general budget line item for White House management.[15]

The White House offices have traditionally been divided into two wings—the "feminine" East Wing, staffed by the first lady's personnel and considered the social and domestic side of the White House, and the "masculine" West Wing, where the president's staff has been housed. When Hillary Rodham Clinton entered the White House, she inherited the established office for the first lady in the East Wing. Power is considered to be centered in the West Wing.

> The first floor of the *West Wing* is reserved for people with real clout. The
> Oval Office is here, along with the White House Press Office. So are the
> offices of the White House chief of staff and the national security adviser
> . . . the West Wing is where every presidential appointee longs to be. One
> would rather have a windowless, unventilated closet on the first floor of the
> West Wing than a suite in any of the other executive quarters near the
> White House.[16]

Upon becoming first lady, Hillary Rodham Clinton immediately sig-
naled her intention to be a public presidential policy adviser by taking an
office in the West Wing. Her office is a "small room at the center of the sec-
ond-floor work space in the West Wing of the White House, surrounded not
by social secretaries but by the largely anonymous policy experts who will
lay out the new administration's domestic programs."[17] How have recent
first ladies used their office to assist the president in his "duties and responsibilities"?

The Public Policy Role of the First Lady

I now give examples of how contemporary first ladies have used their role
to serve as public policy making assistants to the president. The various
times and ways in which they have been "allowed" to serve as public advisers to the president and reactions to their performance of such a role address
the nature of gender in the area of masculinist presidential politics. I begin
by considering three instances in which first ladies have played a role in foreign policy by acting as emissaries for the president to other heads of state
and by performing other foreign policy duties.

Foreign Policy Representative

Women have been handicapped as actors in the foreign policy arena because
of notions of that arena's masculinity (see Chapter 7). Geraldine Ferraro, for
example, was treated harshly as a vice-presidential candidate in 1984
because of questions as to whether she could push the nuclear button. Public
opinion polls have traditionally shown voters giving male candidates the
edge in conducting defense and foreign policy matters, although women
candidates are preferred if the issue is framed in terms of peace. Women are
viewed as not tough enough to represent national economic and security
concerns abroad.[18]

I use illustrations of first ladies acting in the area of foreign relations
precisely because such involvement is rather far removed from what we
have come to conceive of as politically appropriate. At the same time, the
examples illustrate instances of first ladies not conducting foreign policy—
the harder side of the domain—but rather affecting foreign relations and, to

an extent, using their intelligence and their charm to win the support and friendship of other heads of state—instances of gendered politics. These case studies allow us to more fully understand how the first lady has been used in the policymaking realm.

Recollections of Eleanor Roosevelt's years in the White House place these contemporary examples in historical context. Eleanor Roosevelt was deeply involved in domestic politics, conducting advocacy on behalf of minorities, women, and laborers. But she also helped in the war effort during World War II.

Particularly relevant for this analysis is that in 1942 she flew to England to visit the U.S. troops and energize the British populace. Eleanor Roosevelt "inspected bombed London, American Red Cross units, women's training centers and voluntary services, the defense grottoes beneath the white cliffs of Dover, a Spitfire factory. . . . At a shipyard, in the cold drizzle, she addressed fifteen thousand workers. She spoke on the BBC. She lunched with women members of Parliament."[19] In 1943 Eleanor flew to the South Pacific to visit the troops stationed there. But when her husband met with Churchill and Stalin in Casablanca, Teheran, and Yalta to discuss war policy and the post–World War II world, Eleanor was not allowed to accompany him. Women were not supposed to be a part of such meetings. When Churchill brought his daughter to Teheran, Franklin Roosevelt took his daughter, Anna, to Yalta, but he still would not let the first lady participate in this event.[20]

In time, things changed somewhat regarding the first ladies' role in foreign affairs as anything other than a ceremonial surrogate for the president by representing the United States at weddings, inaugurations, and funerals. In 1972 Pat Nixon became the only first lady to visit and officially represent the president in Africa. She served as the president's personal diplomatic emissary on a trip to Liberia for the inauguration of its president and on a tour of Ghana and the Ivory Coast.

The importance of the trip for our purposes here is that Pat Nixon conferred privately and substantively with the leaders of these nations. Prior to embarking on the trip, the first lady was briefed by Henry Kissinger, then President Nixon's adviser on national security. The State Department prepared talking points for her on issues that included Rhodesian and South African policy and future economic aid, and she was updated on the president's planned trips to Peking and Moscow. She played a political role, reporting back to the president, among other things, that the Ivory Coast president did not believe in using force against South Africa. Presidential assistant Chuck Colson sent a seven-page memo about her trip to the president, stating that "Mrs. Nixon has now broken through where we have failed. . . . People, men and women—identify with her—and in return with you."[21]

The trip was primarily a ceremonial goodwill tour, and I am not presenting a revisionist history of the limited role Pat Nixon was allowed to play in her husband's administration. But as *Time* magazine pointed out, it was the first time a first lady had conferred with a head of state on behalf of the president.[22] This activity should not be ignored if we are to construct an accurate accounting of the first lady's role in public policy and to fully understand the presidential advisory system. We must note that the foreign relations excursions first ladies have undertaken on behalf of their husbands' administrations have been exclusively to countries not considered in the "first tier" of diplomatic and strategic importance. And future research should determine whether U.S. presidents have ever received the spouse of another nation's head of state as an official representative sent with substantive messages and diplomatic discussion points.

Pat Nixon's diplomatic foray produced no negative media reaction. This was not the case in the initial press coverage when Rosalynn Carter made a foreign relations trip to confer with the heads of seven Latin American nations in summer 1977. According to Rosalynn Carter's memoirs, her husband had asked her to go on this mission. In announcing the trip, President Carter described his wife as a "'political partner of mine' who would conduct substantive talks with the leaders of those countries and bring back a report on how we might strengthen our ties."[23] He noted that she was well versed in policy matters. The press release from the First Lady's Office said the "visit was on *behalf of the President to express his friendship and good will* and to conduct substantive talks with the leaders of those nations on issues of bilateral, regional and global importance (emphasis added)."[24] Rosalynn Carter pointed out that she would not be conducting negotiations with any of these heads of state.

In articles regarding the prospective trip, both the *New York Times* and the *Washington Post* reported on the "substantive talks" Mrs. Carter planned with government representatives during her visit. Both of these newspapers placed quotation marks around the term *substantive talks*. The *New York Times* continued to refer to the talks in this manner, thus suggesting its skepticism in the days leading up to her departure.

The culture of Latin American states regarding the role of women was not particularly receptive to a diplomatic mission by the president's wife, and some of the leaders of the countries Mrs. Carter was to visit expressed displeasure that "Carter would send a woman, particularly one who is not an expert on inter-American affairs, to discuss serious policy issues."[25] One Brazilian journalist described the situation as one of being promoted from "the backyard of U.S. foreign policy . . . to the kitchen."[26] It was believed she would not be taken seriously.

But Rosalynn Carter spent many hours being briefed for her meetings and taking Spanish lessons. She ended up discussing trade relations, drug trafficking, nuclear proliferation, national security problems, and human rights issues with the heads of state of the seven nations she visited. Her meetings often extended longer than initially scheduled, which indicated that the leaders had begun to take her more seriously and were impressed with her ability to represent the president. Upon her return, President Carter welcomed her home, "obviously pleased with the results of the trip and with his wife's success as a fledgling diplomat."[27] She later reported to congressional committees. The Senate sent a unanimously congratulatory telegram regarding her trip.

Americans supported Rosalynn Carter's trip, at least in retrospect. After her return, the president's pollster, Pat Caddell, reported to the president that "70 percent of Americans rated her journey as excellent or good."[28] At the conclusion of her trip, the *New York Times* editors decided that participating in foreign affairs was not beyond the range of activities in which the spouse of the president could appropriately be involved and accepted the fact that Rosalynn Carter had done a creditable job.

> The initial reports suggest that Mrs. Carter did very well indeed at explaining her husband's interest, concern and policies and at eliciting extensive comments of both support and disagreement from her hosts. It is the quality of her ambassadorship that should concern us, not the range of subjects on which the President might wish to exploit her prestige and proximity.[29]

Rosalynn Carter, then, had apparently convinced a skeptical media that a first lady could perform creditably in the foreign policy arena. Politically, however, it was still unwise to suggest that the spouse of the president should be a foreign policy adviser. During the 1992 campaign, Hillary Rodham Clinton made it a point to stress that she would not be involved in the foreign relations arena in a Clinton White House at the same time she was emphasizing a domestic policy and a political partnership. In the aftermath of the failed Health Care Task Force in 1994—to which President Clinton had appointed her as head at the beginning of his administration—and the devastating midterm elections for Democrats in 1994, the first lady turned to a role as spokesperson for outsiders, particularly women and children. She had long been involved in children's issues and during the 1992 campaign had stressed that she wished to focus on women and children during her tenure in the White House. Her return to this interest after the 1994 elections led her to travel extensively abroad. Her trips were not made as an emissary of the president, but they did include a foreign relations aspect beyond being goodwill missions.

The theme of these trips has been "human rights are women's rights and women's rights are human rights." In commenting on her visit to Pakistan, India, Bangladesh, and Sri Lanka in spring 1995, one favorable editorial noted that it

> was easily the most meaningful international journey so far by anyone associated with the Clinton administration—or, for that matter, the Bush

and Reagan administrations. In focusing attention on the condition of women in a region where their oppression remains rampant, and in speaking frankly about the positive role of U.S. development aid for the poorest nations in the world, Clinton delivered one of the most coherent and humane international policy statements since the days of Jimmy Carter.[30]

The first lady's most notable foreign foray has been the human rights speech she gave at the United Nations Conference on Women in Beijing, China, in September 1995. What she would say and how she would say it were important to U.S. diplomatic relations with the repressive Chinese government. Her attendance at the conference had been the subject of political debate. The first lady gave a ringing endorsement of women's rights and strongly condemned abuses against women. She cataloged the mistreatment of women as an abuse of human rights. "It is violation of human rights when babies are denied food or drowned or suffocated or their spines broken simply because they are born girls," she stated.[31]

Hillary Rodham Clinton is extremely popular overseas. According to Ann Devroy of the *Washington Post,* "[If Hillary Rodham Clinton] is not widely popular at home, she is treated virtually like a folk heroine abroad, particularly by women."[32] An Associated Press wire story from China reported,

> While Americans debate what the First Lady's role should be, women in other countries delight in her prominence. Hillary Clinton wowed the women's conference in China, where she gave an impassioned speech declaring that the time has come to stop the abuse of women around the world. Women emerging from the hall after Hillary Clinton's address were effusive with praise. "Give 'em hell, Hillary," women activists shouted when she showed up the next day for a speech in Huariou, 30 miles outside of Beijing. At one conference panel, she was introduced as "the First Lady of the world." Many people seem to see her as the voice of women's struggle for access to education, health care, jobs and credit, as well as freedom from violence.[33]

As part of her visit to Mongolia following her appearance at the United Nations Conference on Women, Hillary Rodham Clinton announced the provision of an aid package to that country. In addition, she had gone to Mongolia to show U.S. support for fledgling democracies in "Third World" countries. A month later, while attending a conference of Latin American leaders' wives, the first lady announced $11.7 million in U.S. aid for measles eradication. Announcing aid programs for the administration appears to be a new feature in the first lady's role, inching her toward becoming a more formal government representative.

Although they do not suggest involvement in foreign policy making per se, the official nature of these announcements—as opposed to acting in the foreign arena only (but importantly) as a personal representative of the president—makes the first lady part of the executive branch apparatus. Mrs. Clinton made these announcements because of her great interest in foreign aid programs. But unlike Rosalynn Carter, Hillary Rodham Clinton has made it a point not to engage in any substantive discussions with heads of state.[34] She knows that for her to do so would bring criticism to an administration already struggling to create support for a domestic policy advisory role for her.

In March 1996, Hillary Rodham Clinton added another element to her international presence when, recalling Eleanor Roosevelt, she visited U.S. troops in Bosnia. Her trip was undertaken more for domestic political consumption than as a foreign policy foray, however. She once again announced a U.S. aid package in a meeting with international relief organizations.

These examples illustrate a contemporary history, although infrequent in occurrence, of first ladies performing a public policy role we have seldom envisioned for them—publicly assisting their husbands in the foreign policy domain.

Domestic Policy Adviser

Smithsonian Institution curator Edith Mayo has described Hillary Rodham Clinton as "but the latest in a long line of politically astute women who have been intimately involved with their husbands' political careers and administration."[35] The role Clinton has adopted as domestic policy adviser has taken the first lady to a new level within the advisory system, however.

Contemporary first ladies have varied greatly in the extent to which they have sought to be publicly involved in domestic policy making. Eleanor Roosevelt left a substantial legacy in this regard. She was an outspoken advocate for a number of causes, most notably for the rights of blacks, migrant workers, laborers, and women. She testified before Congress regarding public policy issues. But although she traveled extensively to obtain information for her husband, she was not involved in the making of proposed legislation. She lobbied her husband along with others.

Eleanor Roosevelt was followed by two first ladies—Bess Truman and Mamie Eisenhower—who exercised influence only out of the public view. But Lady Bird Johnson saw Eleanor Roosevelt as a role model she greatly admired. According to Norma Foreman, "Both First Ladies said they were acting as 'eyes and ears' for their husbands. They used many of the same techniques in their leadership of public opinion and relations with the press—access for reporters, trips to government projects, use of mass media, and public speaking engagements."[36] One difference, however, was that "Mrs. Johnson never took stands contrary to those of the President nor introduced ideas differing from his. Her actions and words were always an underscore, never a counterforce to the President."[37]

Lady Bird Johnson's involvement began most visibly with a whistle-stop tour through the South, which she took on her own during the 1964 presidential election. This trip dramatically broke new ground for a first lady in the area of campaigning and winning votes.[38] The trip's aim was to win back the South, which felt Lyndon Johnson—a Texan—had betrayed it through his forceful support of civil rights for blacks. Although Lady Bird made no substantive speeches but rather offered "homey" greetings to the crowds, she and her press secretary, Liz Carpenter, were effective at working with the press and getting local Democratic dignitaries to meet with them.[39]

Lady Bird Johnson is best known for her work in the area of beautification. On the surface this may seem to be an example of the noncontroversial type of cause we have come to associate with first ladies. But whereas Lady Bird consciously chose an issue that would not interfere with but instead would complement her husband's agenda, the manner in which she promoted this issue represents an engagement in substantive politics.

"In the summer and fall of 1965, for example, she sat in on strategy conferences, called personally to swing votes in Congress, and rallied groups that favored the Highway Beautification Act."[40] Her advocacy had strong opposition, to the extent that "Impeach Lady Bird" billboards were erected. Overall, Lady Bird Johnson "demonstrated that a First Lady could now do more than serve as a feminine conscience or fact-finder of a president. It was now conceivable she could be a functional and integral part of the office itself."[41] Meg Greenfield, writing in the *Reporter,* described the transformation Lady Bird Johnson had made in the role of the first lady in terms of

> integrat[ing] the traditionally frivolous and routine aspects of the East Wing life into the overall purposes of the administration and . . . enlist[ing] the peculiar assets of First Ladyhood itself in the administration's behalf. They are assets no one fully understood until Mrs. Johnson moved into the White House—or at least no one fully understood their potential political clout.[42]

Rosalynn Carter broke ground for first ladies when she served as Jimmy Carter's emissary to several Latin American nations, as discussed earlier, and in her role as "the president's partner." Her tenure rated a cover story in *Newsweek* in 1979 titled "The President's Partner," which described her as the "most influential First Lady of modern times."[43] She was a joint policymaker with the president and even sat in on cabinet meetings, which caused a stir in the media.

On the domestic scene, Rosalynn Carter chaired her own presidential commission on mental health, through which she helped to initiate legislation and testified before Congress. She was instrumental in the passage of the Mental Health Systems Act of 1980. Mental health was an issue in which Rosalynn had a long-term interest, and she had taken leadership in that area when her husband was governor of Georgia. Because the issue was not new for her and was not a central concern of the Carter presidency, her activity in this area falls into the noncontroversial issue advocacy role most contemporary first ladies have adopted. But her leadership on this issue and her lobbying efforts on its behalf paralleled Lady Bird Johnson's activism and showed her as an engaged policymaker. First lady historian Lewis Gould characterized Rosalynn Carter as taking the position of first lady as surrogate, partner, and advocate to the current limits of its capacity in our system of government.[44]

Hillary Rodham Clinton and the Health Care Task Force

When President Clinton appointed Hillary Rodham Clinton to head his Health Care Task Force in January 1993, he took spousal assistance to an entirely new plane by involving his wife in the making of policy on an issue of central importance to his presidency. Never before had a first lady been put in charge of a major administrative initiative. Public reaction would be crucial both to her success and for the institutionalization of a major policy-making role for presidential spouses if they desired one. Thus, in this section I examine public response to Hillary Rodham Clinton in that role and the public's assessment of her performance.

Since health care reform was a major priority of the Clinton administration, and given the complexity of altering the health care system, the president needed to generate a public focus on the issue immediately after taking office. He had to delegate responsibility to someone to spearhead the effort. A health care policy expert might be able to sort through the thorny policy problems that surrounded the issue, and a Washington political expert might deal best with mobilizing support within Washington—that is, getting the votes in Congress necessary for passage—but it was unlikely that policy and political expertise would be combined in the same person. According to news accounts, Clinton considered Vice President Al Gore for the job, but he turned it down; Senator Bill Bradley was also considered, but he felt it was an inappropriate role for him to assume.[45]

Clinton was reported to have been unhappy prior to the inauguration with what his advisers were saying about the possibilities of achieving the type of reform he desired. Thus, to push the reforms he wanted and to achieve the necessary national focus, he turned to his wife to lead the effort, as he had done as governor of Arkansas when implementing educational reforms.[46] Hillary Rodham Clinton was neither a health care policy expert nor a Washington insider, but her leadership signified that the issue was a presidential priority. The appointment won initial praise in editorials around the country.[47] But critics suggested the appointment was an error because the president would be unable to fire the first lady if she did not produce a successful plan; further, there would be no accountability for her actions.[48]

Pollsters quickly moved to gauge public opinion regarding the appointment. They asked whether the people felt it was appropriate to appoint Mrs.

Clinton to the position, what difference her appointment would make in reforming the health care system, and what kind of job she was doing. Polls showed early support. Approximately six of ten Americans approved, supported, or thought it was appropriate (depending on the question) for the president to name his wife head of the Health Care Task Force, whereas about three in ten opposed, disapproved, or thought the appointment was inappropriate.[49] The public also initially expressed confidence in the first lady's ability to handle the job. When she testified on the administration's health care plan before House and Senate committees at the end of September 1993, 60 percent of those surveyed in a Gallup poll approved of her handling of health care policy and 29 percent disapproved,[50] whereas a Harris poll showed 74 percent rating her as doing an excellent or a pretty good job.[51]

Gwen Ifill's special to the *New York Times* on September 22, 1993, ran with the headline "Role in Health Care Expands Hillary Clinton's Power." Ifill declared that

> Mrs. Clinton is solidifying her position as the power beside, rather than behind, the throne. In doing so, Mrs. Clinton has completed a remarkable public relations transformation, turning the personal qualities that were considered political liabilities in the Presidential campaign into political assets now. . . . No previous First Lady has occupied center stage so aggressively or disarmed her critics more effectively. And with each success, her role has been expanded far beyond that of previous Presidents' wives.[52]

By spring 1994, support for the job Hillary Rodham Clinton was doing regarding health care had plummeted; the plan had undergone numerous attacks, and White House attention had been diverted by the Whitewater affair and foreign policy problems in Haiti and Bosnia. In April, a Gallup poll showed approval of the job she was doing had dropped to only 47 percent, and an equal percentage expressed disapproval of the way she was handling health care policy.[53] In July 1994, Harris found a majority still gave the first lady high marks, with 54 percent saying she had been doing an excellent or a good job, but this represented a substantial drop from earlier findings.[54]

As the health care debate continued to be played out in the 103rd Congress (and ultimately ended in defeat for the Clintons), a majority (55 percent) still felt Hillary Rodham Clinton was helping to improve the nation's health care system, whereas 36 percent believed she was hurting efforts.[55] The public was also divided on whether putting her in charge had made health care reform more likely, had made reform less likely, or had made no difference—24 percent said she had made health care reform more likely, 35 percent said reform was less likely, and 38 percent said she had made no difference.[56]

In November 1994, CBS asked in a national poll, "Do you think having Hillary Clinton chair the health care reform commission was one of the reasons why Congress did not pass health care reform legislation last year, or don't you think so?" The public was split on assigning the first lady blame for this failure—43 percent responded her involvement was one of the reasons for the failure, whereas 49 percent said it was not one of the reasons.[57] Julia Malone reported in a Cox News Service release, "A majority, 56 percent, say First Ladies should not take on policy roles. But most don't blame Hillary Clinton's role for the administration's failure to get health reform through Congress."[58]

In November 1994, the White House announced that Hillary Rodham Clinton would no longer head the Health Care Task Force. The president's wife and her task force had created an enormously complex scheme to revamp the U.S. health care system. They had developed much of the plan in secret, although the first lady had traveled extensively around the country listening to U.S. citizens as she led the task force. Secrecy and complexity had worked against the Clintons' ability to sell the plan.

Had health care reform passed Congress, the first ladyship would have been transformed into an office in which the occupant could, with less cultural conflict, be considered a legitimate presidential policy adviser. Initial polls showed the administration did not have to battle public opinion for the first lady to be able to do her assigned job—the public supported her in this role and had confidence in her ability to do the job. Even in the end, the public did not seem overwhelmingly opposed to her efforts.

The failure to get a vote on the floor of either house of Congress and criticism of Hillary Rodham Clinton for the health care plan's demise make it very unlikely, however, that a first lady will be assigned a similar task in the near future. First ladies will be hesitant to play such a public policy advisory role and will likely revert to private, behind-the-scenes influence. They will see the risk of failure as great. The media would remind them of Hillary's failure if any flirted with the idea of becoming a public policy adviser.

Conclusion

When asked in polls, the public has preferred a more traditional role for the first lady (70 percent in a *U.S. News and World Report* January 1993 poll),[59] and only a minority supported the idea of Hillary Rodham Clinton sitting in on cabinet meetings when that possibility was discussed in the media prior to the inauguration (37 percent in favor, 58 percent opposed). But whereas a majority opposed her appointment to an official position in the Clinton administration (59 percent opposed, 32 percent in favor), a majority (63 percent) also believed Hillary Rodham Clinton had the knowledge and personal characteristics to be an adviser to her husband (24 percent said she was not qualified).[60]

In the first year of the Clinton administration, Hillary Rodham Clinton fairly successfully combined the traditional public hostess role and the public policy adviser role as far as popular opinion was concerned. Although the polls showed that the public preferred a more traditional role for the first lady, respondents did not oppose Mrs. Clinton's more substantive involvement when questions were posed in terms of both her and her activities. The polls indicated that Americans tended to be favorably impressed, as reflected in responses to questions about her Health Care Task Force position described earlier. By the end of the first year of the administration, journalists were describing her as a very popular first lady. This positive response is important to keep in mind as we assess the first ladyship in contemporary American politics.

The liberal feminist movement in the United States has been, among other things, about choice and individual achievement for women in gaining equality with men. Those who have been critical of limiting the first lady to the national hostess and first homemaker have focused on these concepts of choice and individualism in their revaluation of the first ladyship. Whereas liberal feminists would be more comfortable with Hillary Rodham Clinton running for office herself rather than being a political partner with her husband, they have argued that the first lady should be free to choose whatever role—or no role—she wants.

Hillary Rodham Clinton herself has articulated this position; in fact, it was a central theme of her meeting with several members of the press at the end of her trip to Latin America in October 1995. "First Ladies," she said, "are caught in an 'inevitable double bind,' attacked if they are too active and if they are not active enough." Her plea for her successors, she said, "is that they be allowed to work out any kind of conventional or unconventional role in a world where women's roles are changing." "A First Lady," she said, "should be allowed to be an activist or not do anything at all. . . . If you didn't want to do anything . . . this should be your choice."[61]

It is the activist in the White House as a quasi-staffer to the president that relates to the theme of this book. The issue I have been addressing is the first lady's participation in her husband's administration. This is a distinctive problem for the first ladyship because rather than seek independence from his work, which is what liberal feminism advocates, she uses her private relationship with the president to become a policymaker. Rather than separate the private and public roles, they become merged. But what if we seek to reconcile these two perspectives—the independence perspective of liberal feminism and the involvement-as-presidential-adviser perspective of some first ladies?

If it is accepted that every woman should choose what is best for her, why shouldn't the first lady be able to choose to be a political partner of and policymaking adviser to the president? Can the first lady have a legitimate claim to be a presidential adviser? Must a person necessarily be precluded from a policymaking role because of his or her personal relationship to the president? Many presidential advisers are in those roles because of long-standing personal relationships. Presidents need to have people they know and trust to help them. But with the first lady it is the gender issue steeped in sexuality because of her intimate connection to the president that makes it so difficult for observers to accept her as a presidential adviser.

The other issue often raised by journalists when the first lady serves as a presidential adviser is that of a lack of accountability. Maureen Dowd, for example, argued in an October 1995 *New York Times* editorial, in response to Hillary Rodham Clinton's remarks to the press during her Latin America trip quoted earlier, that "when she came to Washington, Mrs. Clinton appeared to willfully ignore the political dangers of assigning herself so much power with no accountability. . . . She thinks Americans fear the part-nership with her husband. What they really fear is a bargain that ignores accountability. It's not about being a woman. It's about not being elected."[62] Or note Meg Greenfield's much earlier comment regarding Rosalynn Carter's public policy advisory role: "Mrs. Carter, by her very seriousness of purpose, is inviting an end to this facade of deference. She is asking to be part of the political and governing process, and the answer to whether or not she *should* do that is this: only if she agrees to make herself accountable in the ordinary way."[63]

In advocating in favor of a role for a political wife in the public policy-making process, we must explore how the first lady can be held accountable. But we must also note that the issue of accountability has surrounded presi-dential staff in general since presidents have acted on the Brownlow Committee's charge that they needed help.[64] The issue is not unique to the first lady.

There is one distinction, however, for the first lady as a staff adviser. A major element of accountability in an institution is receiving a salary and being subject to firing for not performing the job according to the chief executive's wishes. The nation has chosen not to provide a salary for the spouse of the president for the performance of her overall duties as hostess plus adviser; further, because of the "Bobby Kennedy" law, she cannot be paid for any particular task she undertakes for the president.[65] No formal way of firing her exists, either. But she can be dismissed from a position, as Hillary Rodham Clinton essentially was from the Health Care Task Force.

A second means of holding an adviser accountable is by that person's being subject to being called before a congressional committee to explain positions and policy. First ladies have advocated for policies before such committees, but as with the president and his personal advisers, tradition-ally first ladies are not readily subject to being called before those committees.

Thus, this element of accountability is not present for the first lady or other high-level staffers. Congressional committees do hold oversight hearings, however, that affect personnel operations in the White House.

The first lady is held accountable in other ways, probably even more so than most presidential advisers. First, she is the person closest to the president; thus, her activities reflect the most directly on him and his presidency. Her performance will affect evaluation of the president more immediately than that of any other adviser; similarly, her incompetency, particularly given the gendered context in which it will be viewed, will harm the president politically to a greater degree than other administration blunders.

Second, the first lady's actions receive immense press scrutiny. She does little that is not publicized and analyzed in news stories, editorials, and nightly news commentary—far more than are the activities of many high-level members of the White House staff. This indirect form of accountability plays a major role in keeping the first lady accountable for her actions. If she advises only behind the scenes, within the facade of the hostess role, much less accountability exists because the press has greater difficulty reporting on her involvement than when she acts as a public adviser.[66]

Most agree that the presidency would be weakened institutionally if presidents could not choose their own advisers. Ultimately, it is presidents who are held accountable for the decisions of their administrations.

Notes

1. Edith Mayo. "The Influence and Power of First Ladies." *Chronicle of Higher Education,* September 15, 1993: A52.

2. Karen O'Connor, Bernadette Nye, and Laura van Assendelft. 1995. "Wives in the White House: Alternative Routes to Power." Paper presented at the Annual Meeting of the Midwest Political Science Association, Chicago, Illinois, p. 12.

3. See Edith Mayo and Denise Meringolo. 1994. *First Ladies: Political Role and Public Image.* Washington, D.C.: National Museum of American History.

4. Carl S. Anthony. 1991. *First Ladies: The Saga of the Presidents' Wives and Their Power, 1961–1990.* New York: William Morrow; and Betty Caroli. 1987. *First Ladies.* New York: Oxford University Press.

5. Anthony, *First Ladies,* and Caroli, *First Ladies,* trace its institutionalization to the Theodore Roosevelt administration.

6. Hugh Heclo and Lester Salamon. 1981. *The Illusion of Presidential Government.* Boulder, Colo.: Westview Press.

7. George Edwards and Stephen Wayne. 1985. *Presidential Leadership.* New York: St. Martin's Press.

8. The White House Clerk's Office provided the chart for the Bush administration.

9. For example, see Chapter 6 in George C. Edwards III and Stephen J. Wayne. 1994. *Presidential Leadership: Politics and Policymaking,* 3d ed. New York: St. Martin's Press.

10. Caroli, *First Ladies,* p. 218.

11. James Rosebush. 1987. *First Lady, Public Wife: A Behind-the-Scenes History of the Evolving Role of the First Ladies in American Life.* Lanham, Md.: University Press of America, p. 32.

12. This figure is for 1995. It represents a slight increase from the first two years of the administration.

13. Rosalynn Carter. 1984. *First Lady from Plains.* Boston: Houghton Mifflin, p. 168.

14. *Congressional Quarterly Almanac, 1978.* 1979. Washington, D.C.: Congressional Quarterly, p. 797.

15. Rosebush, *First Lady, Public Wife,* p. 32. It should not be ignored that this law was passed during Rosalynn Carter's activist first ladyship.

16. Sheryl McCarthy. "For Hillary, Cookie Days Are Over." *Newsday,* January 25, 1993, p. 13.

17. James M. Perry and Jeffrey H. Birnbaum. "'We' the President: Hillary Clinton Turns the First Lady Role into a Powerful Post." *Wall Street Journal,* January 28, 1993, sec. A.

18. See Barbara C. Burrell. 1994. *A Woman's Place Is in the House: Campaigning for Congress in the Feminist Era.* Ann Arbor: University of Michigan Press.

19. Anthony, *First Ladies,* p. 494.

20. Doris Kearns Goodwin. 1994. *No Ordinary Time: Franklin and Eleanor Roosevelt: The Home Front in World War II.* New York: Simon and Schuster.

21. Anthony, *First Ladies,* p. 197. Also Nan Robertson. "Mrs. Nixon Starts 8-Day Trip to Africa." *New York Times,* January 2, 1972, sec. A.

22. "African Queen for a Week." *Time,* January 17, 1972, pp. 12–14.

23. "Rosalynn's Turn at Diplomacy 'Family Style.'" *U.S. News and World Report,* June 6, 1977, p. 36.

24. Laura Foreman. "Mrs. Carter Leaves on Latin Tour Today." *New York Times,* May 30, 1977, sec. A.

25. Susanna McBee. "'Substantive' Talks Are Slated for Mrs. Carter on Latin Trip." *Washington Post,* May 25, 1977, sec. A.

26. Susanna McBee. "Mrs. Carter's Trip Carefully Crafted to Make Policy Points." *Washington Post,* May 29, 1977, sec. A.

27. Laura Foreman. "Mrs. Carter Home, Gets Husband's Seal of Approval." *New York Times,* June 13, 1977, sec. A.

28. Faye Lind Jensen. 1990. "An Awesome Responsibility: Rosalynn Carter as First Lady." *Presidential Studies Quarterly* 20: 770.

29. "Rosalynn Carter Elected." *New York Times,* June 8, 1977, sec. A.

30. "A First Lady's Global View." *Capital Times,* April 8, 1995, sec. A.

31. *The Capital Times* (Madison, Wis.), Sept. 5, 1995, p. 1.

32. Ann Devroy. "First Lady's Softer Focus Follows Drop in Popularity." *Washington Post,* October 15, 1995, sec. A.

33. "Overseas, Women See Hillary Clinton as Their Champion." *Arkansas Democrat Gazette,* September 10, 1995, sec. A.

34. Interview with Neil Lattimore, deputy press secretary to Hillary Clinton, by the author, 1995.

35. Mayo, "The Influence and Power of First Ladies."

36. Norma Ruth Holly Foreman. 1971. "The First Lady as a Leader of Public Opinion: A Study of the Role and Press Relations of Lady Bird Johnson." Ph.D. dissertation, University of Texas, Austin, p. 283.

37. Ibid.

38. Prior to this time, when first ladies and would-be first ladies appeared on

the campaign trail, they primarily stood at the candidate's side. Eleanor Roosevelt was something of an exception, breaking ground especially when she gave a speech at the 1940 Democratic National Convention urging delegates to support Franklin Roosevelt's choice for his vice-presidential running mate. Goodwin, *No Ordinary Time.*

39. Foreman, "The First Lady as a Leader of Public Opinion."

40. Lewis Gould. 1985. "Modern First Ladies in Historical Perspective." *Presidential Studies Quarterly* 15: 535.

41. Ibid.

42. Quoted in Caroli, *First Ladies,* p. 242.

43. Tom Morganthau. "The President's Partner." *Newsweek,* November 5, 1979, p. 36.

44. Gould, "Modern First Ladies in Historical Perspective," p. 536.

45. Bob Woodward. 1994. *The Agenda: Inside the Clinton White House.* New York: Simon and Schuster.

46. Hillary Rodham Clinton had played a similar role fairly successfully in Arkansas when she headed the governor's educational reform effort. Robert Pear. "Hillary Clinton Gets Policy Job and New Office." *New York Times,* January 22, 1993, sec. A; and Robert Rosenblatt and Edwin.Chen. "Clinton Seeks First Lady's Help on New Health Plan." *Los Angeles Times,* January 22, 1993, sec. A.

47. See "First Lady's First Job Is Vital." *Miami Herald,* January 26, 1993, sec. M; and "Hillary Clinton Goes to Work." *Hartford Courant,* January 24, 1993, sec. C.

48. Perry and Birnbaum, "'We' the President: Hillary Clinton Turns the First Lady Role into a Powerful Post."

49. For a summary of specific questions and their results, see Barbara C. Burrell. 1997. *Public Opinion, the First Ladyship and Hillary Clinton.* New York: Garland Press.

50. Public Opinion Online: Roper Center, University of Connecticut. Accession No. USGALLUP422014.Q03.

51. Public Opinion Online: Roper Center, University of Connecticut. Accession No. USHARRIS.101193.R5.

52. Gwen Ifill. "Role in Health Care Expands Hillary Clinton's Power." *New York Times,* September 22, 1993, sec. A.

53. Gallup Poll, Survey GO422045.

54. Public Opinion Online: Roper Center, University of Connecticut. Accession No. USHARRIS.082294.R04.

55. Public Opinion Online: Roper Center, University of Connecticut. Question ID: USABC.071894.R07G.

56. Public Opinion Online: Roper Center, University of Connecticut. Question ID: USCBSNYT.091294.R56.

57. Public Opinion Online: Roper Center, University of Connecticut. Accession No. 0225034, Question 036.

58. Julia Malone. "Hillary Clinton Is Pressured to Rethink Her Role." *Austin American Statesman,* November 30, 1994, sec. A.

59. Kenneth T. Walsh. "Now, the First Chief Advocate." *U.S. News and World Report,* January 5, 1993, pp. 46–50.

60. Michael Fusby. "A Large Role for Mrs. Clinton No Longer Troubles Most Americans." *Wall Street Journal,* December 15, 1992, sec. A.

61. Ann Devroy. "First Lady Denounces Her Critics." *Milwaukee Journal Sentinel,* October 10, 1995, sec. A.

62. Maureen Dowd. "Return to Gender." *New York Times,* October 19, 1995, sec. A.

63. Meg Greenfield. "Mrs. President." *Newsweek,* June 20, 1977, p. 100.

64. See, for example, John Hart. 1995. *The Presidential Branch: From Washington to Clinton,* 2d ed. Chatham, N.J.: Chatham House.

65. The Postal Revenue and Federal Salary Act of 1967, passed in response to President John F. Kennedy's appointment of his brother Bobby as attorney general, forbids a public official from appointing, employing, promoting, or advancing a relative in an agency in which he or she is serving or over which he or she exercises jurisdiction or control.

66. For example, Hillary Rodham Clinton's rumored involvement in the firing of the White House travel staff in 1993 was a throwback to the manipulating, behind-the-scenes, unaccountable role of first lady. It had nothing to do with her being a presidential policy adviser.

11

The Solicitor General and Gender: Litigating the President's Agenda and Serving the Supreme Court

Richard L. Pacelle, Jr.

In the past half century, the Supreme Court has thrust itself into the center of some of the most controversial issues in American politics—religion, busing, obscenity, affirmative action, and reproductive rights—thus belying its characterization as "the least dangerous branch of government."[1] Under checks and balances, however, the Court does not act in a vacuum; indeed, policymaking by the Court is inexorably connected to the other branches of government. The Court may be asked to interpret the actions of the legislative and executive branches. Court decisions may require congressional support or executive implementation, and they may provoke the ire of the other branches.

The executive and judicial branches in particular are closely linked as policymakers. The executive branch influences the judiciary in two direct ways. First, presidents nominate judges who translate cases into policy (see Chapter 9). Second, the president, with the consent of the Senate, selects the solicitor general (SG), the attorney who sets litigation priorities for the U.S. government.[2] In this chapter, I examine the role the executive has played through the solicitor general's office in constructing judicial doctrine in women's rights.[3] The linkages between the executive and judicial branches are important in understanding the evolution of women's rights policy.

The Relationship Between the Executive and the Judiciary

One of the most important connections between the executive and judicial branches is extraconstitutional. That nexus occurs through the Department of Justice, the cabinet department most proximate to the judiciary. Within the Justice Department, the solicitor general has the greatest ties to the federal courts. The solicitor general is a political appointee who is organizationally responsible to the attorney general.

In practical terms, however, the solicitor general has a level of independence from the Justice Department. The SG is responsible for deciding which of the government's cases should be appealed to the next level of the judiciary. Although this is a formidable power and gives the solicitor general a major voice in the construction of judicial policy, the impact of the office extends further. The SG often enters cases the government is not involved in through an amicus curiae brief, which is filed by a group that is not a party to the case but that may be affected by the outcome. Such briefs give the SG the opportunity to expand or contract issues in the case, provide expertise, and conduct an informal tally of public opinion.[4] This permits the SG to influence the structure of doctrine and advocate a position even though the government is not a party to the case.

The SG's office has thousands of cases it can appeal to the Court, but it screens petitions to bring only the most promising cases.[5] Over time, the solicitor general has earned a high degree of credibility with the justices. The Court grants a higher percentage of the SG's petitions than it grants for any other litigant, and the government is more successful on the merits than any other litigant (winning over two-thirds of its cases).[6] More significantly, the Court often adopts, sometimes verbatim, the arguments the solicitor general propounds in oral arguments and amici briefs. Given the excellence of its attorneys, its knowledge of the justices, and the sheer number of cases, the solicitor general's office has an unmatched opportunity to litigate strategically.[7]

The success of the solicitor general raises two questions. Is the solicitor general so persuasive that the office's arguments are adopted because of their excellence? Or does the expertise of the solicitor general lie in the ability to predict what the justices will consider acceptable and tailor arguments in that direction? The answer is a combination of the two factors.

The primary task of the SG is to represent the executive branch, yet the office also owes responsibility to the Supreme Court. The SG is a respected adviser and gatekeeper for the Court. Indeed, the solicitor general is often referred to as the "tenth justice of the Supreme Court" because of the office's proximity to and influence in the Court. To most solicitors general, the office's relationship with the Court is more important than winning individual cases.[8] That influence is particularly evident when justices turn to the SG for assistance on legal issues and ask the office to submit briefs stating the government's position.

In a handful of cases each term, the Court formally asks the SG to submit an amicus brief and argue a position. In those cases, the SG is acting not as an agent of the executive branch but as a legal adviser to the Supreme Court. In this capacity the solicitor general is less the "tenth justice" and more the "fifth clerk." Just as a justice's clerk would provide legal research without espousing policy views, the SG is expected to provide the Court with a legal analysis without advocating a policy position. The SG may also be responsible to Congress if the office has to defend legislation before the Court.

Given the competing demands on the solicitor general, the question is, who does the office serve—the president, the Court, Congress, or the public? Despite the fact that the SG is appointed by the president, the office must defend legislation and cultivate a relationship with the Court. Thus, to push the president's agenda too aggressively risks alienating the Court, which expects the SG to be the advocate of the people.

Some analysts contend that the office has become increasingly politicized in recent years. The charge has been leveled that Reagan's Solicitors General Rex Lee and Charles Fried attempted to pursue a conservative policy agenda through the federal courts when the administration's policies were blocked in Congress.[9] This attempt to use the Court to further a political agenda threatened the relationship between the SG's office and the Court. This situation is relevant for this chapter because some of the "agenda cases," the cases the solicitor general participated in to advance the administration's political goals,[10] directly involved issues that were central to women's rights—most notably attempts to limit affirmative action and to overturn *Roe v. Wade* (1973).

The Environment for the
Solicitor General in Women's Rights

The discretion of the solicitor general's office varies by the type of case. When the office voluntarily enters a case with an amicus brief, the solicitor general has the most discretion. These cases allow the office to follow the president's agenda. When the Court "invites" the SG to enter a case, the office's flexibility is constrained. In these cases, to use Drew Days's description, the Solicitor General acts as the fifth of the Chief Justice's four clerks.[11] The Solicitor General is thus an agent of the Court. The third category, cases in which the United States is a party, provides the SG with an intermediate level of discretion. In these cases, the SG may be required to support congressional policy. The SG has been involved in all three types of cases in women's rights litigation.[12]

The roles assumed by the solicitor general in gender discrimination and reproductive rights cases were a function of three factors: the evolution of reproductive rights and gender discrimination policy, the composition of the Supreme Court, and the agenda and structure of the solicitor general's office.

The Evolution of Gender Discrimination
and Reproductive Rights Policy

The solicitor general does not litigate in a vacuum. The office's activity is constrained by legislation, precedent, and judicial doctrine. The solicitor general may be obligated to defend legislation that conflicts with the administration's position. In addition, the solicitor general needs to attend to its institutional relationship with the Supreme Court.

Policy construction in the Supreme Court is done by analogy and is an evolutionary process. Newly emergent issues result from ancillary issues and are shaped by related precedents and existing interpretations of proximate constitutional provisions. Gender doctrine resulted from a legal analogy to race litigation under the Fourteenth Amendment. Yet, reliance on the race-based paradigm, which was also used by the solicitor general, could not capture the complexities of gender.[13] Most damaging from a women's rights perspective was the fact that the legal analogies that were the foundation for gender doctrine had been constructed by men.

Women's rights have been divided into two doctrinal streams. Gender discrimination was attacked under the Fourteenth Amendment, whereas reproductive rights were part of the privacy doctrine created by the Court in *Griswold v. Connecticut* (1965) from the shadows and penumbras cast by the First, Third, Fourth, Fifth, and Ninth Amendments.[14] The use of privacy as a basis for reproductive rights constrained the development of the issue. Many argued that reproductive rights would be on firmer ground if they were based on the Fourteenth Amendment.[15]

The separation of issues has hurt women's rights in two ways. First, by dividing the rights between two sets of constitutional provisions, the Court ensured that favorable precedents would not be mutually reinforcing. In other words, a favorable Fourteenth Amendment decision might have symbolic spillover effects for reproductive rights but would not directly contribute to the development of that doctrine. Expansive gender equality precedents could not prevent limitations from being placed on reproductive rights. Second, ultimately the Court retreated in each area. Although the Fourteenth Amendment is a strong vehicle for fighting discrimination, the Court refused to use strict scrutiny to ensure gender equality.[16] Similarly, the Court held that privacy was a fundamental right that triggered strict scrutiny, but reproductive rights have seldom been granted that level of protection. The separation of the constitutional bases of gender equality and reproductive rights allowed the SG to pursue the president's agenda in abortion cases without undermining gender discrimination doctrine and incurring the wrath of Congress.

Many of the gender discrimination cases were not argued or decided on constitutional grounds but involved interpretations of statutory provisions. The statutory basis for many gender cases is the Civil Rights Act of 1964, most notably Title VII, which prohibits employment discrimination. The Civil Rights Act of 1964 also created the Equal Employment Opportunity Commission (EEOC). In 1972 Congress amended Title VII and added Title IX, which prohibited sex discrimination in educational programs receiving federal funds.[17]

The solicitor general and the Court have been called upon to interpret these statutory provisions in a number of factual situations. Congress poses a shifting constraint on the other branches. In interpreting statutory intent, the solicitor general and the Court often need to respond to the current Congress rather than to the one that passed the legislation.[18] After all, it is the current Congress that can respond to a solicitor general's interpretation or to a Court decision that is too narrow or too broad. Indeed, Congress has passed legislation that strengthens civil rights provisions in response to a number of Court decisions it opposed.

Composition of the Supreme Court

The shape of gender and reproductive rights policies is a function of the composition of the Supreme Court. The ideological and doctrinal predilections of the justices provide a context for groups that use the judiciary. The strategies, tactics, and issue analogies used by the solicitor general and groups that litigate women's rights issues have been shaped in part by the composition of the Supreme Court.[19] The solicitor general's agenda must be practical. The office cannot push cases or arguments that are out of line with the ideological tenor of the Court.

Over the past two decades, changes in the composition of the Supreme Court have created an increasingly negative environment for gender discrimination and reproductive rights cases.[20] Of the Republican appointments since the Court began to protect gender and reproductive rights, only Justice Stevens has supported civil liberties and civil rights in more than half the cases he has decided.[21] Conservative appointments appeared to create a critical mass that had the votes to dismantle the precedents that had expanded civil rights. Yet, as the Court became more conservative and the cases became more difficult, judicial support for gender equality did not decline.[22] At the same time, reproductive rights were sharply curtailed.

Appointments to the Solicitor General's Office

One means for the executive to influence the Court is to initiate changes through the solicitor general's office. The president selects the solicitor general and the top deputies, who set the office's legal and policy priorities. But the office has an institutional memory. Some attorneys remain through changes in administration and can affect the ability of political appointees to achieve their goals.

The relationship between the political appointees and the staff attorneys has been noteworthy in gender discrimination and reproductive rights. For decades, the solicitor general's office supported a broad view of civil rights. Indeed, the Eisenhower, Nixon, and Ford solicitors general pushed cases and policies that were more liberal than the stated priorities of their administrations.[23] That was a function of pragmatic solicitors general recognizing what was possible before a Court that was more liberal than the president. The civil rights decisions created supportive precedents that later solicitors general tried to limit or undermine. This situation caused problems for the staff attorneys in the office who had helped to establish and buttress those precedents.

Over time, changes in the priorities of the SG's office did not augur well for women's rights. The agenda cases for the Reagan administration focused on reproductive rights. The Justice Department tried to reassign some staff attorneys because of a fear that they would undermine the SG's agenda. During the Reagan administration, when charges that the solicitor general had become politicized surfaced, a number of attorneys—some of them women—left the office.[24] This exodus occurred in part as a result of attempts to overturn *Roe v. Wade.*

The Solicitor General and Women's Rights Policy

To evaluate the work of the solicitor general, I examined the gender discrimination and reproductive rights cases decided since 1971. A number of other issues concern women's rights, such as obscenity, but they are beyond the scope of this chapter. My primary concern is with those cases the solicitor general argued because the government was a party, was asked to enter, or voluntarily joined with an amicus brief.[25] I examine the position taken by the solicitor general and the Supreme Court's response.

Like the Court, the solicitor general operated differently in two of the realms that comprise women's rights litigation: gender discrimination and reproductive rights. Although the office often adhered to gender equality precedents, the solicitor general went to extremes to limit and overturn *Roe v. Wade.* In gender discrimination, the office sought to narrow issues by avoiding the constitutional provisions and confining cases to statutory grounds. The SG took the opposite approach in reproductive rights cases, seeking to expand the cases by raising constitutional issues.

I coded decisions that favored reproductive rights and ended programs that discriminated against women as pro–women's rights (liberal). I coded support for benign programs based on stereotypes as opposed to gender equality (conservative).[26] I divide analysis here between gender discrimination and reproductive rights to reflect differences in both their constitutional foundations and treatment by the solicitor general and the Supreme Court.

The Solicitor General and Gender Discrimination

The positions and arguments of the solicitor general in gender issues varied on three dimensions. First, there was variation by president and policy goals as the SG's office became more conservative. Second, as issues evolved from the first cases that involved overt discrimination to the more difficult second-generation cases that involved compensatory programs, the solicitor general had to make different arguments. Finally, the position advocated by the SG's office varied according to the different categories of cases: whether the office argued the case directly because the government was a party, was asked by the Court to participate, or voluntarily filed an amicus brief.

Table 11.1 shows how often the individual solicitors general supported and opposed women's rights in gender discrimination cases, and Table 11.2 shows their success before the Court. The tables show variation among types of cases in evaluating the SG's activities in cases in which the United States was a party, cases in which participation of the solicitor general was requested, and voluntary amici cases. The variation across these types of cases seems most interesting because it is tied to the issue of who the office serves and the relative influence of the SG in the gender cases.

Table 11.1   Positions Adopted by Solicitors General in Gender Discrimination Cases, by Type of Involvement in Case

	Direct[a]		Request[b]		Amici[c]	
	Pro[d]	Con[e]	Pro	Con	Pro	Con
Griswold (1967–1973)	0	1	0	0	1	0
Bork (1973–1977)	1	6	1	0	3	0
McCree (1977–1981)	1	3	3	0	3	2
Lee (1981–1985)	4	2	3	1	0	2
Fried (1985–1989)	0	1	1	1	0	4
Starr (1989–1993)	1	0	0	1	1	0
Days (1993–1996)	1	0	0	0	1	0

Notes: a. Cases in which the U.S. government is a direct party. b. Cases in which the solicitor general is asked to participate by the Court. c. Cases in which the solicitor general voluntarily files an amicus curiae brief. d. In favor of women's rights in the case. e. Opposing women's rights in the case.

Table 11.2   Success of Solicitors General in Gender Discrimination Cases, by Type of Involvement in Case

	Direct[a]		Request[b]		Amici[c]	
	Won[d]	Lost[e]	Won	Lost	Won	Lost
Griswold (1967–1973)	0	1	0	0	1	0
Bork (1973–1977)	5	2	0	1	2	1
McCree (1977–1981)	2	2	2	1	5	0
Lee (1981–1985)	4	2	4	0	2	0
Fried (1985–1989)	0	1	0	2	1	3
Starr (1989–1993)	1	0	0	1	1	0
Days (1993–1996)	1	0	0	0	1	0

Notes: a. Cases in which the U.S. government is a direct party. b. Cases in which the solicitor general is asked to participate by the Court. c. Cases in which the solicitor general voluntarily files an amicus curiae brief. d. The Court decided in favor of the party the solicitor general supported. e. The Court decided in favor of the party the solicitor general opposed.

Arguing for Congressional and Administrative Policies: Government as Party. In cases in which the government is a party, the SG may be obligated to argue for legislation or administrative policies that are antithetical to the president's agenda or the office's priorities. This category has been especially important for women's rights litigation. First, many cases involved statutory interpretation. Second, the priorities of the executive and legislative branches have occasionally been at odds, which puts the SG in a difficult position. The Reagan and Bush administrations, for example, were not interested in pushing the frontiers of gender equality. Congress, on the other hand, when controlled by Democrats, has supported women's rights.

Table 11.3 represents a summary of positions taken in gender discrimination cases that involved the government as a party and the frequency with which the solicitor general won. In these cases, the SG supported gender equality only 41 percent of the time (nine of twenty-two cases), many in EEOC cases. Many of the SG's arguments supported benign classifications designed to help women. The Court agreed with the solicitor general 64 percent of the time (fourteen of twenty-two cases), which is about the SG's average rate of success.

Table 11.3   Solicitor General Direct Participation and Supreme Court Reaction in Gender Discrimination Cases

Supreme Court Position	Solicitor General Position		Total
	Liberal[a]	Conservative[b]	
Liberal[a]	7	6	13
Conservative[b]	2	7	9
Total	9	13	22

Notes: a. In favor of women's rights. b. Opposing women's rights.

The solicitor general's influence in these cases was not dramatic. The office was often constrained by the policies of Congress in arguing the cases. But one should not dismiss the impact of the SG, whose arguments shaped doctrine and precedent. Indeed, the SG helped to establish the standards used to evaluate gender-based classifications.

In *Frontiero v. Richardson* (1973), Nixon's Solicitor General Erwin Griswold was obligated to support congressional and military policies regarding differential benefits for servicemen and servicewomen. Griswold helped to structure the Court's consideration of the underlying standard, arguing that the Court should uphold the provision and adopt a low level of scrutiny. He urged the justices to wait for the outcome of the Equal Rights Amendment (ERA). The Court rejected the existing policy but agreed to defer consideration of an overriding standard. The Court ultimately decided on the middle-level standard in *Craig v. Boren* (1976).

In general, the solicitor general has urged judicial deference to the elected branches and avoided constitutional grounds, even when the other party in the case attempted to expand the issue. If most of the cases did not create landmark decisions, they did help to structure and shape the evolving doctrine.

The solicitor general has often argued on behalf of benign classifications established by Congress to help women. The Court has often accepted the arguments of the chief advocate, which has created harmful precedents for women's groups. Many of the challenged policies designed to overcome past discrimination were rooted in stereotypic views and paternalistic attitudes toward women.[27] In its brief in *Craig v. Boren,* the American Civil Liberties Union (ACLU) argued that seemingly benign classifications are part of a cultural message that distinguishes men from women. The harm of such stereotypes and the malevolent effects of benign classifications have never been captured adequately in the arguments of the SG, decisions of the Court, or traditional equal protection analysis.[28]

Two cases were noteworthy. In *Rostker v. Goldberg* (1981), Carter Solicitor General Wade McCree defended the male-only military draft from charges of sex discrimination. The Court adopted his argument, urging deference to the elected branches and the military. The other case, *Grove City College v. Bell* (1984), was significant because the Court ignored congressional intent and the arguments of Reagan Solicitor General Rex Lee and narrowed the interpretation of Title IX. The SG's office argued for a position that was antithetical to the administration and lost anyway. The majority ruled that individual units within the college could discriminate without threatening federal aid received by other departments. The effect was to weaken sanctions against gender discrimination.

In the wake of *Grove City,* Congress sought to restore teeth to Title IX. For two years, Senate opponents filibustered the Civil Rights Restoration Act. In 1987 the act passed Congress but was vetoed by President Reagan. Both houses of Congress were able to muster the votes to override the veto and overrule the *Grove City* case, thus restoring the intended force of Title IX.[29]

Request for Intervention.   These cases involve requests by the Court to the SG to file a brief in a case the government would not otherwise have entered. In some of the cases, the Court takes the extraordinary step of allotting time for the solicitor general to argue a position, even though the government is not a party. These cases are the most difficult for the SG for two reasons. First, the request for a legal argument asks the SG to balance the administration's position with an analysis of law and precedent. This is closer to the original intent of the amicus brief, which was a legal analysis by a neutral party.[30] Second, the Court requests a legal argument because these cases present difficult second-generation questions that do not have clear relevant precedents. Thus, as the "fifth clerk," the SG is asked to survey the legal terrain and help the Court fill the gap.

Table 11.4 shows a summary of the positions argued by the solicitors general when the office was asked to participate in gender discrimination cases, as well as the Supreme Court's treatment of those cases. The solicitors general were asked to join eleven gender discrimination cases. In eight of those cases, the SG answered the Court's request by filing briefs in favor of women's rights (the Court agreed with five). Overall, the Court agreed with the solicitor general in six of the eleven cases it asked the office to enter, a low rate of success. This is understandable because these cases tend to raise uncertain second-generation questions that confuse both the Court and the solicitor general.

Table 11.4   Solicitor General Behavior When Participation Was Requested and Supreme Court Reaction in Gender Discrimination Cases

Supreme Court Position	Solicitor General Position		Total
	Liberal[a]	Conservative[b]	
Liberal[a]	5	2	7
Conservative[b]	3	1	4
Total	8	3	11

Notes: a. In favor of women's rights. b. Opposing women's rights.

The impact of the cases tended to be far-reaching. The major cases involved pregnancy and Titles VII and IX. The influence of the solicitor general on the outcome was less clear. Five of the six cases in which the Court and the SG agreed were relatively minor.

One of the first of these requests for SG intervention was *General Electric v. Gilbert* (1976), a Title VII case involving a denial of disability benefits for pregnant women. In *Gilbert,* the Court asked Ford's Solicitor General Robert Bork to submit an amicus brief and argue the administration's position on providing disability benefits for pregnancy. His brief, which argued that such benefits should cover pregnancy, was considered weak and hurt the case, thus structuring the long-term construction of doctrine.[31]

The Court justified its decision in *Gilbert* on the grounds that pregnancy was a special disability. The Court held that the policies created a distinction between pregnant and nonpregnant people rather than a gender-based distinction. Even more problematic, the decision created an adverse precedent that might spill over to other gender cases. Congress expressed disapproval of the decision and amended Title VII with the Pregnancy Discrimination Act, which expanded the definition of sex discrimination to cover pregnant workers. The act protected pregnant workers but did not remove the negative precedent.[32]

In *Hishon v. King and Spalding* (1984) and *Anderson v. City of Bessemer* (1985), Solicitor General Lee was asked to formulate a legal position on the use of Title VII to challenge alleged discrimination in hirings and firings. In each case, Lee argued a position that was not entirely compatible with the policies of the Reagan administration but was more closely aligned with congressional designs. In both cases, the Court adopted an expansive view of Title VII. When the Court requests the intervention of the SG, it seeks a legal argument rather than a policy position, and Lee fulfilled that stipulation in these two cases.

In the most important of these cases, the Supreme Court requested that Reagan Solicitor General Charles Fried intervene in *Johnson v. Transportation Agency, Santa Clara County* (1987), an affirmative action case. Opposition to affirmative action was a central component of the Reagan administration's agenda cases. But the Court was seeking a legal analysis rather than a policy position. Fried was not pleased with the request, claiming the case had terrible facts for the government to overcome (the promoted employee in the case was the first woman to hold such a position, the program was voluntary, and she was very qualified).[33] Fried would have preferred a case involving mandatory affirmative action in which a less qualified woman was promoted over a man, which would have allowed the SG to make a legal argument against affirmative action that was consistent with the administration's policies. Fried claimed the Justice Department looked for ways to make the case "go away."[34] He argued against the affirmative action program because there was no evidence of past discrimination. The Court rejected his position, thereby upholding the affirmative action program.

In a number of cases argued by Fried and Kenneth Starr, Bush's solicitors general, the office took a position that the Court deemed more policy oriented than legal. The Court's response was to repudiate the solicitor general.

The Solicitor General as Amici.   Because the SG has discretion in cases the office voluntarily enters through an amicus brief, these cases are arguably the most important. The issues before the Court are structured by others, but the solicitor general seeks to expand the issue beyond the parties in the case. The role of the solicitor general and the questions regarding which masters the office serves are sharply brought into focus in the sex discrimination cases the SG voluntarily joined as amici. Table 11.5 shows that in the aggregate, the solicitor general had the most success with these briefs. This is not surprising, given that the solicitor general acts strategically and is not

Table 11.5   Solicitor General Amicus Behavior and Supreme Court Reaction in Gender Discrimination Cases

Supreme Court Position	Solicitor General Position		
	Liberal[a]	Conservative[b]	Total
Liberal[a]	7	3	10
Conservative[b]	1	5	6
Total	8	8	16

Notes: a. In favor of women's rights. b. Opposing women's rights.

likely to file an amicus brief and risk an adverse precedent in cases the office considers questionable. Indeed, the Court agreed with the solicitor general in twelve of the sixteen cases in this category.

The voluntary amici filed in gender discrimination cases were evenly divided: eight in favor of women's rights and eight opposed. The Court agreed with the solicitor general in seven of the eight cases filed in favor of women's rights and in five of the eight briefs that opposed the women's rights position. What the table does not show is that the positions taken by the solicitor general became progressively more conservative over time.

A number of possible explanations might account for the reason the SG's position has become more conservative. Certainly, one could point to the identity of the president, but that is only a partial answer. Wade McCree, Carter's solicitor general, took the conservative side more often than Robert Bork, a Nixon appointee. Rex Lee and Charles Fried, Reagan's solicitors general, were responsible for most of the conservative amici briefs.

Alternatively, issue evolution could be responsible for the changes.[35] Simple cases arise first, leading the SG to a relatively easy position that favors women's rights. As second-generation cases become more difficult, classifications become less obvious, and support for women's rights in the solicitor general's briefs would be expected to decline. The easy cases that involve discrimination against women gave way to benign classifications that favor women and affirmative action programs.

Another possible explanation is the SG's need to be pragmatic. The amici positions urged by the solicitor general have tended to parallel the increased conservatism of the Court. Perhaps the SG was responding to the ideological direction of the Court. The ultimate answer is probably a combination of these three factors.

Although Solicitor General McCree filed three voluntary amici in favor of women's rights and was on the winning side in all of those cases, his contribution to gender issues is best remembered for the two amici he filed against gender equality. The Court agreed with McCree in both cases. The two cases, *Personnel Administrator of Massachusetts v. Feeney* (1979) and *Michael M v. Sonoma County Court* (1981), had multidimensional components that led the solicitor general to downplay the discrimination issue in favor of the competing interests.

In *Feeney,* the Court upheld a Massachusetts law that provided employment preference for Vietnam veterans. The law had the effect of discriminating against women because the vast majority of veterans were males. McCree argued that the statute discriminated between veterans and nonveterans, not between men and women. The Court had used similar reasoning about distinctions between pregnant and nonpregnant people (rather than women and men) in *Gilbert.*

The *Michael M* case involved a statutory rape provision that imposed criminal sanctions on males who had intercourse with underage females but did not punish females who had sexual relations with underage males. The SG argued that differential treatment was justified by biological differences between men and women. McCree's brief and the Court's opinion assumed that the "harmful consequences of pregnancy are 'by nature' only visited upon women."[36] Upholding the distinction tended to reinforce stereotypes of male aggressiveness and female vulnerability. The latter provided support for policies and Court decisions that perpetuated harmful stereotypes and were in accord with the motivations of protective legislation. As Deborah Rohde has argued: "The stereotypes underpinning such exemptions are not easily confined. Assumptions about females' physical incapacities and maternal responsibilities spill over to other areas of social life and reinforce traditional expectations about gender roles and hierarchies."[37]

Reagan's first solicitor general, Rex Lee, neither argued nor filed amici in any significant gender discrimination cases. During his tenure, gender discrimination cases were not percolating through the courts.[38] Lee did begin the administration's attack on affirmative action in race cases. Clearly, spillover effects from restrictive precedents reached gender cases later. Lee also began the assault on *Roe* that defined the Reagan agenda cases. Reportedly, Lee resigned because of increasing attempts by Attorney General Meese to politicize the SG's office, which Lee feared would damage the relationship between the solicitor general and the Court.[39]

Meritor Savings Bank v. Vinson (1986) was not part of the Reagan agenda cases, but attorneys from the Justice Department thought it was important enough to advance to the attention of the solicitor general. The case involved a bank employee who was sexually harassed by her boss. Fried argued for a narrow interpretation of sexual harassment, which the Court, in a unanimous opinion, firmly rejected.[40] In general, Fried was remarkably unsuccessful in the gender discrimination cases and was on the losing side in three of the four cases he entered. More than in other areas, Fried seemed out of step with the Court in these cases.

Bush's solicitor general, Kenneth Starr, filed only one amicus brief in gender discrimination cases. *United Automobile Workers v. Johnson Controls* (1991) presented the SG with a difficult balancing task.[41] Johnson Controls had a fetal protection policy that banned all women, except those who could prove infertility, from jobs that involved exposure to lead, which was at higher than safe levels. The administration opposed abortion and considered whether to support the policy for its protection of the unborn. Ultimately, Starr argued that the policy was discriminatory because it did not consider the effects on men exposed to lead, perhaps assuming the Court leaned in that direction. The Court, sensitive to the difficulty of balancing the rights of the unborn with those of the workers, adopted Starr's analysis.[42]

President Clinton's solicitor general, Drew Days III, has entered two gender discrimination cases as an amicus. *Harris v. Forklift Systems* (1993) raised the issue of whether Title VII required that a female employee must prove psychological damage to demonstrate an abusive work environment. Days argued that the employee was not required to prove harmful effects to her psychological well-being or clear injury to demonstrate sexual harassment. There were concerns that the justices would undermine the *Meritor* precedent. Instead, the Court unanimously agreed with the solicitor general's analysis, thus extending *Meritor.*

At the end of the 1995 term, the Supreme Court announced its decision in *United States v. Commonwealth of Virginia,* ruling that the Virginia Military Institute must admit qualified women or forfeit state funding. The Court viewed the effort to establish a military program at a nearby women's college as failing to provide equal educational opportunities for women. More notable than the ruling, however, was Solicitor General Drew Days's argument that the Court should use this case to establish the strict scrutiny test in regard to gender discrimination. Days's recommendations were rejected by the Court, its ruling in favor of the government notwithstanding, causing the implications of this case to still be debated by legal scholars.

Filing a voluntary amicus provides the SG with the chance to pursue the administration's goals. Although solicitors general have exploited these opportunities in abortion cases, they have been less inclined to use them in gender discrimination cases. First, gender discrimination cases have not been priorities on the office's agenda. Second, few constitutional issues have been percolating through the courts to use as vehicles for pursuing policy goals.[43] Third, although the Court has become more conservative, it has not systematically attempted to dismantle existing precedents. Finally, solicitors general have been concurrently attacking affirmative action and reproductive rights, cases that had consequences for women.

The Solicitor General and Reproductive Rights Doctrine

The reproductive rights cases provide a contrast to the gender discrimination cases. Because the solicitor general became involved in few of these cases,

I examine virtually all of them. The solicitor general's position in reproductive rights cases has been significantly different from the office's activities in gender discrimination cases. Initially, the solicitor general's office only became involved in reproductive rights cases at the Court's request. During the Reagan administration, the solicitors general took the offensive in seeking to overturn *Roe v. Wade.*

At the Court's request, Solicitor General Bork addressed questions of whether states could restrict funding under Medicaid guidelines in a trilogy of 1977 cases—*Beal v. Doe, Maher v. Roe,* and *Poelker v. Doe.* Bork argued: "The fact that a woman has a qualified right to an abortion does not imply a correlative constitutional right to free treatment."[44] Bork's argument was echoed in the opinion. Bork attacked the trappings of reproductive rights rather than the right itself, but his position was important in helping the Court retreat from *Roe.* The decision set a precedent for *Harris v. McRae* (1980).

In *Harris v. McRae* Solicitor General McCree argued for the government to uphold the Hyde Amendment, which prohibited use of Medicaid funds for abortion. Representative Henry Hyde and a right-to-life group Americans United for Life (AUL) did not trust the Carter administration to argue persuasively for the law, so they intervened and submitted an amicus. Indeed, the AUL brief was more thorough than McCree's and raised additional arguments in support of the law.[45] The Court upheld its constitutionality. When law and policy collide, as in the early abortion cases, the solicitor general's brief is often less than compelling.

The Reagan solicitors general took a more aggressive tack, voluntarily entering cases to further an agenda. In *City of Akron v. Akron Reproductive Health Services* (1983), the government became directly involved for the first time in abortion litigation that did not involve a funding issue. Solicitor General Lee filed an amicus brief and asked for time to argue orally as well. Although some members of the administration wanted him to attack *Roe,* Lee did not take the extreme path. Rather, he argued that since *Planned Parenthood of Central Missouri v. Danforth* (1976), the Court had been allowing exceptions to *Roe.* The Court permitted restrictions unless they unduly burdened the right to an abortion. Lee argued that in determining whether a regulation was unduly burdensome, justices should defer to the judgment of the state legislatures. Even though he did not ask the Court to overturn *Roe,* his solution would have had that effect.

In response, the Court gave pro-choice groups their strongest victory since *Roe.* The decision was considered an embarrassment for the Reagan administration, but Lee did not view it as a complete loss. Indeed, Justices O'Connor, White, and Rehnquist adopted some of the points made by Lee. In particular, O'Connor began to advocate Lee's undue burden argument.[46]

In *Thornburgh v. American College of Obstetricians and Gynecologists* (1986), the SG asked the Court to overturn *Roe* directly. During the genesis of the case, Lee left the solicitor general's office. It is unclear whether he resigned or was fired, but apparently Lee did not want to go through with the case. Charles Fried was named acting solicitor general, an unusual appointment. According to some accounts, Attorney General Meese would remove the "acting" title only after Fried filed an amicus in *Thornburgh* requesting that the Court overturn *Roe*. This was widely viewed as compromising the independence of the solicitor general's office.

In his brief, Fried abandoned the undue burden standard, claiming *Roe* violated the intent of the framers of the Constitution.[47] Fried requested time to argue the government's position, but Pennsylvania refused to share its time and the Court denied his request. The Court's decision, a stinging rebuke of Fried's position, emphatically upheld *Roe*. In dissent, White and Rehnquist agreed with Fried that *Roe* should be overturned. O'Connor refused to go that far. She returned to the undue burden standard but went further, noting problems caused by *Roe*.

Fried admitted having raised rationales to give allies on the Court ammunition to insert new arguments into the debate and to create a foundation for future cases.[48] Fried announced that he would not make a "pest" of himself before the Court by pressing the abortion issue again, thus hoping to avoid damaging the relationship between the SG's office and the Supreme Court.[49]

But Fried filed an amicus brief for the government in *Webster v. Reproductive Health Services* (1989), again urging the Court to reconsider *Roe*. Fried was not solicitor general at the time, but the Bush administration requested that he argue the case. Reportedly, no one in the new administration wanted to deal with the case. Fried argued that *Roe* could be safely excised like a "single thread" without tearing at the fabric of law that had been constructed from privacy and abortion precedents. The Court upheld state regulations but failed to overturn *Roe*.[50]

Solicitor General Starr had his first chance to intervene with an amicus brief in *Hodgson v. Minnesota* (1990), a parental consent case. Although it was not relevant to the case, Starr took the unusual step of urging the justices to go beyond the question of the constitutionality of parental consent to the core issue of abortion itself, thus attacking the right itself rather than its trappings. The Court declined the invitation, although it upheld the parental consent provisions.

In *Planned Parenthood of Southeastern Pennsylvania v. Casey* (1992), Starr filed an amicus to argue that the undue burden standard did not provide a meaningful guide for assessing the weight of competing interests. Starr pressed the argument that *Roe* had been wrongly decided and should be overturned. If the Court would not go that far, Starr felt the Court should clarify the standard of review for abortion regulations and make clear that the liberty interest did not rise to the level of a fundamental right, thereby triggering strict scrutiny.[51]

With the retirements of Justices Brennan and Marshall, there appeared to be enough votes to overturn *Roe.* Yet, the Court did not provide the result Reagan and Bush solicitors general had been seeking. A majority refused to overturn *Roe,* but the Court did allow state regulations and lowered the standard of protection for reproductive rights.

Abortion was clearly one of the agenda issues for the Reagan solicitors general. Unable to reverse *Roe,* the solicitors general attacked reproductive rights both directly and indirectly.[52] The solicitor general's office clearly damaged reproductive rights. Bork began the process of limiting *Roe.* Lee and Fried attempted to expedite that process, but their impact may have been counterproductive. Their open attempts to overturn *Roe* may have done more harm than good to their cause. Their briefs armed opponents of reproductive rights with resolve but may have cost the administration the votes of supposedly conservative justices like O'Connor, Kennedy, and Souter.[53]

Conclusion

In the area of reproductive rights, it is not difficult to answer the question of whose interest the solicitor general has served. In the funding cases, the solicitors general appeared to be serving the interests of Congress and the Court by providing the justices with arguments about second-generation abortion-related questions. But when the direct attacks on *Roe* began, Lee and Fried were clearly serving the administration's goals and pursuing its policy agenda cases.

In the gender discrimination cases, the solicitor general's impact was less certain. The Court, with the blessing of the SG, proceeded slowly in early gender discrimination cases in hopes that the passage of the ERA (which had appeared likely) would settle the question of the appropriate level of review. The lack of constitutional grounds in many cases limited the progress in some ways but may have been prudent in view of the Court's increasing conservatism. The SG's success is in part a function of bringing appropriate cases, given the temper of the Court. The solicitor general's position on the compensatory policy cases and the briefs on pregnancy introduced doctrinal obstacles to gender equality.

Some of these problems were a function of the SG's need to serve many masters. At times, the solicitor general's office needed to follow congressional dictates, in other cases the president's agenda dominated, and in a few cases the need to help justices formulate coherent standards made the Court the primary constituency. This situation created inconsistencies for the solicitors general in arguing cases and exacted costs in issue development and doctrinal equilibrium.

These problems were particularly acute for the Reagan solicitors general, and the inconsistencies were evident in their approach to the different types of participation. When they argued on behalf of the government after the Democrats had regained control of the Senate, Lee and Fried often had to argue for broader definitions of gender discrimination than the administration supported. When the Court requested his involvement, Lee made efforts to provide a legal brief, even though the position often contradicted the administration's policy position. Left to their own devices, however, Lee and Fried voluntarily entered cases with conservative amici briefs to further the stated positions of the Reagan administration. This apparent working at cross purposes created confusion in the office and took a toll on doctrinal consistency.

Increasingly, the SG did not play a central role in gender discrimination cases, in part as a function of the issues presented. The solicitor general typically wants to enter cases in which major political issues are litigated. Gender discrimination cases have been increasingly limited in scope and involve statutory interpretation. The office is more interested in cases that make a significant contribution by presenting a new approach. Most gender discrimination cases have not provided such opportunities.

Interestingly, during the Reagan administration the SG's office did little directly to short-circuit gender discrimination doctrine. Instead, attempts were made to undermine gender doctrine by attacking equal protection in other areas. The office presided over the narrowing of Fourteenth Amendment protections for race. Solicitors General Lee and Fried had success attacking affirmative action by using race cases as the basis. These precedents may be transplanted at some future time to limit or reverse the gains made by women's rights advocates.[54]

Even as the Court became more conservative, the SG pushed arguments that reinforced gender equality. Part of the reluctance to restrict gender equality may have resulted from a wariness in Congress. The solicitor general and the Court may have been aggressive in broadly interpreting Title VII because they feared congressional reaction. Indeed, following the Civil Rights Restoration Act, the Court responded with "feminist extensions of civil rights statutes."[55] Although there is a focus on the executive branch and its priorities and the ideological composition of the Court, analysts also need to consider Congress and its willingness to become involved in the issue. With the 1992 and 1994 elections, the presidency, the solicitor general, and Congress have undergone significant changes. The Court has also changed somewhat. These changes could alter the evolution of women's rights.

Notes

1. Alexander Hamilton referred to the judiciary as the least dangerous branch in *Federalist 78.*

2. Robert Scigliano. 1971. *The Supreme Court and the Presidency.* New York: Free Press, p. vii.

3. For a previous study of the solicitor general and gender issues, see Jeffrey Segal and Cheryl Reedy. 1988. "The Supreme Court and Sex Discrimination: The Role of the Solicitor General." *Western Political Quarterly* 41: 553–568.

4. Richard Pacelle. 1991. *The Transformation of the Supreme Court's Agenda: From the New Deal to the Reagan Administration.* Boulder, Colo.: Westview Press, p. 31.

5. Rebecca Salokar. 1992. *The Solicitor General: The Politics of Law.* Philadelphia: Temple University Press.

6. Jeffrey Segal. 1988. "*Amicus Curiae* Briefs by the Solicitor General During the Warren and Burger Courts: A Research Note." *Western Political Quarterly* 41: 135–144.

7. Kevin T. McGuire. 1993. *The Supreme Court Bar: Legal Elites in the Washington Community.* Charlottesville: University Press of Virginia.

8. Karen O'Connor. 1983. "The *Amicus Curiae* Role of the U.S. Solicitor General in Supreme Court Litigation." *Judicature* 66: 260.

9. Lincoln Caplan. 1987. *The Tenth Justice: The Solicitor General and the Rule of the Law.* New York: Vintage Books.

10. Salokar, *The Solicitor General: The Politics of Law,* p. 76.

11. This analogy was drawn by Solicitor General Drew Days III during an address at the St. Louis University School of Law, 1995.

12. In this chapter I use the term *gender discrimination* to refer specifically to equal protection cases involving women. The term *reproductive rights* refers specifically to abortion cases. I use the term *women's rights* inclusively to refer to both gender discrimination and reproductive rights cases.

13. Deborah Rohde. 1991. *Justice and Gender: Sex Discrimination and the Law.* Cambridge, Mass.: Harvard University Press, p. 90.

14. Justice Douglas's opinion found privacy at the intersection of amendments. Freedom of association from the First Amendment, prohibitions against the forcible quartering of troops in the Third Amendment, the Fourth Amendment rights to be free from unwarranted searches, and due process guarantees of the Fifth Amendment cast shadows that suggest a right to privacy. Douglas also adopted the Planned Parenthood argument for the inclusion of the Ninth Amendment, which states that the enumeration of some rights does not foreclose the exercise of others. Thomas Emerson. 1965. "Nine Justices in Search of a Doctrine." *Michigan Law Review* 64: 219–234.

15. Eva R. Rubin. 1987. *Abortion, Politics, and the Courts: Roe v. Wade and Its Aftermath.* Westport, Conn.: Greenwood Press, p. 4.

16. Many laws, such as that involving the drinking age, make distinctions based on classifications. The Court uses one of three levels of scrutiny to assess whether the distinction is legal—minimum, moderate, or strict. Under minimum scrutiny, the government needs to show only a rational purpose in passing the law. At the other end of the continuum, the Court ruled that the government must show a compelling reason for race-based distinctions. Virtually no laws can survive this strict scrutiny. Moderate scrutiny was created for gender. Ruth Bader Ginsburg. 1983. "The Burger Court's Grappling with Sex Discrimination." In *The Burger Court: The Counter-Revolution That Wasn't,* ed. Vincent Blasi. New Haven: Yale University Press. Gender-based distinctions must further an important governmental objective, which is easier for the government to meet than the compelling standard.

17. Sally Kenney. 1992. *For Whose Protection? Reproductive Hazards and*

Exclusionary Policies in the United States and Britain. Ann Arbor: University of Michigan Press, p. 142.

18. William Eskridge. 1994. *Dynamic Statutory Interpretation.* Cambridge, Mass.: Harvard University Press.

19. Segal and Reedy, "The Supreme Court and Sex Discrimination: The Role of the Solicitor General"; Karen O'Connor and Lee Epstein. 1983. "Beyond Legislative Lobbying: Women's Rights Groups and the Supreme Court." *Judicature* 67: 134–143; and Tracey George and Lee Epstein. 1991. "Women's Rights Litigation in the 1980s: More of the Same?" *Judicature* 74: 314–321.

20. Lawrence Baum. 1988. "Measuring Policy Change in the U.S. Supreme Court." *American Political Science Review* 82: 905–912; and Jeffrey Segal, Lee Epstein, Charles Cameron, and Harold Spaeth. 1995. "Ideological Values and the Votes of U.S. Supreme Court Justices Revisited." *Journal of Politics* 57: 812–823.

21. Lee Epstein, Jeffrey Segal, Harold Spaeth, and Thomas Walker. 1994. *The Supreme Court Compendium.* Washington, D.C.: Congressional Quarterly, pp. 428–429.

22. George and Epstein, "Women's Rights Litigation in the 1980s: More of the Same?"

23. Stephen Puro. 1981. "The United States as *Amicus Curiae.*" In *Courts, Law, and Judicial Processes,* ed. S. Sidney Ulmer. New York: Free Press; and Segal, "*Amicus Curiae* Briefs by the Solicitor General During the Warren and Burger Courts: A Research Note."

24. Caplan, *The Tenth Justice,* pp. 218–223.

25. I attribute participation to the solicitor general even though assistants may have argued the case. For instance, Lawrence Wallace, who served through a number of presidential administrations, often argued women's rights cases for the office.

26. Early women's rights cases involved laws that clearly discriminated against women. As the Court found these laws unconstitutional, attention turned to the structural barriers to gender equality. Those issues often involved compensatory programs to remedy past discrimination. I distinguish between "invidious" and "helpful" programs. Judith Baer. 1983. *Equality Under the Constitution: Reclaiming the Fourteenth Amendment.* Ithaca: Cornell University Press. I coded support for compensatory programs, such as benefits for widows that are denied widowers, as opposed to gender equality. Support for protective legislation that denied jobs to women was categorized as conservative and against gender equality. In coding protective regulation cases, I adopted the perspectives of the women's groups litigating these cases. I coded support for affirmative action as pro–women's rights. I coded cases that did not recognize differences attendant to pregnancy as conservative and opposed to gender rights. Liberal feminist litigation, designed to eradicate male-created categories, was the dominant strategy of women's organizations' litigators. Cultural feminists, on the other hand, argued that differences between the sexes had to be recognized. Pure equality would reinforce traditional barriers to long-term equality. (For a discussion of the schools of feminist thought, see Patricia Cain. 1993. "Feminism and the Limits of Equality." In *Feminist Legal Theory: Foundations,* ed. D. Kelly Weisberg. Philadelphia: Temple University Press.)

27. Joan Hoff. 1991. *Law, Gender, and Injustice: A Legal History of U.S. Women.* New York: New York University Press, p. 273.

28. Rohde, *Justice and Gender: Sex Discrimination and the Law,* p. 256.

29. Hoff, *Law, Gender, and Injustice: A Legal History of U.S. Women,* pp. 242–256.

30. Salokar, *The Solicitor General: The Politics of Law,* pp. 142–143.

31. Karen O'Connor. 1980. *Women's Organizations' Use of the Courts.* Lexington: Lexington Books, p. 131.

32. Hoff, *Law, Gender, and Injustice: A Legal History of U.S. Women,* p. 296.

33. Martha Minow. 1993. "The Supreme Court 1986 Term: Justice Engendered." In *Feminist Legal Theory: Foundations,* ed. Weisberg, p. 307.

34. Charles Fried. 1991. *Order and Law: Arguing the Reagan Revolution—A Firsthand Account.* New York: Simon and Schuster, p. 117.

35. Baum, "Measuring Policy Change in the U.S. Supreme Court."

36. Rohde, *Justice and Gender: Sex Discrimination and the Law,* p. 102.

37. Ibid., p. 101.

38. Leslie Friedman Goldstein and Diana Stech. 1995. "Explaining Transformations in Supreme Court Policy." *Judicature* 79: 80–85.

39. Caplan, *The Tenth Justice,* p. 107.

40. Ibid., pp. 253–254.

41. David Savage. 1992. *Turning Right: The Making of the Rehnquist Supreme Court.* New York: John Wiley & Sons, p. 373.

42. Kenny, *For Whose Protection? Reproductive Hazards and Exclusionary Policies in the United States and Britain.*

43. Goldstein and Stech, "Explaining Transformations in Supreme Court Policy."

44. Lee Epstein and Joseph Kobylka. 1992. *The Supreme Court and the Legal Change: Abortion and the Death Penalty.* Chapel Hill: University of North Carolina Press, pp. 222–224.

45. Ibid., p. 227.

46. Caplan, *The Tenth Justice,* p. 106.

47. Former Solicitors General John Davis, Archibald Cox, Erwin Griswold, and Wade McCree condemned the brief as too strident. Rex Lee claimed the SG should not tell the Court it had made errors of constitutional doctrine. Over two hundred lawyers in the Justice Department protested the brief. Epstein and Kobylka, *The Supreme Court and the Legal Change,* p. 254.

48. Fried, *Order and Law.*

49. Epstein and Kobylka, *The Supreme Court and the Legal Change,* p. 260.

50. James Simon. 1995. *The Center Holds: The Power Struggle Inside the Rehnquist Court.* New York: Simon and Schuster, p. 125.

51. Ibid., pp. 155–156.

52. Solicitors general entered cases that did not directly involve reproductive rights but that provided an opportunity to help or harm the broader rights. On the basis of *Harris v. McRae* (1980), Starr argued in *Rust v. Sullivan* (1991) that the government could prohibit doctors in federal clinics from advising patients about the availability of abortion. In *Bray v. Alexandria Women's Health Clinic* (1993), the clinic sued antiabortion protestors, claiming animus against women. The Court agreed with Starr that the protests were not directed toward women as a class but were intended to reverse legalization of abortion. Drew Days III filed briefs in *NOW v. Scheidler* (1993) and *Madsen v. Women's Health Center* (1994), which involved right-to-life protestors, in favor of those who sought to protect a woman's right to have an abortion. In *NOW,* Days supported the use of RICO (Racketeer-Influenced and Corrupt Organizations) statutes to stop abortion protestors. In *Madsen,* a First Amendment case, Days supported a law that kept antiabortion groups from protesting within thirty-six feet of a clinic. In both cases, the Court supported the SG's position.

53. Simon, *The Center Holds: The Power Struggle Inside the Rehnquist Court*, pp. 141, 156–158.

54. Women may not be harmed as badly as African Americans in affirmative action cases. In decisions limiting affirmative action, the Court has held that programs that allow hiring and promotion preferences constitute reverse discrimination against whites. As discriminatory policies based on race, they must be judged by the strict scrutiny standards that apply to programs that discriminate against African Americans. Because gender receives a lower level of scrutiny, affirmative action programs that benefit women may be less constitutionally suspect.

55. Goldstein and Stech, "Explaining Transformations in Supreme Court Policy," pp. 82–83.

12

From the Ballot Box to
the White House?

Clyde Wilcox

Although women have held the chief executive office in nations across the world, the United States appears to be years away from electing its first woman president. No woman has mounted a serious campaign for her party's nomination, and only a few women have even been mentioned as credible candidates.

There are signs, however, that women are poised to move onto the short list of credible candidates in both the Democratic and Republican Parties. Women are increasingly winning election to offices that have traditionally proven to be the incubators of presidents—the U.S. Senate and House and state governorships.[1] The 1994 elections increased the number of Republican women in the Congress and thinned the ranks of female Democrats, thereby providing more partisan balance among women in that body. It is probable that one or even both parties will nominate a woman as vice president in the next decade, an office that is a heartbeat away from the presidency.

Although women are not mentioned as serious contenders for the presidency, their votes are ardently courted by men who seek that office. In 1988 George Bush made a substantial effort to attract women voters, who initially favored Michael Dukakis in large numbers. In 1992 Bill Clinton did far better among women than among men, and his appointments and early policy efforts were geared toward shoring up that constituency. Of course, any future woman presidential candidate will also hope to attract disproportionate numbers of women voters.

To understand the role of women in shaping presidential campaigns and agendas and to consider the likelihood of a woman president in the near future, this chapter considers a number of questions. First, do women have different policy preferences than men? Second, do these preferences translate into a gender gap in partisanship and vote choice? Third, are women more or less likely than men to participate in politics? Fourth, are women more likely than men to support a woman candidate, or do they vote their partisanship and issue positions? Finally, is the public ready to elect a woman as president?

Gender and Policy Preferences

Many feminist theorists have argued that women are likely to hold distinctive policy positions in several areas. First, several strands of feminist theory argue that women can be expected to oppose policies that might threaten the health and welfare of their children.[2] The most frequent application of this principle is in women's opposition to the use of U.S. troops in military combat. In addition, these maternalists have argued that women should be more opposed to all kinds of violence—for example, to the death penalty—and supportive of gun control. Research has generally confirmed the empirical claim, and the findings are remarkably strong and consistent in showing that women are less supportive than men of the use of military force.[3]

Other theorists have suggested that women's greater propensity toward empathy and nurturing should lead them to be more supportive of environmental protection, more sympathetic to the disadvantaged, and more supportive of programs to aid the poor. Empirical investigations of gender differences in environmental attitudes have uncovered weak and conflicting patterns, but most studies show small but consistent differences in support for programs to aid the poor.[4]

In some policy areas in which we might expect gender differences, research has failed to uncover a gender gap. Although significant gender differences exist in attitudes toward gender equality and reproductive liberty in European countries, in the United States men are as supportive as women of gender equality and abortion rights.[5]

Table 12.1 shows gender differences in public policy preferences in 1992, using data from the American National Election Study (NES), and compares the magnitude of those differences to differences between blacks and whites, those with higher and lower levels of education, older and younger citizens, and evangelical Christians and other Americans. The entries are correlation coefficients, which measure the strength of the relationship between these variables and attitudes. The larger the absolute value of the correlation, the stronger the relationship. Negative correlations indicate that those who are scored high on the demographic variable (women, blacks, the better educated, older people, and evangelicals) are more conservative than others; positive correlations indicate that they are more liberal.

The data in this table tell us two things. First, women are slightly more liberal than men on many—but not all—economic, defense, social, and racial issues. Most of these differences are large enough that we are confident they are not the result of sampling error. Thus, women are more

Table 12.1   Demographic Sources of Policy Attitudes, 1992

	Sex	Race	Education	Age	Evangelicalism
Economic Issues					
Guaranteed jobs	0.12**	0.21**	–0.15**	–0.10**	–0.00
Government health insurance	0.10**	0.11**	–0.12**	–0.00	–0.05*
Government services	0.15**	0.23**	–0.17**	–0.08**	–0.00
Spending					
Food stamps	0.09**	0.18**	–0.08**	–0.00	0.00
Homeless	0.12**	0.12**	–0.08**	–0.12**	–0.01
Child care	0.10**	0.16**	–0.04	–0.21**	–0.05*
Foreign and Defense Issues					
Use of force	0.06**	0.06**	0.07**	0.01	–0.09**
Gulf War was worth it	0.19**	0.19**	–0.08**	–0.01	–0.00
Defense spending	0.06**	0.05**	0.18**	–0.04*	–0.13**
Social Issues					
Abortion	–0.01	–0.03	0.24**	0.09**	0.37**
Notify parents	0.03	–0.00	0.15**	–0.06**	–0.14**
Notify spouse	0.11**	–0.02	0.26**	0.03	–0.18**
Gays in military	0.23**	0.04	0.09**	–0.09**	–0.24**
Gay adoption	0.08**	0.00	0.19**	–0.15**	–0.22**
Gay discrimination	0.13**	0.08**	0.11**	–0.03	–0.19**
Family values	–0.02	0.06**	0.12**	–0.23**	–0.15**
Tolerate different lifestyles	0.01	0.07**	0.01	–0.11**	–0.22**
School prayer	–0.01	–0.08**	0.20**	–0.14**	–0.20**
Too much equality	0.04	0.26**	0.14**	–0.11**	–0.07**
Race/Crime Issues					
Aid to blacks	0.06**	0.22**	0.06**	–0.05*	0.00
Integration	0.09**	0.26**	–0.03	–0.06**	0.02
Death penalty	0.15**	0.21**	–0.01	–0.03	–0.05*

Source: American National Election Study, 1992.
Notes: * means that the probability of this result by chance is less than 5%. ** means that the probability of this result by chance is less than 1%.

liberal than men on a range of issues but not on all issues. Sue Tolleson Rinehart has cautioned scholars to avoid oversimplifying the gender gap, with good cause.[6] On some sorts of issues, women take positions that are traditionally considered more conservative—they are more likely than men to favor limits on pornography, on free speech rights of unpopular groups, and on immigration in areas in which jobs are scarce.

Second, the magnitude of the gender gap on most issues is fairly modest. The average correlation between sex and policy preferences is smaller than that for race, education, age, or evangelicalism, and only on retrospective evaluations of the Gulf War and allowing gays in the military are gender differences truly sizable. Black middle-class professional women are more likely to share the attitudes of men in their community than the attitudes of white working-class women on most issues.

To better understand the magnitude of the gender gap, consider the gender gap in support of gay adoption (0.08), which is an average correlation in the table, and that in support of gays in the military (0.23), which is the largest gender gap. Only 7 percent of men strongly support allowing gays and lesbians to adopt children, while 65 percent strongly oppose this policy. In contrast, 15 percent of women strongly favor the policy, whereas 59 percent strongly oppose gay adoption. The gender gap in support of allowing lesbians and gays to serve in the military, in contrast, is substantial. Only 23 percent of men strongly favor this policy, while 41 percent strongly oppose it. Fully 41 percent of women strongly favor allowing gays to openly serve, whereas only 24 percent strongly oppose the policy. Thus, a correlation of 0.08 represents relatively modest gender differences, whereas a correlation of 0.23 represents a major difference in the views of men and women.

Why are gender differences on economic and social issues less substantial than differences among other demographic groups? Race, education, age, and religion are frequently sources of residential segregation and of different economic circumstances and life courses. Blacks and whites often live in largely segregated communities, hold somewhat different jobs, and interact most often with members of their own race. To a lesser extent, this is also true for different educational groups, generations, and religious groups. In contrast, men and women generally live together in families, raise children together, and share a common economic fate. Indeed, given the degree and nature of contact between men and women, in some ways it is surprising that significant gender differences on policy issues exist at all.

Yet, although men and women live together and build common lives, they experience the world through the prism of gender and construct their political lives out of their socialization, experiences, and life circumstances. Even in the most egalitarian families, women generally spend more time than their husbands with children and on common household chores. Men spend more time consuming political media, in part because their wives' extra household labor allows them the leisure to do so.[7] Women experience gender discrimination and sexual harassment and fear violent crime in a way men cannot fully understand, and in most families they establish closer bonds with their children. Women also frequently work in occupations dominated by women and are more likely than men to live in poverty. Moreover, not all women live with men, and among single women the gender gap is far larger than that among married citizens.

Thus, modest gender differences in policy preferences are found consistently in the United States, and these same differences exist in other countries as well. Women are more likely than men to favor spending on social programs, to oppose both spending on the military and the use of force, to oppose homophobic policies, and to oppose the death penalty. These differences are small, but they show up in nearly all surveys, and they do have important political consequences.

Given these differences in policy preferences, it is not surprising that in the United States women are somewhat more likely than men to identify themselves as Democrats and to support Democratic candidates for all levels of office. Figure 12.1 shows the percentage of men and women who have identified themselves as Democrats and Republicans in every presidential election year since 1952. Although both men and women have drifted away from Democratic partisanship during this period, the change has been far larger for men than for women. The percentage of men who consider themselves Democrats declined from 48 percent in 1952 to 32 percent in 1992; for women during that same period the drop was from 49 percent to 40 percent. This means that the gender gap in partisanship has grown in recent years. Figure 12.2 shows the Democratic advantage in partisanship between men and women in each election year between 1952 and 1992. Note that whereas the two parties had almost equal numbers of male partisans in 1992, Democrats enjoyed a substantial lead among women.

Why have women remained more loyal to the Democratic Party during this period while men deserted it in large numbers? One answer is that the parties have staked different positions on those policy issues on which men and women have different positions. In recent elections, Republican presidential candidates have favored cutting spending on social programs that benefit the disadvantaged, increasing spending on military weapons, adopting conservative positions on social issues, and reducing or ending programs targeted to aid minority groups—especially affirmative action. Moreover, although the death penalty is carried out almost entirely at the state level, George Bush made capital punishment a central issue of his 1988 campaign. Each of these policy positions has more appeal to men than to women, and in each case Democratic candidates have taken positions that are more appealing to women.

Indeed, the gender gap in partisanship can be explained entirely by gender differences in policy positions. Men and women who hold similar policy positions do not differ significantly in their partisanship; rather, a gender gap exists in part because men and women hold different positions on key issues. Table 12.2 shows the results of two separate regression analyses. In the first, bivariate (two variable) model, gender differences are statistically significant—that is, they are large enough that we are confident they are not the result of drawing an atypical sample. In the 1992 NES data, women were 10 percent more likely than men to be Democrats, whereas men were 10 percent more likely to be Republicans.

In the multivariate regression results in Table 12.2, the coefficient for sex is not significant when we hold constant attitudes on social issues such as abortion and gays in the military, force issues such as defense spending and the death penalty, compassion issues such as aid to blacks and spending on food stamps, and traditional economic issues such as a governmental guarantee of jobs. This means that when we compare men and women who have identical attitudes, they are equally likely to be Democrats or Republicans. Women are more Democratic than men because they are more liberal on these issues, and sex differences entirely explain the gender gap on partisanship.

Figure 12.1 Gender Differences in Partisanship, 1952–1992

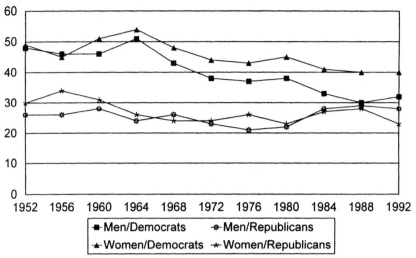

Source: National Election Studies

Figure 12.2 Gender Gap in Net Partisanship, 1952–1992

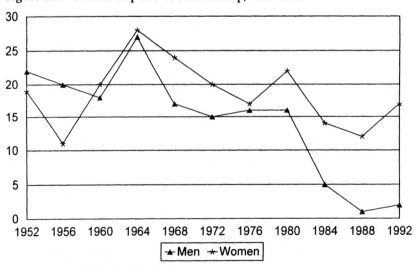

Source: National Election Studies

Table 12.2   Sex and Partisanship, 1992

Variable	b	beta	t
Model 1: Bivariate Regression			
Sex	0.33	0.03	25.511**
N 2,455			
R² 0.01			
Model 2: Multivariate Regression			
Sex	0.10	0.03	1.00
Abortion	0.14	0.07	2.84**
Gays in military	0.18	0.15	5.53**
Death penalty	0.18	0.12	4.92**
Defense spending	0.16	0.11	4.29**
Food stamp spending	0.18	0.07	2.69*
Aid to blacks	0.08	0.06	2.05*
Guaranteed jobs	0.25	0.21	8.04**
N 1,465			
R² 0.20			

Source: American National Election Study, 1992.
Notes: * means that the probability of this result by chance is less than 5%. ** means that the probability of this result by chance is less than 1%.

Moreover, the partisanship of men and women is explained by a slightly different set of issues. Table 12.3 shows the results of separate regression analyses for men and women that predict partisanship from issue positions. Attitudes on defense spending and the death penalty are important predictors of partisanship among men but are less important among women,

Table 12.3   Issues and Partisanship for Men and Women, 1992

	Men			Women		
	b	beta	t	b	beta	t
Abortion	0.16	0.08	2.36**	0.12	0.07	1.75*
Gays in military	0.17	0.14	3.89***	0.19	0.15	3.87***
Death penalty	0.25	0.17	4.62***	0.08	0.06	2.05**
Defense spending	0.20	0.14	2.73***	0.09	0.07	2.20**
Food stamp spending	0.01	0.04	1.04	0.29	0.12	2.84**
Aid to blacks	0.00	0.01	0.44	0.11	0.10	2.38**
Guaranteed jobs	0.30	0.25	6.85***	0.20	0.17	4.48***
N		765			700	
R²		0.21			0.18	

Source: American National Election Study, 1992.
Notes: * means that the probability of this result by chance is less than 10%. ** means that the probability of this result by chance is less than 5%. *** means that the probability of this result by chance is less than 1%.

whereas attitudes toward aid to minorities and spending on food stamps are significant predictors of partisanship among women but not among men. This finding suggests that of those Americans whose partisanship is instrumental (i.e., they identify with a party because of its issue positions), men are more likely to focus on issues of force, whereas women are more likely to focus on issues of compassion. These results add some tentative support for feminist theories that stress the importance of women's greater empathy and compassion toward others.

Of course, it is difficult to sort out the relationship between partisanship and policy views because partisanship influences policy views just as policy views influence partisanship. Strong Democrats may be more likely than others to be persuaded when Bill Clinton advocates allowing gay men and lesbians to serve openly in the military, and those who disagree with Clinton's policy may be more likely to change their partisanship.[8] Yet, it seems likely that the rapid movement of men toward the Republican Party and the greater loyalty of women to the Democrats are in no small part the result of the policy positions of the parties themselves.

Gender and Political Participation

When political scientists first began to study voter turnout using survey data, women were significantly less likely than men to vote. For example, in their classic book *The American Voter,* Angus Campbell, Philip E. Converse, Warren E. Miller, and Donald E. Stokes reported that in the 1952 presidential election, women were 10 percent less likely than men to vote.[9] The authors explained this finding by reference to the political aspects of traditional sex roles and noted that the gender gap was larger in more traditional areas, such as the South, and in rural areas.

Yet, even in 1952 there was evidence that women might overcome this turnout deficit. Campbell and colleagues found that the gender gap was largest among those with little education and was almost nonexistent among those with college degrees. Moreover, among younger citizens with no children, college-educated women were more likely to vote than men with similar educations.[10]

As education levels have risen and new generations have been socialized into more egalitarian gender roles, the gender gap in turnout has disappeared. Indeed, since 1980 women have been more likely than men to vote. Table 12.4 shows the percentages of men and women who have voted in each election since 1964, according to the U.S. Census.

We might imagine that women now vote slightly more often than men primarily because of generational replacement—that is, as older cohorts have died, they have been replaced by younger citizens who were socialized in different gender roles. Alternatively, men and women of all ages may

Table 12.4   Voting Turnout Rates for Women and Men, 1964–1992 (%)

	Women	Men	Difference
1964	67.0	71.9	−4.9
1968	66.0	69.8	−3.8
1972	62.0	64.1	−2.1
1976	58.8	59.6	−0.8
1980	59.4	59.1	+0.3
1984	60.8	59.0	+1.8
1988	58.3	56.4	+1.9
1992	62.3	60.2	+2.1

Source: U.S. Bureau of the Census.

have come to accept that voting is the responsibility of all citizens and is part of a woman's role, however else defined. The data support this second idea: Men and women were essentially equally likely to vote in 1992 across generations, with women sometimes being slightly more likely to do so.[11] Even among those raised in an era when more traditional sex roles were dominant, women voted as often as men.

The fact that women voted more often than men in 1992 is even more important because women constitute a larger share of the potential electorate. Women live longer than men, and there are more women than men in the United States, so if women vote at a higher rate their electoral clout becomes fairly important. The 1990 census revealed that women constituted 51.3 percent of all Americans, compared with 48.7 percent for men. Thus, women make up a sizable majority of voters, and both Bush and Clinton received a majority of their votes from women.

In some other forms of participation, however, women have not caught up with men. For example, men still dominate the funding of presidential campaigns by about the same margin as was the case in the early 1970s.[12] In recent years, organizations such as EMILY's List and WISH List have formed to mobilize women into giving to female candidates.[13] These organizations have had some success, and women will likely soon play a more active role in financing campaigns.[14]

Gender and Presidential Evaluations and Voting

If men and women differ in their policy positions and their partisanship, it should not be surprising that they differ in their evaluations of incumbent presidents. For example, in the midterm American National Election Studies, compared to men, women were far less supportive of Reagan in 1982 and 1986 and of Bush in 1990 and were more supportive of Clinton in 1994.

Throughout the Clinton presidency, women have been more supportive of the president than have men. The visible role of Hillary Rodham Clinton as policy adviser, especially in the area of health care, has also produced a sizable gender gap in evaluations of her role. Surveys have shown that women are significantly more supportive of the first lady than are men, although in 1994 both men and women rated Bill Clinton more warmly than they did Hillary.[15] (See Chapter 10.)

Of course, women should be expected to rate Republican presidents less positively than men because they are more likely than men to be Democrats. Indeed, in most of the NES surveys, women and men who share the same partisanship rate Republican and Democratic candidates the same. Thus, the gender gap in presidential evaluations seems to be entirely explained by differences in policy preferences and partisanship.

Women also rate Republican presidential candidates less favorably and Democratic candidates more warmly than men. Republican candidates have often tried to narrow this gap: George Bush fashioned his "kinder and gentler" theme, with advertising images of him lifting his grandchildren into the air, to try to narrow what was initially a sizable gender gap.[16] Bush succeeded in narrowing the gender gap, although women were more likely than men to support Dukakis in almost every poll conducted throughout the campaign.[17] Earlier, Ronald Reagan had targeted single working women, married working women, and elderly or widowed women in his efforts to narrow the gender gap.[18]

Although a gender gap almost always exists at any given point during a presidential campaign, it waxes and wanes as events occur and issues become more or less salient. Mary Bendyna and Celinda Lake reported that the gender gap in support of Clinton grew and declined as political events unfolded, in particular as Ross Perot withdrew and reentered.[19] In June 1996, Bill Clinton and Bob Dole were running essentially even among men, but Clinton had a huge lead among women voters.

On election day, women are more likely than men to vote for Democratic candidates for the presidency and other offices. The gender gap in presidential voting was significant in 1972, vanished in 1976, and was substantial in 1980 and in all elections since. In some years, the gender gap in presidential voting has been large. In 1980 men voted 55 percent to 36 percent for Reagan over Carter, whereas women preferred Reagan by a narrow 47 percent to 45 percent. In 1992 men gave Clinton a narrow 41 percent to 38 percent advantage over Bush, whereas women provided Clinton with a more comfortable 46 percent to 36 percent margin.[20] Yet, in all presidential elections since 1976, a plurality of both men and women have voted for the winning candidate.

In most presidential elections, the gender gap in voting has been entirely explained by the gender gap in partisanship. That is, Democratic men and women are equally likely to vote for the Democratic candidate, and the same is true for Republican men and women. In 1992, however, men were especially attracted to the Perot campaign, with women somewhat more likely to vote for Clinton. Republican women were slightly more loyal to Bush than were Republican men, but among the 30 percent or so of Republicans who defected from their party's candidate, women were more likely than men to choose Clinton.[21]

Thus far, I have established that women are more liberal and Democratic than men and that they constitute a sizable electoral bloc. They are more supportive of Democratic candidates, forcing Republicans to choose issues and campaign themes to try to narrow the gender gap and forcing Democratic presidents to try to retain the loyalty of this important constituency. Republican candidates and presidents face a more complicated strategic decision, for within their party women are often strongly conservative.

Recent research has shown that women constitute a sizable majority of conservative Christians, who have become a strong force within the Republican Party.[22] Among both Christian conservative and moderate party factions, women are slightly more liberal than men, but women are far more likely than men to be found in the conservative Christian faction.[23] Thus, Republicans who seek to woo liberal women voters risk alienating Phyllis Schafley, Beverly LaHaye, and other leading Christian conservative women. Several pro-life Christian Right women won election to the House as Republicans in 1994, and they are possibly the first of a growing number of such women to run for office.

Thus, Republican candidates and presidents must try to appeal to the larger, more liberal bloc of women voters without alienating an important active constituency among Christian Right women. Moreover, moderate pro-choice Republican women have defected to pro-choice Democrats in a number of recent state elections. Democratic candidates, in contrast, generally actively campaign against the Christian Right and on behalf of choice on abortion, equal protection laws, and other feminist policies, but they face the prospect of losing votes from morally traditional women.

When Women Run

How does this ideological and partisan equation change when women run for office? To date, available research suggests that women voters are motivated more by policy and partisanship than by candidate gender. In 1990, for example, Democratic incumbent Bill Bradley defeated Republican challenger Christine Todd Whitman (now governor of New Jersey) by building a large lead among women voters, whereas Whitman won more narrowly among men. Elizabeth Cook reported that in 1990, women appeared to ignore the candidate's sex and voted their partisan preference, preferring liberal men to conservative women.[24]

In 1992, however, the media attention to the "Year of the Woman," coupled with the large number of Democratic women who sought election to the House and Senate, produced a different pattern. Cook found that in 1992 women were especially likely to vote for female Democratic candidates.[25] Although Democratic men and women alike voted for these candidates, independent and Republican women were more likely than the men who shared their partisanship to cross party lines and vote for the Democratic women. *In that election, both partisanship and candidate gender influenced vote choice among women voters.*

In general, however, women appear to prefer male candidates who share their partisanship and policy views to women candidates from the other party with whom they disagree. This situation is not unique to women: African Americans generally vote overwhelmingly for white Democratic candidates when they are opposed by conservative black Republicans. The members of many distinctive social groups appear to prefer candidates who represent their policy views over those who would provide descriptive representation.

In intraparty primary elections, however, there is some evidence that women prefer female candidates. In the 1992 elections, women who voted in Democratic primaries were significantly more likely than men to vote for women candidates and helped to provide the winning advantage to women Senate candidates in Illinois, California, and Pennsylvania. In their study of hypothetical voting in Los Angeles, Seth Thompson and Janie Steckenrider reported that a small number of voters in each party preferred women candidates over men, and these voters were usually strong partisans who voted in primary elections.[26]

These data suggest that women voters are not especially drawn to Republican women candidates and indeed prefer more liberal male Democrats to conservative Republican women. In 1992 Republican and independent women voters were more likely than their male counterparts to cross party lines to support a Democratic woman. Moreover, in Democratic primary elections in 1992, women were especially drawn to women candidates. These results in 1992 may or may not generalize to other elections.

These data suggest that if a woman were to seek her party's nomination, she would have strong appeal to women voters in that party. Yet, policy concerns will also be important—a pro-choice Republican woman will evoke strong opposition among Christian conservative women, for example. In a general election with a woman candidate, most women voters will support the candidate of their party, but a few may cross party lines to send a woman to the Oval Office.

Is America Ready to Elect a Woman President?

Is it possible for a woman to be elected president in the United States? In national surveys, a substantial majority of women and men have indicated that they would vote for a qualified woman candidate for president from their party. Figure 12.3 shows that the percentage of Americans who say they would vote for a woman for president has climbed steadily over time, from more than 70 percent in 1972 to more than 90 percent in 1994. Roughly equal numbers of men and women indicated they were willing to vote for a woman.

Figure 12.3 Willingness to Vote for a Woman for President, 1972–1994

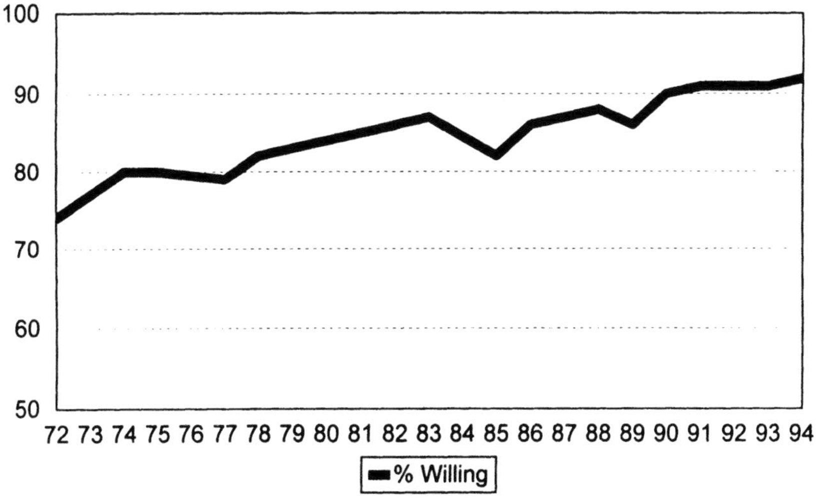

Source: General Social Survey, 1972–1994

The absence of a gender gap in the general public masks two offsetting gender gaps among the oldest and youngest citizens. Table 12.5 shows the percentages of men and women who indicated they would vote for a woman for president in General Social Surveys conducted during the 1990s. Among the very oldest respondents, women were significantly less likely than men to say they would vote for a woman, whereas among the youngest respondents, women would be more likely to vote for a woman for president. For both men and women it is the oldest citizens who are unwilling to vote for a woman; this means that over time, as younger Americans replace those oldest cohorts, the public will likely become even more willing to support a woman for president.[27]

Table 12.5   **Willingness to Vote for a Woman for President, by Sex and Cohort (%)**

Cohort	Men	Women
Great Depression	82	72*
World War II	81	82
Feminine Mystique era	88	87
Feminist era	93	95
Reagan-Bush era	90	96*
1990s	94	98

Source: General Social Surveys.
Note: * means that the probability of this result by chance is less than 5%.

Of course, people often tend to answer surveys in ways that make them appear to be fair, unbiased citizens. Because racism and sexism are not socially accepted in American public life, most citizens are reluctant to confess to interviewers that they would not vote for women or blacks. Indeed, in several elections in the 1980s, black candidates did markedly worse on election day than they had in polls the previous evening, which suggests that at least some respondents were unwilling to admit they would not vote for a black candidate.[28]

This means we cannot accept at face value the overwhelming willingness of the American electorate to vote for a woman for president, although such willingness does constitute some positive evidence. How else might we discern the willingness of the electorate to vote for a woman for president? One approach would be to determine how willing voters are to support women who run for other offices—for seats in the U.S. House and Senate and for governorships.

Research has revealed that voters are willing to support qualified women who run for the U.S. House or Senate. In a comprehensive study of voting for women candidates, R. Darcy, Susan Welch, and Janet Clark concluded that "sex is not relevant to congressional elections."[29] Although women lose more House elections than men, this occurs primarily because men are more likely to be incumbents. When we control for candidate status, women are as likely to win as men. In her exhaustive study of women candidacies for the U.S. House, Barbara C. Burrell concluded that women win as often as men; therefore, the best way to increase the number of women in the House is to recruit more women candidates.[30] By analogy, the best way to elect a woman to the White House might be to recruit a few qualified women to seek the office.

Yet, the lessons from congressional elections may not be determinative. Although women have made substantial gains in legislative office, few hold governorships. Voters may regard the job of single executive differently from that of legislator, and women may therefore suffer some disadvantage in presidential elections. No woman has run for the presidency as the nominee of a major party, so it is impossible to know whether the first to do so will face any disadvantages. There is some evidence, however, that voters use different stereotypes to evaluate male and female candidates.

Researchers have suggested that voters perceive men as more competent than women at handling issues that deal with force, such as crime and foreign policy, whereas women are perceived as better at dealing with compassion issues, such as poverty, education, unemployment, and health care.[31] Women are perceived as more sensitive and caring, whereas men are thought to be aggressive and tough.[32] In some years, the mix of issues appears to advantage women; in others, it advantages men. In 1992, for example, some analysts have argued that women who ran for the House and Senate were given an advantage by their status as outsiders and by their perceived strengths on education and health care, issues that were highly salient in that election. In contrast, in 1990, as the United States was poised to engage in war in the Gulf, male candidates (especially those with military records) were advantaged.

Women often campaign on themes that help them overcome the perception that they are compassionate but not tough. Dianne Feinstein's longtime support of the death penalty is an obvious example. Leonard Williams reported that in 1992 women felt free to emphasize their advantage on compassion issues and sought to portray themselves as competent through "connected activity"—that is, working concretely for people.[33] Overall, in legislative races these voter stereotypes do not appear to disadvantage women, for Burrell has demonstrated that women suffer no significant discrimination at the ballot box.[34] Yet, for executive office these stereotypes might be more important.

Although in some presidential elections compassion issues, such as health care and education, are among the most salient to voters, the president's unique role as commander in chief makes defense and foreign policy issues important in almost all presidential elections. Even in 1992, when the public was primarily concerned with health care, unemployment, education, and related issues, George Bush argued that Bill Clinton was unfit to serve as commander in chief because he had never served in the military and had actively avoided the draft during the Vietnam War. Although Clinton came to office emphasizing domestic issues, he has acted as commander in chief in Haiti, Bosnia, and Iraq, and has been involved in foreign policy in the Middle East and Ireland. Moreover, in recent elections Republican candidates have successfully run on issues such as the death penalty, and many observers believe Bush scored points against Michael Dukakis when the latter was unable to forcefully respond to a question about the death penalty in a presidential debate.

If the electorate has special concerns about the president's ability to defend U.S. citizens from foreign and domestic aggression, then women who run for the presidency will have to overcome doubts about their role as commander in chief and chief law enforcement officer. Such doubts are unwarranted, for women prime ministers around the world have proven tough on foreign policy in many settings. Margaret Thatcher's role in the war with Argentina over the Falkland Islands is only one case in point. Yet clearly, the issue will be raised.

Ultimately, such issues may not be decisive. In 1992, although citizens were apparently concerned about Clinton's lack of foreign policy experience, they elected him to help solve domestic economic problems. Moreover, many women, such as Dianne Feinstein, project images of strength, and others such as Barbara Boxer have substantive expertise in military issues and foreign policy. Boxer served on the House Armed Services Committee, and during her Senate election she frequently displayed her knowledge of arcane issues relating to military technology. This suggests that some women might be able to use the focus on military and crime issues to their advantage.

One final way to assess the willingness of American voters to support a woman for president is to examine the vice-presidential campaign of Geraldine Ferraro in 1984. The Mondale-Ferraro campaign was somewhat quixotic, for the short-lived economic surge of 1984 made Reagan temporarily rather popular. The 1984 National Election Study showed that men and women rated Ferraro more positively than her opponent, George Bush, on both strength and caring early in the campaign. A significant gender gap was found in reactions to Ferraro, with women of both parties more positive than their male counterparts.

During the campaign, issues surfaced about Ferraro's husband's business dealings and other personal matters. Ultimately, the Mondale campaign concluded that Ferraro had hurt the ticket, although this was not confirmed by exit poll data. Ferraro was asked during the vice-presidential debate whether she was tough enough to push the button, which suggests that such questions will surely be posed to a female presidential candidate.

Overall, it appears Americans are ready to vote for a woman for president. They overwhelmingly tell survey researchers they will do so, and they vote for women in House and Senate races as often as they do for similarly qualified men. But the first woman candidate may have to deal with lingering stereotypes about toughness and her ability to act as military commander in chief. Depending on the issues that are salient in the election, this may or may not prove a difficult hurdle.

How to Get There from Here: Electing the First Woman President

Over the past forty years, our presidents have been drawn primarily from a pool of governors, senators, and vice presidents. A president has not been elected directly from a seat in the House in over a hundred years, and although increasing numbers of candidates have had no previous elected experience (for example, Pat Robertson, Jesse Jackson, Ross Perot, Steve Forbes, Pat Buchanan), thus far none has come close to winning. We might therefore define the eligibility pool for the presidency as those Americans who have served in the Senate, as governor of a state, or as vice president.

At the start of the 104th Congress, eight women were serving in the U.S. Senate. In 1996 one woman held a governorship, and the vice president was a man. Thus, the pool of eligible women is currently fairly small. The offices of senator, governor, and vice president, in turn, have their own eligibility pools, which include women in state legislatures and in the U.S. House. These pools are larger, and more women will likely soon be found in the U.S. Senate and in governors' mansions across the country.

In the near future, the most likely route to the presidency for a woman may be through the vice presidency. In 1984 Walter Mondale chose Geraldine Ferraro, then a House member from New York, as his running mate. In 1996 Christine Todd Whitman (the governor of New Jersey) was briefly touted as a potential Republican vice-presidential candidate, although she withdrew from consideration. Opposition to her candidacy was raised by many pro-life Republican women, who objected to her pro-choice views.

For a woman to be elected president, women must first agree to run for the office. Presidential elections are grueling marathons held over many months with endless speeches, dinners, and fund-raising and close media scrutiny of every word the candidate utters. It should not be surprising that many qualified women (and men) choose not to run.

The first woman to seek a major party's nomination will face additional media scrutiny, which will give her free publicity but will also provide additional problems. Moreover, some kinds of events will likely evoke double standards among the electorate. When Newt Gingrich cried under the stress of negative publicity, the event attracted only limited attention.[35] When Pat Schroeder teared over when she withdrew from her short-lived presidential bid, it was the subject of endless media scrutiny.[36] Similarly, if a sex scandal breaks out about a woman presidential candidate, the media will almost certainly treat it somewhat differently than the stories about Clinton and Bush were handled in 1992.

Yet ultimately, ambitious women will run, and one will win the presidency. Voters appear to be ready to support a woman, and there are growing numbers of contributors to fund such a campaign. Until then, women will continue to constitute a vital constituency for both Republican and Democratic presidential candidates.

Although the Democratic Party is more closely allied with feminist groups, the first woman president may well be a Republican. The Democratic Party is viewed by voters as more compassionate but less assertive in foreign policy—stereotypes voters apply to women candidates as well. Thus, Democratic women candidates may be perceived as weak in the case of military crisis and perhaps as too compassionate. For Republican women, on the other hand, the party stereotype may counter gender expectations. Just as only Nixon could go to China, perhaps only the Republicans can elect a woman president in the near future.

Notes

1. Elizabeth Adell Cook, Sue Thomas, and Clyde Wilcox, eds. 1994. *The Year of the Woman: Myths and Realities.* Boulder, Colo.: Westview Press.

2. Nancy C. Hartsock. 1985. *Money, Sex, and Power: Toward a Feminist Historical Materialism.* Boston: Northeastern University Press; and Sara Ruddick. 1980. "Maternal Thinking." *Feminist Studies* 6: 342–367. Note, however, that socialization theories also predict this result.

3. Robert Y. Shapiro and Harpreet Mahajan. 1986. "Gender Differences in Policy Preferences: A Summary of Trends from the 1960s to the 1980s." *Public Opinion Quarterly* 50: 42–61; Pamela Johnston Conover. 1988. "Feminists and the Gender Gap." *Journal of Politics* 50: 985–1010; and David Fite, Marc Genest, and Clyde Wilcox. 1990. "Gender Differences in Foreign Policy Attitudes: A Longitudinal Analysis." *American Politics Quarterly* 18: 492–513.

4. Conover, "Feminists and the Gender Gap"; and Elizabeth Adell Cook and Clyde Wilcox. 1991. "Feminism and the Gender Gap: A Second Look." *Journal of Politics* 53: 1111–1122.

5. April Morgan and Clyde Wilcox. 1992. "Anti-Feminism in Western Europe, 1975–1987." *West European Politics* 15: 151–169; Ted G. Jelen, Sue Thomas, and Clyde Wilcox. 1994. "The Gender Gap in Comparative Perspective: Gender Differences in Abstract Ideology and Concrete Issues in Western Europe." *European Journal of Political Research* 25: 171–186; and Elizabeth Adell Cook, Ted G. Jelen, and Clyde Wilcox. 1992. *Between Two Absolutes: Public Opinion and the Politics of Abortion.* Boulder, Colo.: Westview Press.

6. Sue Tolleson Rinehart. 1994. "The California Senate Races: A Case Study in the Gendered Paradoxes of Politics." In *The Year of the Woman: Myths and Realities,* eds. Cook, Thomas, and Wilcox.

7. Doris Graber. 1984. *Processing the News: How People Tame the Information Tide.* White Plains, N.Y.: Longman.

8. Clyde Wilcox and Robin Wolpert. 1996. "President Clinton, Public Opinion, and Lesbians and Gays in the Military." In *Gay Rights, Military Wrongs: Political Perspectives on Lesbians and Gays in the Military,* ed. Craig Rimmerman. New York: Garland Publishers.

9. Angus Campbell, Philip E. Converse, Warren E. Miller, and Donald E. Stokes. 1960. *The American Voter.* New York: John Wiley & Sons.

10. For a discussion, see Mary Bendyna and Celinda Lake. 1994. "Gender and Voting in the 1992 Presidential Election." In *The Year of the Woman: Myths and Realities,* eds. Cook, Thomas, and Wilcox.

11. For this analysis, I isolated those who came of age before World War II, those who came of age during the era described as the "feminine mystique," those who came of age during the period of feminist mobilization, and those who came of age during the Reagan backlash.

12. Clifford Brown Jr., Lynda Powell, and Clyde Wilcox. 1995. *Serious Money: Contributing and Fundraising in Presidential Nomination Campaigns.* New York: Cambridge University Press.

13. EMILY's List gives to Democratic women pro-choice candidates, and WISH List gives to Republican women pro-choice candidates. Both groups bundle substantial amounts of cash, along with their contributions, and help to recruit candidates as well. EMILY's List is an acronym for Early Money Is Like Yeast, emphasizing the importance of giving early to help women candidates launch their campaigns. WISH List is an acronym for Women in the Senate and House.

14. Candice J. Nelson. 1994. "The Business-Industry PAC: Trying to Lead in an Uncertain Business Climate." In *Risky Business? PAC Decisionmaking in Congressional Elections,* ed. R. Biersack, P. Herrnson, and C. Wilcox. Armonk, N.Y.: M. E. Sharpe; and Craig A. Rimmerman. 1994. "New Kids on the Block: The WISH List and the Gay and Lesbian Victory Fund in the 1992 Elections." In *Risky Business,* eds. Biersack, Herrnson, and Wilcox.

15. Source: My analysis of 1994 National Election Study data.

16. The Willie Horton campaign was also aimed at women. The Republicans hoped women would feel Bush was more likely to protect them from violent crime.

17. Note that although most accounts of the gender gap portray it as a serious problem for Republicans, Republicans often have an easier time attracting women's votes than Democrats have winning the votes of men.

18. Linda Witt, Karen M. Paget, and Glenna Matthews. 1994. *Running as a Woman: Gender and Power in American Politics.* New York: Free Press.

19. Bendyna and Lake, "Gender and Voting in the 1992 Presidential Election."

20. A similar data analysis was performed by Mary E. Bendyna and Celinda C. Lake. See Bendyna and Lake. 1994. "Gender and Voting in the 1992 Presidential Election."

21. Actually, Republican women were almost as likely to defect to Perot as they were to vote for Clinton.

22. Clyde Wilcox. 1992. *God's Warriors: The Christian Right in 20th Century America.* Baltimore: Johns Hopkins University Press.

23. Bendyna and Lake, "Gender and Voting in the 1992 Presidential Election."

24. Elizabeth Adell Cook. 1994. "Voter Responses to Women Senate Candidates." In *The Year of the Woman: Myths and Realities,* eds. Cook, Thomas, and Wilcox.

25. Ibid.

26. Seth Thompson and Janie Steckenrider. Forthcoming. "The Relative Irrelevance of Candidate Sex." *Women and Politics.*

27. If we hold constant demographic factors, there is no significant gender gap in willingness to vote for a woman for president. If we also hold constant more general attitudes toward women in politics, however, women are significantly more likely to express a willingness to vote for a woman.

28. Indeed, in exit polls conducted in Virginia in 1989, when black candidate Douglas Wilder won the governorship, it appears many voters could not admit they had voted against him even on an anonymous survey ballot.

29. R. Darcy, Susan Welch, and Janet Clark. 1994. *Women, Elections, and Representation,* 2d ed., revised. Lincoln: University of Nebraska Press, p. 94.

30. Barbara C. Burrell. 1994. *A Woman's Place Is in the House: Campaigning for Congress in the Feminist Era.* Ann Arbor: University of Michigan Press.

31. Virgina Sapiro. 1981–1982. "If U.S. Senator Baker Were a Woman: An Experimental Study of Candidate Images." *Political Psychology* 2: 61–83.

32. Leonie Huddy and Nayda Terkildsen. 1993. "Gender Sterotypes and the Perception of Male and Female Candidates." *American Journal of Political Science* 37: 119–147.

33. Leonard Williams. 1994. "Political Advertising in the Year of the Woman: Did X Mark the Spot?" In *The Year of the Woman: Myths and Realities,* eds. Cook, Thomas, and Wilcox.

34. Burrell. 1994. *A Woman's Place Is in the House: Campaigning for Congress in the Feminist Era.*

35. Michael Weisskopf and David Maraniss. "Stung and Beset, Speaker Breaks Down and Weeps." *Washington Post,* January 18, 1996, sec. A (electronic).

36. Pat Schroeder's weeping occurred in 1987 when she withdrew from the 1988 presidential campaign. Patricia Schroeder. "Women Are the Losers in the Political Weep Stakes." *Washington Post,* May 17, 1996, sec. B (electronic).

13

Conclusion

MaryAnne Borrelli

The contributors to this volume have investigated the circumstances of women as officeholders in and constituents of the U.S. national executive branch. To understand the interplay of these realities, the authors have drawn upon their expertise in presidency studies and in women and politics research, as well as their knowledge of public policy, legislative-executive and executive-judicial relations, political theory, and comparative politics. Their research methodologies are unusually diverse, encompassing qualitative and quantitative, institutional, behavioral, historical, and theoretical approaches. Because the diversity and richness of their findings confound easy summarization, this conclusion merely notes some of the themes that run throughout the text and draws the reader's attention to the consistency of the associated findings.

Perhaps the most fascinating of these themes is representation, a topic frequently overlooked by presidency scholars. Indeed, applying Hanna Pitkin's now classic typology to this branch reveals the complexity of an issue that is too often addressed only in glib campaign promises. To deepen this analysis of executive branch representation, the authors have also utilized concepts from gender and women studies. Thus, their investigation of descriptive representation leads to a consideration of sex differences in career development. Assessing symbolic representation leads to an enhanced awareness of the impact of gender on executive politics. Finally, the investigation of substantive representation reveals the pressures that shape officeholders' actions and decisions. Formal representation is considered in every study. The result of this work is a nuanced and complex presentation of the national executive branch.

Descriptive Representation: Who Are the Other Elites?

In studying women in the executive branch, one's attention is immediately

231

drawn to the first ladies. Still, their service as advisers to the president has been highly informal. Turning to women with formal executive authority, one finds the Franklin D. Roosevelt administration was distinguished by an extensive network of women presidential appointees, including Frances Perkins, the first woman cabinet secretary. Without diminishing the accomplishments of these women, the fact remains that not until the Carter administration were women appointed to high-level offices in significant numbers. As a result, the authors have focused most closely on the four presidential administrations that governed from 1977 to 1996.

The institutional context of women's entry into the executive branch was also carefully considered. Three developments were viewed as particularly significant. First, authors took account of the "thickening of government," the increasing numbers of offices at every layer of the executive branch. Under these circumstances, one must record both the number and the percentage of offices held by women in (and even during) each administration.

Second, contributors weighed the effects of partisan succession on appointees' career paths and on the appointee pool for any particular president. Republican control of the White House for the eight years preceding Bush's election, for example, dramatically affected Bush's appointments practices. Third, and finally, the authors took care not to overgeneralize their findings, recognizing that a great deal of differentiation exists among the various departments, agencies, and offices.

Janet M. Martin then begins her analysis of presidential appointments by noting that the percentage of appointments going to women increased steadily during these years, with downward swings occurring only in the Nixon and Reagan administrations. Martin then examines how women's access to education and to college networks may have contributed to these gains. She also considers patterns of geographic mobility among women and men nominees to see how family responsibilities influence appointees' career decisions. She finds women appointees are highly educated and are often members of an "old girls'" network of graduates of the Seven Sisters colleges. Women are also becoming more mobile and may, in time, be increasingly recruited from outside the Washington Beltway. These patterns are significantly influenced, however, by the extent to which a president resists or relies upon the Washington community for appointees.

In studying the distribution of women's appointments, Martin finds that increasing proportions of women are named to the lower posts. No subsequent administration has equaled the Carter administration, when 13.0 percent of women appointees held the rank of secretary, deputy secretary, or under secretary. The Carter administration is also unequaled in appointing 44.4 percent of its women nominees to the rank of assistant secretary. However, the proportional decreases at this level have been less marked.

Whether this development will deepen the pool of women candidates for higher-level appointments or create a presidential glass ceiling awaits future events.

As Kathryn Dunn Tenpas demonstrates, White House staff developments are similarly complex. The sheer number of women on the White House staff is increasing, both throughout the staffing hierarchies and across the various offices. Again, however, this increase coincides with an increase in the number of offices; further research is necessary to determine the effects of this "thickening" on White House women staffers. Women at the highest levels, however, clearly do not necessarily wield the same degree of formal or informal power as their male colleagues. Dee Dee Meyers, for example, found her role was diluted and her authority circumscribed even in her earliest days as deputy assistant to the president and press secretary. Tenpas also notes that women are seldom considered for the advising positions closest to the president. With the White House staff frequently drawn from the ranks of campaign advisers and presidential intimates, *comitatus*, as explicated by Georgia Duerst-Lahti, may be having an inhibitory effect.

Women presidential appointees and White House staff members are incontestably elites. Their educational background and political resources distinguish them from other citizens and thus raise questions about their descriptive representation. As political elites, these women may have little in common with other women in the wider polity. Or their dilemmas—juggling family and professional responsibilities, countering tokenism, and breaking the glass ceiling—may highlight enduring concerns in women's lives. An examination of the potential of the descriptive representative to serve as a role model and a facilitator of change draws us to a discussion of symbolic representation.

Symbolic Representation: What Are the Other Elites?

Assessments of symbolic representation oblige a researcher to determine what significance attaches to the sex and gender of the political actor. Notably, the researcher must investigate whether this meaning is imposed upon or claimed by the woman.

Historically, women's place and role have been in the private sphere of home and family. The expectation that the husband's career will determine where and how the family will live is a conception that, as Janet M. Martin demonstrates, has significantly influenced the careers of executive branch women. Perhaps the strongest and most symbolic presentation of the belief that a woman is best suited to the private sphere, though, is evidenced in the Office of the First Lady.

The first lady has traditionally served as the president's supportive wife and the nation's gracious hostess. As such, the first lady was a role model of private-sphere womanhood. Barbara C. Burrell, however, explores how first ladies have assumed more public governmental and advisory roles. In diplomatic relations, first ladies have conducted state visits, consulted with chief executives, and delivered influential speeches. In regard to domestic policy, where first ladies have routinely pursued "a cause," Hillary Rodham Clinton's leadership of the Health Care Task Force represented a greater degree of activism. The failure of the Clinton medical reform initiative inevitably led to criticism of this first lady. Still, the public was comparatively accepting of her leadership. Commenting on the failed legislation, for example, 43 percent of respondents to a CBS poll found Hillary Rodham Clinton partially responsible. This response suggests that the voters are at once able to hold the first lady accountable and yet also are aware that congressional-presidential negotiations involve more than one person.

Clyde Wilcox provides further evidence of a gradually emerging acceptance of women political activists and decisionmakers. With the possible exception of the 1992 election, in which candidates were sometimes elected for their gender, voters generally choose candidates for their issue positions. Under these circumstances, elected offices show promise of becoming transgendered. This development includes the presidential office, as younger voters are more receptive to the election of a woman chief executive. Still, women candidates for the presidency will have to counter traditionally gendered expectations and reservations, especially in regard to their "toughness" and their capacities as military leaders.

Resistance to and uncertainty about women in the executive branch may be greater among the (men) elites than within the public. Of course, elites are more aware of how a more inclusive government will affect their own political resources. In regard to executive and judicial appointments, for example, presidential and legislative expectations have clashed on more than one occasion.

In their case study of the Roberta Achtenberg nomination, Jean Reith Schroedel, Sharon Spray, and Bruce D. Snyder analyze the Senate response to a president's willingness to create a more inclusive definition of "elites." This nomination paid a campaign debt to an individual supporter and to a voting group and was therefore an indicator of the ascendant power of gay and lesbian voters. At her confirmation hearing, Achtenberg explicitly challenged enduring presumptions that presidential appointees would be heterosexual, identifying herself as a lesbian woman who had the credentials for a presidential appointment. During the floor debate, however, Achtenberg's supporters sought to avoid discussion of her lesbian identity. Her confirmation, then, was not indicative of support for or even acceptance of her presence as an elite. Instead, it was the product of another tradition—one of Senate deference to presidential executive staffing decisions.

In regard to judicial appointments, as Richard L. Pacelle, Jr., details, recent presidents have restructured selection procedures. In so doing they have sometimes diminished senators' ability to advance particular candidates for lower court appointments and reduced the influence of the American Bar Association in evaluating candidates. The Carter administration was especially dedicated to making these reforms, and appointed a higher percentage of women to the district and appellate courts than had previous administrations. Although these numbers dropped sharply during the Reagan years, they have subsequently increased during the Bush and Clinton administrations.

These chapters clearly demonstrate that the president's willingness to appoint and consult women is an important factor in women's entry into the executive and judicial branches. No less important are the structures and processes by which the president institutionalizes this receptivity. Exploring this theme, Nancy E. McGlen and Meredith Reid Sarkees detail how State and Defense Department policymakers have excluded women through discriminatory appointment and personnel practices. Although there is evidence of some reform, the effects of these practices remain. Women are also excluded from policymaking by virtue of presidential tendencies to work only or principally with those who share the president's ideology and with whom the president is personally comfortable. This was especially evident during the Reagan and Bush years. During the Clinton administration, a more scrambled ("spokes-in-a-wheel") management style has further complicated the advisory process and marginalized women. Once again, the fact that women were present in the executive branch did not necessarily mean they were engaged in wielding its power.

As even these brief overviews demonstrate, the symbolic representation afforded by executive branch women upsets long-rooted conceptions of women as unsuited to the public sphere. If women are to be rich and complex symbols of political activism, however, they will need access to the formal and informal powers of their offices. In other words, they will have to be fully enfranchised members of the policymaking process. This brings us to substantive representation.

Substantive Representation: Why Are There Other Elites?

Substantive representation is the politics of "acting for" a constituent, advancing her or his interests within the government. It is from within this classic frame that Richard L. Pacelle, Jr., approaches his study of the solicitor general and women's rights litigation. He examines how this actor, caught between institutional obligations to the Supreme Court and Congress and political allegiance to the president, litigates on behalf of the government's interest. Discerning and expressing those interests in women's rights cases have led to major legal developments and intrabranch conflicts and have decisively altered women's equal protection and abortion rights.

The authors of this volume argue that policy and institutional processes are crucial to our understanding of the political system. In other words, political "outcomes" include both policies and persons—a democratic republic articulates laws and regulations while socializing its citizens and officeholders. Both undertakings are part of substantive representation. This understanding obliges us to inquire about the dynamics that produce an "other" among citizens and elites.

Georgia Duerst-Lahti in particular investigates why women are designated "other," as not the norm and therefore suspect. Utilizing the analytic insights of gender and women's studies, Duerst-Lahti analyzes how masculinism and feminism function as meta-ideologies, setting the political agenda at the most fundamental level. Among the ways the executive branch manifests its masculinist precepts is through the (somewhat contradictory) insistence on presidential autonomy and White House comity.

Although she predicts that any change will be slow and difficult, Duerst-Lahti concludes that such change is likely to take three forms. First, some positions may be "revalued" as they are held by women, acquiring lesser or greater significance. Second, gender dichotomies may be reinforced in some posts, with women and men presumed (and even instructed) to behave in keeping with their traditional gender roles, notwithstanding their apparent professional similarities. This "regendering" occurs, for example, when women managers are expected to nurture subordinates and men managers are expected to command obedience. Regendering may be enforced through formal or informal means. Alternatively, a position may be "transgendered," held by women and men who are perceived as equally capable.

Measuring gender is no easy task, and setting the standards to assess gendered change appears overwhelming. We are beginning to discern, however, the patterned responses to women's holding executive offices, as seen in the previously described assessments of descriptive and symbolic representation.

MaryAnne Borrelli also examines the process and progress of gendered change in her chapter on cabinet building. Through a detailed examination of Clinton's initial cabinet appointments, Borrelli uncovers the conflicting responses that greet "diversity" secretaries-designate. On the one hand, presidents are obliged to acknowledge and pay their campaign debt to voting groups of women and people of color. Organizations such as the Coalition for Women's Appointments act to ensure this responsiveness. On the other hand, presidents want appointees whose first loyalty is to themselves and who will be trusted presidential surrogates. Where comity is valued, difference is viewed as dangerous. Certainly, the media coverage of the Clinton cabinet appointments reveals profound uncertainties about these appointees. Although one's identity as "other" may no longer preempt the possibility of being appointed, it remains the cause of extended scrutiny and debate.

Piper A. Hodson then uses case studies of three South Asian chief executives—Benazir Bhutto, prime minister of Pakistan; Chandrika Kumaratunga, president of Sri Lanka; and Khaleda Zia, prime minister of Bangladesh—to test the cultural relativity of Western theories about women's political ambition and to challenge prevailing Western assessments of these women's political leadership. Although she acknowledges the ways in which women chief executives benefit from their membership in the political elite and gives due consideration to the distinctive opportunities for their leadership in newly independent states, Hodson argues that these women are innovative and powerful rulers. To hold their offices, they have competed against family members (in claiming their right to "inherit" the name recognition earned initially by their parents or spouses) and political opponents (including those whose regimes assassinated their family members). Hodson argues that political effectiveness must be judged by a trans-gendered standard.

Politics is about ideas, persons, and policies. Reduced to such basic elements, every chapter in this book clearly examines the substance of politics and thus touches upon the principal concern of substantive representation—the pursuit and protection of constituent interests. The three chapters outlined above, however, highlight the problematics of such advocacy when it is performed by the "other elites." Georgia Duerst-Lahti identifies the extent to which being "other" places these elites apart from the communications and relationships that typify masculinist institutions. MaryAnne Borrelli notes the effects of mass and elite uncertainties about the capabilities and allegiances of other elites. And Piper Hodson suggests that political scientists may need to reconsider their interpretations of women leaders, particularly in the "developing" nations. Women executives' performance of substantive representation, therefore, promises to be an increasingly intriguing research topic for political scientists across the discipline.

The Other Elites

The findings recorded in these chapters provoke all of the frustrations typically associated with transitions. The mechanisms and the pace of change are always the most difficult to analyze when one is in the midst of their working, but a significant degree of agreement is found among the contributors this volume. In brief, women are gaining access to offices throughout the executive branch, although the pace of this development can often be described only as excessively deliberate. It seems women will remain the other elites for some time into the future.

In reaching this conclusion, one should be very clear about the authors' contribution to our understanding of women in the executive branch. First, the authors have ascertained that sex differences and gendered distinctions do exist among executive branch officeholders. The significance of these contrasts has been carefully detailed. Second, the authors have addressed the full range of relationships between citizens and officeholders and have also critically examined relations among officeholders. Although their research agendas are precisely circumscribed, the implications of their findings are far-reaching.

This book is not about "otherness," nor is it about "elites." Neither of these terms alone can adequately describe the circumstances of women in the U.S. executive branch. This collection has therefore provided a series of investigations into the interactions between these two realities. The patterned experience of difference and of membership has proven to be a fascinating and controversial subject of study. Consequently, the editors will be well pleased if the chapters in this book .engage readers in debate and reassessment, thereby contributing to this research.

Select Bibliography

Aberbach, Joel D., and Bert A. Rockman. 1990. "What Has Happened to the U.S. Senior Civil Service?" *Brookings Review* 8(4, Fall): 35–41.

Abraham, Henry. 1992. *Justices and Presidents: A Political History of Appointments to the Supreme Court,* 3rd ed. New York: Oxford University Press.

Acker, Joan. 1990. "Hierarchies, Jobs, Bodies: A Theory of Gendered Organizations." *Gender and Society* 4(2): 139–158.

Aliotta, Jilda. 1995. "Justice O'Connor and the Equal Protection Clause: A Feminine Voice?" *Judicature* 78: 232–235.

Allen, David, and Diane Wall. 1993. "Role Orientations and Women State Supreme Court Justices." *Judicature* 77: 156–165.

Althusser, Louis. 1979. *For Marx.* Trans. Ben Brewster. London: Verso.

Andersen, Kristi, and Stuart Thorson. 1984. "Congressional Turnover and the Election of Women." *Western Political Quarterly* 37: 143–156.

Anthony, Carl S. 1991. *First Ladies: The Saga of the Presidents' Wives and Their Power, 1961–1990.* New York: William Morrow.

Baer, Judith. 1983. *Equality Under the Constitution: Reclaiming the Fourteenth Amendment.* Ithaca: Cornell University Press.

Bailey, Christopher J. 1986. "The United States Senate: The New Individualism and the New Right." *Parliamentary Affairs: A Journal of Comparative Politics* 39(3): 354–367.

Ball, Howard. 1987. *Courts and 'Politics: The Federal Judicial System,* 2d ed. Englewood Cliffs, N.J.: Prentice-Hall.

Barthes, Roland. 1991. *Mythologies.* Trans. Annette Lavers. New York: Noonday Press.

Bartol, K. M. 1978. "The Sex Structuring of Organizations: A Search for Possible Causes." *Academy of Management Review* 3: 805–815.

Baugh, Joyce Ann, Christopher E. Smith, Thomas R. Hensley, and Scott Patrick Johnson. 1994. "Justice Ruth Bader Ginsburg: A Preliminary Assessment." *University of Toledo Law Review* 26: 1–34.

Baum, Lawrence. 1988. "Measuring Policy Change in the U.S. Supreme Court." *American Political Science Review* 82: 905–912.

Berkson, Larry. 1979. "The U.S. Circuit Judge Nominating Commission: The Candidate's Perspective." *Judicature* 62: 466–482.

Berkson, Larry, and Susan Carbon. 1980. *The United States Circuit Judge Nominating Commission: Its Members, Procedures, and Candidates.* Chicago: American Judicature Society.

Berman, Maxine. 1994. *The Only Boobs in the House Are Men: A Veteran Woman Legislator Lifts the Lid on Politics Macho Style.* Troy, Mich.: Momentum Books.

Bhutto, Benazir. 1989. *Daughter of Destiny: An Autobiography.* New York: Simon and Schuster.

Biersack, R., P. Herrnson, and Clyde Wilcox, eds. 1994. *Risky Business? PAC Decisionmaking in Congressional Elections.* Armonk, N.Y.: M. E. Sharpe.

Binion, Gayle. 1993. "The Nature of Feminist Jurisprudence." *Judicature* 77: 140–143.

Blakesley, Lance. 1995. *Presidential Leadership from Eisenhower to Clinton.* Chicago: Nelson-Hall Publishers.

Blasi, Vincent, ed. 1983. *The Burger Court: The Counter-Revolution That Wasn't.* New Haven: Yale University Press.

Borrelli, MaryAnne. Forthcoming. "Gender, Credibility, and Politics: The Senate Nomination Hearings of Cabinet Secretaries-Designate, 1975–1993." *Political Research Quarterly.*

Brown, Clifford, Jr., Lynda Powell, and Clyde Wilcox. 1995. *Serious Money: Contributing and Fundraising in Presidential Nomination Campaigns.* New York: Cambridge University Press.

Brown, Wendy. 1988. *Manhood and Politics: A Feminist Reading in Political Theory.* Totowa, N.J.: Rowman and Littlefield.

Burrell, Barbara C. 1994. *A Woman's Place Is in the House: Campaigning for Congress in the Feminist Era.* Ann Arbor: University of Michigan Press.

Burrell, Barbara C. 1997. *Public Opinion, the First Ladyship and Hillary Clinton.* New York: Garland Press.

Calkin, Homer. 1978. *Women in the Department of State: Their Role in American Foreign Affairs.* Washington, D.C.: Department of State.

Campbell, Angus, Philip E. Converse, Warren E. Miller, and Donald E. Stokes. 1960. *The American Voter.* New York: John Wiley & Sons, Inc.

Campbell, Colin, and Bert A. Rockman eds. 1996. *The Clinton Presidency: First Appraisals.* Chatham, N.J.: Chatham House Publishers.

Cannon, Lou. 1991. *President Reagan: The Role of a Lifetime.* New York: Simon and Schuster.

Caplan, Lincoln. 1987. *The Tenth Justice: The Solicitor General and the Rule of the Law.* New York: Vintage Books.

Caroli, Betty. 1995. *First Ladies.* Expanded Edition. New York: Oxford University Press.

Carp, Robert, and C. K. Rowland. 1983. *Policymaking and Politics in the Federal District Courts.* Knoxville: University of Tennessee Press.

Carroll, Susan. 1984. "The Recruitment of Women for Cabinet-Level Posts in State Government: A Social Control Perspective." *Social Science Journal* 21(1): 91–107.

Carroll, Susan. 1984. "Women Candidates and Support for Feminist Concerns: The Closet Feminist Syndrome." *Western Political Quarterly* 37: 307–323.

Carroll, Susan. 1994. *Women as Candidates in American Politics,* 2d ed. Bloomington: Indiana University Press.

Carroll, Susan, and Barbara Geiger-Parker. 1983. *Women Appointed to the Carter Administration: A Comparison with Men.* New Brunswick, N.J.: Center for the American Woman and Politics, Eagleton Institute of Politics, Rutgers University.

Carter, Rosalynn. 1984. *First Lady from Plains.* Boston: Houghton Mifflin.

Cederbaum, Miriam Goldman. 1993. "Women on the Federal Bench." *Boston University Law Review* 73: 39–45.

Chubb, John, and Paul Peterson, eds. 1985. *The New Direction in American Politics.* Washington, D.C.: Brookings Institution.

Clarke, Duncan L. 1992. *American Defense and Foreign Policy Institutions: Toward a Sound Foundation.* New York: University Press of America.

Clatterbaugh, Kenneth. 1990. *Contemporary Perspectives on Masculinity: Men, Women, and Politics in Modern Society.* Boulder, Colo.: Westview Press.

Cohen, Jeffrey E. 1988. *The Politics of the U.S. Cabinet: Representation in the Executive Branch, 1789–1984.* Pittsburgh: University of Pittsburgh Press.

Conover, Pamela Johnston. 1988. "Feminists and the Gender Gap." *Journal of Politics* 50: 985–1010.

Cook, Beverly. 1982. "Women as Supreme Court Candidates: From Florence Allen to Sandra O'Connor." *Judicature* 65: 314–326.

Cook, Beverly, Leslie Friedman Goldstein, Karen O'Connor, and Susette Talarico. 1988. *Women in the Judicial Process.* Washington, D.C.: American Political Science Association.

Cook, Elizabeth Adell, and Clyde Wilcox. 1991. "Feminism and the Gender Gap: A Second Look." *Journal of Politics* 53: 1111–1122.

Cook, Elizabeth Adell, Ted G. Jelen, and Clyde Wilcox. 1992. *Between Two Absolutes: Public Opinion and the Politics of Abortion.* Boulder, Colo.: Westview Press.

Cook, Elizabeth Adell, Sue Thomas, and Clyde Wilcox, eds. 1994. *The Year of the Woman: Myths and Realities.* Boulder, Colo.: Westview Press.

Crapol, Edward P., ed. 1987. *Women and American Foreign Policy: Lobbyists, Critics, and Insiders.* New York: Greenwood Press.

Cronin, Thomas. 1980. *The State of the Presidency,* 2d ed. Boston: Little, Brown.

Darcy, R., and Sarah Slavin Schramm. 1977. "When Women Run Against Men." *Public Opinion Quarterly* 41: 1–12.

Darcy, R., Susan Welch, and Janet Clark. 1994. *Women, Elections, and Representation,* 2d ed., revised. Lincoln: University of Nebraska Press.

Davis, Sue. 1993. "The Voice of Sandra Day O'Connor." *Judicature* 77: 134–139.

Davis, Sue, Susan Haire, and Donald Songer. 1993. "Voting Behavior and Gender on the U.S. Court of Appeals: The Votes of Women Circuit Court Judges in Employment Discrimination and Search and Seizure Cases Differ from Those of Their Male Counterparts." *Judicature* 77: 129–133.

Deering, Christopher J. 1989. *Congressional Politics.* Pacific Grove, Calif.: Brooks/Cole.

Diamond, Irene. 1977. *Sex Roles in the State House.* New Haven: Yale University Press.

Di Stefano, Christine. 1991. *Configurations on Masculinity: A Feminist Perspective on Modern Political Theory.* Ithaca: Cornell University Press.

Dodson, Debra L., Susan J. Carroll, Ruth B. Mandel, Katherine E. Kleeman, Ronnee Schreiber, and Debra Liebowitz. 1995. *Voices, Views, Votes: The Impact of Women in the 103rd Congress.* New Brunswick, N.J.: Center for the American Woman and Politics, Eagleton Institute of Politics, Rutgers University.

Drew, Elizabeth. 1994. *On the Edge: The Clinton Presidency.* New York: Simon and Schuster.

Duerst-Lahti, Georgia. 1987. "Gender Power Relations in Public Bureaucracies." Ph.D. dissertation, University of Wisconsin.

Duerst-Lahti, Georgia. 1989. "The Government's Role in Building the Women's Movement." *Political Science Quarterly* 104(2): 249–268.

Duerst-Lahti, Georgia, and Cathy Marie Johnson. 1990. "Gender and Style in Bureaucracy." *Women and Politics* 10(4): 67–120.

Duerst-Lahti, Georgia, and Rita Mae Kelly, eds. 1995. *Gender Power, Leadership, and Governance.* Ann Arbor: University of Michigan Press.

Durkheim, Emile. 1983. *Durkheim and the Law,* ed. Steven Lukes and Andrew Scull. Oxford: Basil Blackwell.

Dworkin, Andrea. 1988. *Letters from a War Zone.* New York: E. P. Dutton.

Edwards, George, and Stephen Wayne. 1994. *Presidential Leadership: Politics and Policymaking,* 3rd ed. New York: St. Martin's Press.

Eisenstein, Zillah. 1993. *The Radical Future of Liberal Feminism.* Boston: Northeastern University Press.

Elazar, Daniel J. 1984. *American Federalism: A View from the States,* 3rd ed. New York: Harper and Row.

Elshtain, Jean Bethke. 1993. *Public Man, Private Woman: Women in Social and Political Thought,* 2d ed. Princeton, N.J.: Princeton University Press.

Elshtain, Jean Bethke. 1995. *Women and War.* Chicago: University of Chicago Press.

Emerson, Thomas. 1965. "Nine Justices in Search of a Doctrine." *Michigan Law Review* 64: 219–234.

Epstein, Lee, and Joseph Kobylka. 1992. *The Supreme Court and the Legal Change: Abortion and the Death Penalty.* Chapel Hill: University of North Carolina Press.

Eskridge, William. 1994. *Dynamic Statutory Interpretation.* Cambridge, Mass.: Harvard University Press.

Fenno, Richard F. 1959. *The President's Cabinet, An Analysis in the Period from Wilson to Eisenhower.* Cambridge, Mass.: Harvard University Press.

Fenno, Richard F. 1989. "The Senate Through a Looking Glass: The Debate over Television." *Legislative Studies Quarterly* 14: 313–348.

Ferguson, Kathy E. 1984. *The Feminist Case Against Bureaucracy.* Philadelphia: Temple University Press.

Fite, David, Marc Genest, and Clyde Wilcox. 1990. "Gender Differences in Foreign Policy Attitudes: A Longitudinal Analysis." *American Politics Quarterly* 18: 492–513.

Foreman, Norma Ruth Holly. 1971. "The First Lady as a Leader of Public Opinion: A Study of the Role and Press Relations of Lady Bird Johnson." Ph.D. dissertation, University of Texas, Austin.

Foucault, Michel. 1979. *Discipline and Punishment: The Birth of the Prison.* New York: Vintage.

Fowler, W. Gary. 1984. "Judicial Selection Under Reagan and Carter: A Comparison of Their Initial Recommendation Procedures." *Judicature* 67: 265–283.

Fried, Charles. 1991. *Order and Law: Arguing the Reagan Revolution—A Firsthand Account.* New York: Simon and Schuster.

Funderburk, Charles. 1982. *Presidents and Politics: The Limits of Power.* Monterey, Calif.: Brooks/Cole Publishing Company.

Genovese, Michael A., ed. 1993. *Women as National Leaders.* Newbury Park, Calif.: Sage Publications.

George, Tracey, and Lee Epstein. 1991. "Women's Rights Litigation in the 1980s: More of the Same?" *Judicature* 74: 314–321.

Gilligan, Carol. 1982. *In a Different Voice.* Cambridge, Mass.: Harvard University Press.

Goldman, Sheldon. 1978. "A Profile of Carter's Judicial Nominees." *Judicature* 62: 246–254.

Goldman, Sheldon. 1979. "Should There Be Affirmative Action for the Judiciary?" *Judicature* 62: 488–494.

Goldman, Sheldon. 1981. "Carter's Judicial Appointments: A Lasting Legacy." *Judicature* 64: 344–355.

Goldman, Sheldon. 1983. "Reagan's Judicial Appointments at Mid-Term: Shaping the Bench in His Own Image." *Judicature* 66: 335–347.

Goldman, Sheldon. 1985. "Reaganizing the Judiciary: The First Term Appointments." *Judicature* 68: 313–329.

Goldman, Sheldon. 1987. "Reagan's Second Term Judicial Appointments: The Battle at Midway." *Judicature* 70: 324–339.

Goldman, Sheldon. 1989. "Reagan's Judicial Legacy: Completing the Puzzle and Summing Up." *Judicature* 72: 318–330.

Goldman, Sheldon. 1991. "The Bush Imprint on the Judiciary: Carrying on a Tradition." *Judicature* 74: 294–306.

Goldman, Sheldon. 1995. "Judicial Selection Under Clinton: A Midterm Examination." *Judicature* 78: 276–291.

Goldman, Sheldon, and Matthew Saronson. 1994. "Clinton's Nontraditional Judges: Creating a More Representative Bench." *Judicature* 78: 68–73.

Goldstein, Leslie Friedman, and Diana Stech. 1995. "Explaining Transformations in Supreme Court Policy." *Judicature* 79: 80–85.

Goodwin, Doris Kearns. 1994. *No Ordinary Time: Franklin and Eleanor Roosevelt: The Home Front in World War II*. New York: Simon and Schuster.

Gottschall, Jon. 1983. "Carter's Judicial Appointments: The Influence of Affirmative Action and Merit Selection on Voting on the U.S. Courts of Appeals." *Judicature* 67: 164–173.

Gottschall, Jon. 1986. "Reagan's Appointments to the U.S. Courts of Appeals: The Continuation of a Judicial Revolution." *Judicature* 70: 48–54.

Gould, Lewis. 1985. "Modern First Ladies in Historical Perspective." *Presidential Studies Quarterly* 15: 532–540.

Graber, Doris. 1988. *Processing the News: How People Tame the Information Tide*, 2d ed. Lanham, Md.: University Press of America.

Gramsci, Antonio. 1971. *Selections from the Prison Notebooks of Antonio Gramsci*. Trans. Quintin Hoare and Geoffrey Nowell Smith. New York: International Publishers.

Grant, Judith. 1993. *Fundamental Feminism: Contesting the Core Concepts of Feminist Theory*. New York: Routledge.

Gugin, Linda C. 1986. "The Impact of Political Structure on the Political Power of Women: A Comparison of Britain and the United States." *Women and Politics* 6: 37–56.

Guy, Mary Ellen, ed. 1992. *Women and Men of the States: Public Administrators at the State Level*. Armonk, N.Y.: M. E. Sharpe.

Hakim, S. Abdul. 1992. *Begum Khaleda Zia of Bangladesh: A Political Biography*. New Delhi: Vikas Publishing House.

Hall, Elaine. 1993. "Waitering/Waitressing: Engendering the Work of Table Servers." *Gender and Society* 7(3): 329–346.

Hart, John. 1995. *The Presidential Branch: From Washington to Clinton*, 2d ed. Chatham, N.J.: Chatham House.

Hartsock, Nancy C. 1985. *Money, Sex and Power: Toward a Feminist Historical Materialism*. Boston: Northeastern University Press.

Heclo, Hugh, and Lester Salamon. 1981. *The Illusion of Presidential Government*. Boulder, Colo.: Westview Press.

Hess, Stephen. 1988. *Organizing the Presidency*. Washington, D.C.: Brookings Institution.

Hibbing, John R., and Sue Thomas. 1990. "The Modern United States Senate: What Is Accorded Respect." *Journal of Politics* 52: 126–145.

Hinckley, Barbara. 1985. *Problems of the Presidency: A Text with Readings.* Glenview, Ill.: Scott, Foresman.

Hinckley, Barbara. 1994. *Less Than Meets the Eye: Foreign Policy Making and the Myth of the Assertive Congress.* Chicago: University of Chicago Press.

Hoff, Joan. 1991. *Law, Gender, and Injustice: A Legal History of U.S. Women.* New York: New York University Press.

Holm, Jeanne. 1993. *Women in the Military: An Unfinished Revolution.* Revised Edition. Novato, Calif.: Presidio.

Hoover, Kenneth. 1994. *Ideology and Political Life,* 2d ed. Belmont, Calif.: Wadsworth Publishing.

Horner, Constance. 1993. "The Politics of Presidential Appointment: The Old and New Culture of Job Seeking in Washington." *American Enterprise* 4: 20–24.

Huddy, Leonie, and Nayda Terkildsen. 1993. "Gender Stereotypes and the Perception of Male and Female Candidates." *American Journal of Political Science* 37: 119–147.

Iannello, Kathleen P. 1992. *Decisions Without Hierarchy: Feminist Interventions in Organization Theory and Practice.* London: Routledge.

Jackson, Donald. 1974. *Judges.* New York: Atheneum.

Jacoby, Henry. 1973. *The Bureaucratization of the World.* Berkeley: University of California Press.

Jamieson, Kathleen Hall. 1995. *Beyond the Double Bind: Women and Leadership.* New York: Oxford University Press.

Jayawardena, Kumari. 1986. *Feminism and Nationalism in the Third World.* London: Zed Books.

Jelen, Ted G., Sue Thomas, and Clyde Wilcox. 1994. "The Gender Gap in Comparative Perspective: Gender Differences in Abstract Ideology and Concrete Issues in Western Europe." *European Journal of Political Research* 25: 171–186.

Jensen, Faye Lind. 1990. "An Awesome Responsibility: Rosalynn Carter as First Lady." *Presidential Studies Quarterly* 20: 769–775.

Jewell, Malcolm, and Marcia Lynn Whicker. 1994. *Legislative Leadership in the American States.* Ann Arbor: University of Michigan Press.

Johnson, Charles A. 1976. "Political Cultures in American States: Elazar's Formulation Examined." *American Journal of Political Science* 20: 491–509.

Jones, Charles O. 1994. *The Presidency in a Separated System.* Washington, D.C.: Brookings Institution.

Jost, Kenneth. 1994. "Religion and Politics." *Congressional Quarterly Researcher* 4: 891–911.

Kalt, Joseph P., and Mark A. Zupan. 1984. "Capture and Ideology in the Economic Theory of Politics." *American Economic Review* 74: 279–300.

Kanter, Rosabeth Moss. 1977. *Men and Women of the Corporation.* New York: Basic Books.

Kegley, Charles W., and Eugene R. Wittkopf. 1996. *American Foreign Policy: Pattern and Process,* 5th ed. New York: St. Martin's Press.

Kelly, Rita Mae. 1991. *The Gendered Economy: Work, Careers, and Success.* Newbury Park, Calif.: Sage Publications.

Kelly, Rita Mae, and Mary Boutilier, eds. 1978. *The Making of Political Women: A Study of Socialization and Role Conflict.* Chicago: Nelson-Hall.

Kenney, Sally. 1992. *For Whose Protection? Reproductive Hazards and*

Exclusionary Policies in the United States and Britain. Ann Arbor: University of Michigan Press.

Kincaid, Diane. 1978. "Over His Dead Body: A Positive Perspective on Widows in the U.S. Congress." *Western Political Quarterly* 31: 96–104.

Light, Paul C. 1995. *Thickening Government: Federal Hierarchy and the Diffusion of Accountability.* Washington, D.C.: Brookings Institution.

Lorber, Judith. 1993. "Believing Is Seeing: Biology as Ideology." *Gender and Society* 7(4): 568–581.

Mackenzie, G. Calvin. 1981. *The Politics of Presidential Appointments.* New York: Free Press.

Mackenzie, G. Calvin, ed. 1987. *The In-and-Outers: Presidential Appointees and Transient Government in Washington.* Baltimore: Johns Hopkins University Press.

Martin, Elaine. 1982. "Women on the Federal Bench: A Comparative Profile." *Judicature* 65: 306–313.

Martin, Elaine. 1987. "Gender and Judicial Selection: A Comparison of the Reagan and Carter Administrations." *Judicature* 71: 136–142.

Martin, Elaine. 1990. "Men and Women on the Bench: Vive la Difference?" *Judicature* 73: 204–208.

Martin, Janet M. 1985. "Cabinet Secretaries from Truman to Johnson: An Examination of Theoretical Frameworks for Cabinet Studies." Ph.D. dissertation. The Ohio State University.

Martin, Janet M. 1988. "Frameworks for Cabinet Studies." *Presidential Studies Quarterly* 18: 795–814.

Martin, Janet M. 1989. "The Recruitment of Women to Cabinet and Subcabinet Posts." *Western Political Quarterly* 42: 161–172.

Martin, Janet M. 1991. "An Examination of Executive Branch Appointments in the Reagan Administration by Background and Gender." *Western Political Quarterly* 44: 173–184.

Martin, Janet M. 1992. "George Bush and the Executive Branch." In *Leadership and the Bush Presidency,* ed. Ryan J. Barilleaux and Mary E. Stuckey. Westport, Conn.: Praeger.

Matalin, Mary, and James Carville, with Peter Knobler. 1995. *All's Fair: Love, War, and Running for President.* New York: Random House.

Matthews, Donald R. 1960. *U.S. Senators and Their World.* New York: Vintage Books.

Mayo, Edith, and Denise Meringolo. 1994. *First Ladies: Political Role and Public Image.* Washington, D.C.: National Museum of American History.

McGlen, Nancy E., and Meredith Reid Sarkees. 1993. *Women in Foreign Policy: The Insiders.* New York: Routledge.

McGuire, Kevin T. 1993. *The Supreme Court Bar: Legal Elites in the Washington Community.* Charlottesville: University Press of Virginia.

Medved, Michael. 1979. *The Shadow Presidents: The Secret History of the Chief Executives and Their Top Aides.* New York: Times Books.

Meese, Edwin. 1992. *With Reagan: The Inside Story.* Washington, D.C.: Regnery Gateway.

Milkis, Sidney. 1993. *The President and the Parties.* New York: Oxford University Press.

Minault, Gail, ed. 1981. *The Extended Family: Women and Political Participation in India and Pakistan.* Delhi: Chanakya Publications.

Minow, Martha. 1990. *Making All the Difference: Inclusion, Exclusion, and American Law.* Ithaca: Cornell University Press.

Mitchell, Alison. 1995. "Assessing the Influence of the Women's Network on the

C‑H

Electoral and Legislative Processes: A Case Study of Women and Participation in the Massachusetts General Court." Honors Thesis in Government, Connecticut College.

Morgan, April, and Clyde Wilcox. 1992. "Anti-Feminism in Western Europe, 1975–1987." *West European Politics* 15: 151–169.

Morgan, David R., and Sheilah S. Watson. 1991. "Political Culture, Political System Characteristics, and Public Policies Among the States." *Publius* 21(2): 31–48.

Nathan, Richard P. 1986. *The Administrative Presidency.* New York: Macmillan.

Neff, Alan. 1981. *The United States District Judge Nominating Commissions: Their Members, Procedures, and Candidates.* Chicago: American Judicature Society.

Neustadt, Richard E. 1990. *Presidential Power and the Modern Presidents: The Politics of Leadership from Roosevelt to Reagan.* New York: Free Press.

O'Brien, David. 1988. *Judicial Roulette: Report of the Twentieth Century Fund Task Force on Judicial Selection.* New York: Priority Press.

O'Brien, David. 1995. *The Supreme Court: The 1995 Term.* New York: Norton.

O'Brien, David. 1996. *Storm Center: The Supreme Court in American Politics,* 4th ed. New York: Norton.

O'Connor, Karen. 1980. *Women's Organizations' Use of the Courts.* Lexington, Mass.: Lexington Books.

O'Connor, Karen. 1983. "The *Amicus Curiae* Role of the U.S. Solicitor General in Supreme Court Litigation." *Judicature* 66: 256–264.

O'Connor, Karen, and Lee Epstein. 1983. "Beyond Legislative Lobbying: Women's Rights Groups and the Supreme Court." *Judicature* 67: 134–143.

O'Connor, Karen, Bernadette Nye, and Laura van Assendelft. 1995. "Wives in the White House: Alternative Routes to Power." Paper presented at the Annual Meeting of the Midwest Political Science Association, Chicago, Illinois.

Pacelle, Richard. 1991. *The Transformation of the Supreme Court's Agenda: From the New Deal to the Reagan Administration.* Boulder, Colo.: Westview Press.

Pacelle, Richard, and Patricia Pauly. 1996. "The Freshman Effect Revisited: An Individual Based Analysis." *American Review of Politics* 17: 1–22.

Palmer, John L., and Isabel V. Sawhill, eds. 1984. *The Reagan Record: An Assessment of America's Changing Domestic Priorities.* Cambridge, Mass.: Ballinger Publishing Company.

Perry, Barbara. 1991. *A "Representative" Supreme Court? The Impact of Race, Religion, and Gender on Appointments.* New York: Greenwood Press.

Peterson, Paul E., and John Chubb, eds. 1989. *Can the Government Govern?* Washington, D.C.: Brookings Institution.

Pfiffner, James. 1990. "Establishing the Bush Presidency." *Public Administration Review* 50 (January/February): 64–73.

Pfiffner, James, ed. 1991. *The Managerial Presidency.* Pacific Grove, Calif.: Brooks/Cole Publishing Company.

Pfiffner, James P. 1996. *The Strategic Presidency: Hitting the Ground Running,* 2d ed., revised. Lawrence: University Press of Kansas.

Pious, Richard M. 1996. *The Presidency.* Boston: Allyn and Bacon.

Pitkin, Hanna Fenichel. 1972. *The Concept of Representation.* Berkeley: University of California Press.

Polsby, Nelson W. 1978. "Presidential Cabinet Making: Lessons for the Political System." *Political Science Quarterly* 93: 15–25.

Polsby, Nelson W. 1981. "Transformation of the American Political System, 1950–1980." Paper presented at the Annual Meeting of the American Political Science Association, New York.

Pomper, Gerald M. et al. 1993. *The Election of 1992: Reports and Interpretations.* Chatham, N.J.: Chatham House Publishers.

Poole, Keith T., and Howard Rosenthal. 1985. "A Spatial Model for Legislative Roll Call Analysis." *American Journal of Political Science* 29: 357–384.

Poole, Keith T., and Howard Rosenthal. 1991. "Patterns of Congressional Voting." *American Journal of Political Science* 35: 228–278.

President's Committee on Administrative Management ["Brownlow Committee"]. 1937. "Administrative Management in the Government of the United States." Washington, D.C.: United States Government Printing Office.

Rather, Dan, and Gary Paul Gates. 1974. *The Palace Guard.* New York: Harper and Row.

Reagan, Ronald. 1990. *An American Life.* New York: Simon and Schuster.

Renshon, Stanley A., ed. 1995. *The Clinton Presidency: Campaigning, Governing, and the Psychology of Leadership.* Boulder, Colo.: Westview Press.

Rimmerman, Craig, ed. 1996. *Gay Rights, Military Wrongs: Political Perspectives on Lesbians and Gays in the Military.* New York: Garland Publishers.

Rinehart, Sue Tolleson. 1988. "Madam Secretary: The Careers of Women in the U.S. Cabinet, 1932–1988." Paper presented at the Annual Meeting of the Southern Political Science Association.

Rohde, Deborah. 1991. *Justice and Gender: Sex Discrimination and the Law.* Cambridge, Mass.: Harvard University Press.

Roof, Wade Clark, and William McKinney. 1987. *American Mainline Religion: Its Changing Shape and Future.* New Brunswick, N.J.: Rutgers University Press.

Rose, Richard. 1991. *The Postmodern President: George Bush Meets the World,* 2d ed. Chatham, N.J.: Chatham House Publishers.

Rosebush, James. 1987. *First Lady, Public Wife: A Behind-the-Scenes History of the Evolving Role of First Ladies in American Political Life.* Lanham, Md.: University Press of America.

Rossi, Alice, ed. 1973. *The Feminist Papers.* New York: Columbia University Press.

Rossiter, Clinton. 1963. *The American Presidency,* 2d ed. New York: Harcourt, Brace, and World.

Rourke, John T., Ralph G. Carter, and Mark A. Boyer. 1996. *Making American Foreign Policy,* 2d ed. Madison, Wis.: Brown and Benchmark.

Rubin, Eva R. 1987. *Abortion, Politics, and the Courts:* Roe v. Wade *and Its Aftermath.* Revised edition. New York: Greenwood Press.

Ruddick, Sara. 1980. "Maternal Thinking." *Feminist Studies* 6: 342–367.

Rule, Wilma. 1981. "Why Women Don't Run: The Critical Contextual Factors in Women's Legislative Recruitment." *Western Political Quarterly* 34: 60–77.

Rule, Wilma. 1990. "Why More Women Are State Legislators: A Research Note." *Western Political Quarterly* 43: 437–448.

Rule, Wilma, and Joseph F. Zimmerman, eds. 1994. *Electoral Systems in Comparative Perspective: Their Impact on Women and Minorities.* Westport, Conn.: Greenwood Press.

Salokar, Rebecca. 1992. *The Solicitor General: The Politics of Law.* Philadelphia: Temple University Press.

Sapiro, Virginia. 1981–1982. "If U.S. Senator Baker Were a Woman: An Experimental Study of Candidate Images." *Political Psychology* 2: 61–83.

Savage, David. 1992. *Turning Right: The Making of the Rehnquist Supreme Court.* New York: John Wiley & Sons.

Scigliano, Robert. 1971. *The Supreme Court and the Presidency.* New York: Free Press.

Segal, Jeffrey, and Cheryl Reedy. 1988. "The Supreme Court and Sex Discrimination: The Role of the Solicitor General." *Western Political Quarterly* 41: 553–568.

Segal, Jeffrey, and Harold Spaeth. 1993. *The Supreme Court and the Attitudinal Model.* New York: Cambridge University Press.

Segal, Jeffrey, Lee Epstein, Charles Cameron, and Harold Spaeth. 1995. "Ideological Values and the Votes of U.S. Supreme Court Justices Revisited." *Journal of Politics* 57: 812–823.

Shapiro, Robert Y., and Harpreet Mahajan. 1986. "Gender Differences in Policy Preferences: A Summary of Trends from the 1960s to the 1980s." *Public Opinion Quarterly* 50: 42–61.

Sharkansky, Ira. 1969. "The Utility of Elazar's Political Culture: A Research Note." *Polity* 2: 66–83.

Silverstein, Mark. 1994. *Judicious Choices: The New Politics of Supreme Court Confirmations.* New York: Norton.

Simon, James. 1995. *The Center Holds: The Power Struggle Inside the Rehnquist Court.* New York: Simon and Schuster.

Sinclair, Barbara. 1989. *The Transformation of the U.S. Senate.* Baltimore: Johns Hopkins University Press.

Slavin, Sarah, ed. Forthcoming. *Lesbian and Gay Political Behavior in the United States.* New York: Routledge Press.

Slotnick, Elliot E. 1979. "The Changing Role of the Senate Judiciary Committee in Judicial Selection." *Judicature* 62: 502–510.

Slotnick, Elliot E. 1980. "Reforms in Judicial Selection: Will They Affect the Senate's Role?" *Judicature* 64: 60–73.

Slotnick, Elliot E. 1980. "Reforms in the Judicial Selection: Will They Affect the Senate's Role? Part II." *Judicature* 64: 114–129.

Slotnick, Elliot E. 1981. "Federal Appellate Judges Selection During the Carter Administration: Recruitment Changes and Unanswered Questions." *Justice Systems Journal* 6: 283–304.

Slotnick, Elliot E. 1984. "Gender, Affirmative Action, and Recruitment to the Federal Bench." *Golden Gate University Law Review* 14: 519–571.

Slotnick, Elliot E. 1984. "The Paths to the Federal Bench: Gender, Race, and Judicial Recruitment Variation." *Judicature* 67: 370–388.

Snyder, James M. 1992. "Committee Power, Structure-Induced Equilibria, and Roll Call Votes." *American Journal of Political Science* 36: 1–30.

Songer, Donald, Jeffrey Segal, and Charles Cameron. 1994. "The Hierarchy of Justice: Testing a Principal-Agent Model of Supreme Court–Circuit Court Interactions." *American Journal of Political Science* 38: 673–696.

Spray, Sharon. Forthcoming. "The Politics of Confirmations: A Study of Senate Roll Call Confirmation Voting, 1787–1994." Ph.D. dissertation, Claremont Graduate School.

Stanley, David T., Dean E. Mann, and Jameson W. Doig. 1967. *Men Who Govern: A Biographical Profile of Federal Political Executives.* Washington, D.C.: Brookings Institution.

Stehr, Steven D. 1989. "Top Bureaucrats and the Distribution of Influence in Reagan's Executive Branch." Presented at the Annual Meeting of the American Political Science Association, Atlanta, Georgia.

Stiehm, Judith Hicks. 1989. *Arms and the Enlisted Women.* Philadelphia: Temple University Press.

Tate, C. Neal. 1981. "Personal Attribute Models of the Voting Behavior of the U.S. Supreme Court Justices: Liberalism in Civil Liberties and Economic Decisions, 1946–1978." *American Political Science Review* 75: 355–367.

Thomas, Sue. 1991. "The Impact of Women on State Legislative Policies." *Journal of Politics* 53: 958–976.

Thomas, Sue. 1994. *How Women Legislate.* New York: Oxford University Press.

Tilly, Louise A., and Patricia Gurin, eds. 1990. *Women, Politics, and Change.* New York: Russell Sage Foundation.

Tinker, Irene, ed. 1983. *Women in Washington: Advocates for Public Policy.* Beverly Hills: Sage Publications.

Tobias, Carl. 1993. "Closing the Gender Gap on the Federal Courts." *University of Cincinnati Law Review* 61: 1237–1249.

Tobias, Carl. 1994. "Keeping the Covenant on the Federal Courts." *SMU Law Review* 47: 1861–1876.

Walker, Thomas, and Deborah Barrow. 1985. "The Diversification of the Federal Bench: Policy and Process Ramifications." *Journal of Politics* 47: 596–617.

Ware, Susan. 1981. *Beyond Suffrage: Women in the New Deal.* Cambridge, Mass.: Harvard University Press.

Weisberg, D. Kelly, ed. 1993. *Feminist Legal Theory: Foundations.* Philadelphia: Temple University Press.

Weisberg, Herbert F. 1987. "Cabinet Transfers and Departmental Prestige." *American Politics Quarterly* 15: 238–253.

Weisberg, Herbert F., ed. 1995. *Democracy's Feast: Elections in America.* Chatham, N.J.: Chatham House Publishers.

Weko, Thomas J. 1995. *The Politicizing Presidency: The White House Personnel Office, 1948–1994.* Lawrence: University Press of Kansas.

Welch, Susan. 1978. "Recruitment of Women to Public Office: A Discriminant Analysis." *Western Political Quarterly* 31: 372–380.

Welch, Susan. 1985. "Are Women More Liberal Than Men in the U.S. Congress?" *Legislative Studies Quarterly* 10: 125–134.

Wilcox, Clyde. 1992. *God's Warriors: The Christian Right in 20th Century America.* Baltimore: The Johns Hopkins University Press.

Witt, Elder. 1986. *A Different Justice: Reagan and the Supreme Court.* Washington, D.C.: Congressional Quarterly.

Witt, Linda, Karen M. Paget, and Glenna Matthews. 1994. *Running as a Woman: Gender and Power in American Politics.* New York: Free Press.

Woodward, Bob. 1994. *The Agenda: Inside the Clinton White House.* New York: Simon and Schuster.

The Contributors

MaryAnne Borrelli is assistant professor of government at Connecticut College. Her research interests center on the links among gender, leadership, and organizational culture. Her articles have investigated abortion policy-making at the state level and have examined the circumstances of women cabinet members, weighing gender power dynamics during confirmation hearings. She is currently preparing a book-length manuscript entitled *Patterns of Opportunity, Patterns of Constraint: The Nomination and Confirmation of Women Cabinet Members in the United States* (University of Michigan Press).

Barbara C. Burrell is researcher at Wisconsin Survey Research Laboratory. She has published extensively on women, public opinion, and political developments in the United States. Her articles have presented research on party politics, campaign finance, and women as legislative candidates. She is the author of *A Woman's Place Is in the House: Campaigning for Congress in the Feminist Era* (University of Michigan Press, 1994) and *Public Opinion, the First Ladyship and Hillary Clinton* (Garland Press, 1997).

Georgia Duerst-Lahti is associate professor of government at Beloit College. She has researched and published on the challenges confronting women in electoral and bureaucratic politics. Her articles have revealed the links between private lives and public work through a critical examination of career patterns, gender stereotypes and professional opportunities, and management styles and decisionmaking routines. Duerst-Lahti's book on the implications of masculinism for U.S. politics, coedited with Rita Mae Kelly, is entitled *Gender Power, Leadership, and Governance* (University of Michigan Press, 1995).

Piper A. Hodson is a Ph.D. candidate at the University of Illinois at Urbana-

Champaign. Her research and publications have focused on theories of nuclear proliferation and national security decisionmaking; her fieldwork has been conducted in South Asia. She has received the Hubert H. Humphrey Fellowship in Arms Control and Disarmament from the Arms Control and Disarmament Agency (1994) and has been an affiliate of the Program in Arms Control, Disarmament and International Security (1991–1997). Her dissertation tests the applicability of prospect theory to elite decisionmaking in South Asia.

Janet M. Martin is associate professor of government at Bowdoin College. Her research has examined executive appointments to the cabinet and sub-cabinet levels from the presidency of Franklin Delano Roosevelt to the present. Her articles have examined the patterns of presidential selection with reference to appointees' gender and career patterns and have assessed those same individuals' perspectives on their role in the executive branch. A former American Political Science Association congressional fellow, Martin is the author of *Lessons from the Hill: The Legislative Journey of an Education Program* (St. Martin's Press, 1994); she is currently preparing a book-length manuscript entitled *A Place in the Oval Office: Women and the American Presidency.*

Nancy E. McGlen is professor of political science at Niagara University. She has written three books and twenty-two articles assessing the position and contributions of women in U.S. politics. Her research has focused on foreign policy formulation in the Defense and State Departments; interest group activism, also in foreign policy making; the women's rights movement; and the role of women in political science. Her most recent book, coauthored with Professor Karen O'Connor (American University), is entitled *Women, Politics, and American Society* (Prentice Hall, 1995).

Richard L. Pacelle, Jr., is assistant professor of political science at the University of Missouri–St. Louis. His research has examined the role of the judiciary in policymaking, revealing how institutional developments within the Supreme Court affect its decisionmaking processes and thus its case rulings. His articles have considered the "freshman effect" and have assessed Supreme Court authority within the judicial hierarchy; he is currently considering the dynamics of Supreme Court agenda setting through a critical analysis of civil rights and abortion case holdings. Pacelle is the author of *The Transformation of the Supreme Court's Agenda: From the New Deal to the Reagan Administration* (Westview Press, 1991), and he is preparing a book-length manuscript entitled *The Emergence and Evolution of Supreme Court Policy.*

Meredith Reid Sarkees is associate professor of political science at

Niagara University. She has investigated the role of women in U.S. national security and is also an expert on the politics of the Middle East. Her articles include examinations of U.S. foreign policy, policymaking, and policymakers; comparative studies of Yemeni and Syrian foreign relations; and analyses of women in the discipline of political science. She is the author, with Nancy E. McGlen, of *Women in Foreign Policy: The Insiders* (Routledge, 1993).

Jean Reith Schroedel is associate professor of politics and economics at Claremont Graduate School. Her primary research and teaching interests are gender politics and congressional politics. She has written two books, *Alone in a Crowd: Women in Trades Tell Their Stories* (Temple University Press, 1985) and *Congress, The President and Policy-making: A Historical Analysis* (M. E. Sharp, 1994), and numerous articles. Currently, Schroedel is researching fetal abuse policy and gay and lesbian elected officials.

Bruce D. Snyder is a Ph.D. candidate at Claremont Graduate School. Snyder, who received his J.D. from Loyola in 1979, is writing a dissertation on political and policy cycles in federal affirmative action programs. His primary research and teaching interests include constitutional law, the courts, Congress, the presidency, and policymaking. He has published an article in *Studies in American Political Development* and has written several book chapters.

Sharon Spray is an assistant professor of political science and associate dean of students at the University of the South. Her primary research interests are in presidential-legislative relations, focusing on the presidential appointments process.

Kathryn Dunn Tenpas is assistant professor of government and international affairs at the University of South Florida. She has researched the effects of the presidential reelection campaign on the White House, with particular attention to the implications of the president's candidacy for White House staff dynamics. Her articles include specialized studies of the presidential electoral process, third-party presidential candidates, electoral reform initiatives, and the White House Office of Political Affairs. Tenpas, who served on the staff of the 1988 Commission on Presidential Debates, is currently preparing a book-length manuscript entitled *Presidents as Candidates: Inside the White House for the Presidential Campaign.*

Clyde Wilcox is associate professor of government at Georgetown University. He has explored patterns of political participation in recent elections, religious orientations and political attitudes, and gender role attitudes and feminism. He has written four books, including *God's Warriors: The*

Christian Right in 20th Century America (The Johns Hopkins University Press, 1992) and *Serious Money: Fundraising and Contributing in Presidential Nomination Campaigns* (with Clifford W. Brown, Jr., and Lynda W. Powell; Cambridge University Press, 1995). Wilcox has also edited a number of volumes; he is the author of thirteen chapters in volumes other than his own and of nearly one hundred articles in a wide variety of scholarly journals. He is currently preparing two book manuscripts, *God and the GOP in the Old Dominion: Marriage Made in Heaven or Holy War?* and *Onward Christian Soldiers: The Christian Right in American Politics.*

Index

About the Book

The Other Elites features original essays that provide important insights for both presidential studies and the study of women in U.S. politics.

This book represents the first volume on the presidency that addresses the issue of gender. The contributors investigate the circumstances of women as officeholders in and consituents of the U.S. national executive branch. To understand the interplay of these realities, the authors have drawn upon their expertise in presidency studies and women-and-politics research as well as their knowledge of public policy, legislative-executive and executive-judicial relations, political theory, and comparative politics. Their research methodologies are unusually diverse, encompassing qualitative and quantitative, institutional, behavioral, historical, and theoretical approaches. The chapters investigate the election and appointment of women to executive and to judicial office, the effects of presidential decisionmaking styles upon women's influence as policymakers, and the role of gender in popular participation and in executive power.

MaryAnne Borrelli is assistant professor of government at Connecticut College, where she specializes in executive branch politics and women and politics. She is preparing a book entitled *Patterns of Opportunity, Patterns of Constraint: The Nomination and Confirmation of Women Cabinet Members in the United States.* **Janet M. Martin** is associate professor of government at Bowdoin College. She is the author of *Lessons from the Hill: The Legislative Journey of an Education Program.* Her latest book project is *A Place in the Oval Office: Women and the American Presidency.*